Hindu Nationalists in India

Hindu Nationalists in India

The Rise of the Bharatiya Janata Party

Yogendra K. Malik and V. B. Singh

Westview Press

BOULDER • SAN FRANCISCO • OXFORD

Copyright © 1994 by Westview Press, Inc.

Published in 1994 in the United States of America by Westview Press, Inc., 5500 Central Avenue, Boulder, Colorado 80301-2877, and in the United Kingdom by Westview Press, 36 Lonsdale Road, Summertown, Oxford OX2 7EW

Library of Congress Cataloging-in-Publication Data
Malik, Yogendra K.
  Hindu nationalists in India : the rise of the Bharatiya Janata
Party / by Yogendra K. Malik and V. B. Singh.
    p. cm.
  Includes bibliographical references and index.
  ISBN 0-8133-8810-4
  1. Bharatiya Janata Party—History. 2. India—Politics and
government—1977– I. Singh, V. B., 1941– . II. Title.
JQ298.B55M35 1994
324.254'083—dc20
                                                                    94-23352
                                                                    CIP

Printed and bound in the United States of America

The paper used in this publication meets the requirements
of the American National Standard for Permanence of Paper
for Printed Library Materials Z39.48-1984.

10   9   8   7   6   5   4   3   2   1

CONTENTS

TABLES AND FIGURES

ACKNOWLEDGMENTS

In 1987 while collecting material on parties and political finance in India as a Senior Fellow of the American Institute of Indian Studies, I became interested in the ideology, leadership, and organization of the Bharatiya Janata Party (BJP). It was, however, in 1992, while serving as a Senior Fulbright Scholar in India that I was able to complete my research. I am deeply indebted to the American Institute of Indian Studies (AIIS) and Fulbright Foundation for the financial support which enabled me to conduct field research in India. I was granted an affiliation at The Center for the Study of Developing Societies in Delhi which facilitated the approval of the project by the Ministry of Education of the Government of India. Dr. V.B. Singh of the Center agreed to write a chapter on the BJP's electoral performance. While he is primarily responsible for the writing of this chapter, both of us have read each other's chapters and made suggestion for revisions or changes. Thus both of us are responsible for the opinion expressed in the book. Our analysis and statements made in the book do not reflect the positions of the AIIS, Fulbright Foundation, or the Center on the issues raised and discussed.

In India various individuals and organizations were helpful in completing this project. I am especially indebted to Mrs. Sharda Nayak and Mr. O. P. Bhardwaj of the United States Educational Foundation in New Delhi for making our stay in India a very pleasant and fruitful experience. M/S K. R. Malkani, Krishan Lal Sharma and Sundar Singh Bhandari of the Bharatiya Janata Party were very cooperative and helpful in providing very useful information and spending time with me despite their busy schedules. Mr. Malkani was kind enough to provide me the copies of most of his publications including the clippings of his newspaper writings.

Dina Nath Mishra graciously shared his files on the BJP and other political parties with me. Brij Mohan Lal was helpful in establishing my contacts with Professor Devinder Swroop of Deen Dayal Research Institute. Professor Swroop not only provided many of the publications of the Institute, but also spent a number of hours discussing with me his political thinking and the Institute's cultural and social activities. I was also able to attend various seminars and lectures organized by the Institute, which enabled me to discern the diversity in the thinking of the intellectual establishment of the organization.

K. L. Sharma, the chief librarian of the *Times of India* and an old friend, opened up the library files on various dimensions of the activities of the Hindu nationalists. At the Center, Drs. R. K. Srivastva and Harsh Sethi read various sections of the manuscript and made very useful comments. Dr. V. B. Singh was assisted by Mrs. Kanchan Malhotra in the collection and analysis of the statistical data.

Various colleagues and friends in the United States and Canada also read different sections of the manuscript. Carl Lieberman and Jim Sperling of Political Science and Devinder Malhotra of the Economics Department at the University of Akron were kind enough to read some chapters and make very useful suggestions. I am especially indebted to Baldev Raj Nayar of McGill University for reading the introduction and conclusions. He helped me correct some errors in tracing the development of the two versions of nationalism in India. Craig Baxter, a friend and a colleague, was gracious and generous enough to go through the whole manuscript and made very important suggestions in improving its quality. Surender Mohan Bhardwaj, professor of geography at Kent State University, graciously prepared two maps included in the book despite his busy schedule. Mrs. Bonnie Ralston, administrative assistant in the department of Political Science, has typed many of my previous manuscripts with a great degree of patience and efficiency. This manuscript has been no exception. She skillfully and graciously typed many drafts of this manuscript and has prepared the final copy despite an increase in her manifold responsibilities. I sincerely appreciate her help and cooperation. Without the wise counsel and encouragement of senior editor Susan McEachern and her staff at Westview Press, it would have taken a lot longer to finish this project than it did. My thanks to Professor S. Dolly Malik Madan, my daughter, who alerted me to some glaring deficiencies in the first few chapters and made useful suggestions on its improvement. Last but not least, my thanks to my wife, Usha, for her help in conducting the fieldwork and for exercising patience with me during some of the rough periods.

For all our appreciation to those who helped us in the completion of this project, however, the authors alone bear the responsibility for the material presented, analysis made, and opinions expressed in this volume.

Yogendra K. Malik

1

Ideology, Power, and Political Parties

The rise of the Bharatiya Janata Party (BJP), with its emphasis on Hindu nationalism, at the center stage of Indian politics has raised questions about the validity of the secular nationalist ideology which has been the foundation of the Indian state since its independence. The party's rise has also led to heated debate among the politicians and intellectuals about the nature and functions of the Indian state as well as the basis of Indian national identity. The question has even been asked whether the Indian state, as it has been known since its independence, will survive if the BJP comes to power and implements its ideology. The prospect of its coming to power generates strong emotions, creates fear, and raises alarm both inside and outside of India.

We intend to explain the ideological basis of the Bharatiya Janata Party in the context of the evolution of the different versions of nationalism in India, the origin and development of the party, the strategies of its leadership to capture political power, its programs and policies, and its organizational structure. In order to assess its place in Indian politics, we will analyze the circumstances which have led to its emergence as a major contender for political power. In short, we intend to provide an academic analysis of the BJP and what it represents in contemporary Indian politics.

The Ideological Context of Indian Politics

In order to understand the nature of the BJP, it is essential to describe the various dimensions of the ideological basis of Indian politics. Political scientists differ in their definition of ideologies. We believe, however, that in all societies there develop certain patterns of thoughts, norms of behavior, and beliefs concerning the nature of the state, the basis of political authority, and the goals of the government. Such a collection of values, myths, and norms of behavior is used both to exercise control over citizens and to seek their compliance with the laws. We agree with Alexis de Tocqueville that "in order that society should exist . . . it is necessary that the minds of all the citizens should be rallied and held together by certain predominant ideas."[1]   Besides acquiring ideas and beliefs from certain groups of people, believers in a distinct ideology tend to identify themselves with certain heroes, seers, sages, historic persons and events, and sacred works and declarations.[2]

Ideologies are part of a culture or if borrowed, they gradually become integrated into a culture. They determine how the members of a society should act, live, and respond to the demands made on them by the changes taking place in the environment. They are dynamic and reflect the changes constantly taking place in the citizens' and the elites' existing world-views and assumptions.

In the context of political developments in India, the ideology of nationalism, identified with a politically unified Indian state, is of recent origin. In the early stages of Indian history, Indian unity was achieved on the basis of pan-Indian cultural identity and common civilizational values. The core of this value system was the recognition of multiple diversities, both behavioral and normative, and legitimacy of group identities and autonomies. In the absence of a centralized political authority it was "the Indian civilizational enterprise" which "over the centuries achieved a remarkable degree of cohesion and held together different sub-systems in a continental-size society."[3]   The unifying force was Indian civilization rather than a political ideology.

The major component of this civilization was Hinduism. This religion lacked a dominant theology and allowed various sects to flourish within its fold with their own theologies and ways of worship. The variety of castes and communities that formed part of the Hindu social organization also developed their own norms of behavior and traditions. These various traditions of Hinduism led to the development of the pluralistic traits of Indian civilization within which different communities with different traditions and beliefs could coexist.

Islam, Christianity, and Judaism, religions coming from outside the Indian sub-continent, while contributing to Indian civilization and culture, were also deeply influenced by the pluralistic nature of Hindu society and became part of the diversified cultural traditions of India.

Nationalism: Two Versions of a Pan-Indian Ideology

Whether nationalism can be defined strictly as a political ideology or not, in the context of politics in India, nationalism became an ideology *par excellence*. While seeking independence for the country, political leaders and India's intellectual establishment became engaged in a broad-based discussion on the nature and the functions of the state, the potentials and the limits of political authority, the basis of political legitimacy, and the definition of national identity.

There are two predominant versions of nationalism in India: Indian nationalism and Hindu nationalism. Hindu nationalism developed as a reaction against the Indian nationalism. The proponents of the latter were mainly Western-educated Indian elites who were secular and utilitarian in their approach. In the words of Heimsath, "Having at its base an anti-traditional, liberal democratic, secular and politically oriented concept of the nation," the early nationalism developed an ideology which "could properly encompass all Indian cultures and religions."[4] These nationalists sought to distance themselves from the cultural heritage of Hindus.

The origin of Hindu nationalism, on the other hand, is rooted in the Hindu cultural revival and social reform movements of the nineteenth century. Being syncretistic in nature, the movement aimed at social reforms by incorporating Western values and sought their validation through reinterpretation of Hindu sacred texts.

To the Hindu elites in the nineteenth century, the concept of Indian national identity was indistinguishable from Hindu identity. They accepted textual Brahmanism as a potent political force and linked the rising Indian identity to the period of *Vedas* and *Upanishadas* and accepted the role of the state in carrying on the reforms of the religious aspects of Hindu society. Employing a psychological approach to understanding the development of national identity in India, Ashis Nandy observes:

> Brahmanism provided, for the first time, a basis for collective identity, which was more open to new ideas and less fettered by primordial allegiance and fragmentation of the myriad folk cultures of India. Predominantly integrationist and liberal, it was informed by a certain positivist universalism that made sense to a majority of the Indians in the public sphere.[5]

They laid the "foundation of Indian self-image that would not humiliate the country's majority of Hindu inhabitants."[6]

Swami Vivekananda, who became the apostle of Hindu nationalism, recognized the spiritual heritage of Hinduism as the cornerstone of the

country's emerging national identity. In no uncertain terms, he declared
that "The backbone, the foundation, the bedrock of India's national life
was . . . its spiritual genius."[7] Contrasting that with the materialism of the
West, he added, "let others talk of politics, of the glory of acquisition or
of the power and spread of commercialism; these cannot inspire India. . . .
Religion . . . is the one consideration in India."[8] And there is no doubt
that, for Vivekananda, this religion was none other than Hinduism.

Aurobindo Ghosh, another prominent philosopher-thinker of the early
period of the nationalist movement, also closely identified nationalism with
the teachings of Sanatan Dharma, the orthodox version of Hinduism.
Giving an absolutist definition of the newly developing Indian national
identity, he asserted that "nationalism is simply the passionate aspiration
of the realization of the Divine Unity in the nation."[9] For Ghosh, therefore, nationalism is a religion, one which requires pursuit of an active
rather than a meditative life. For him, the Indian nation was an incarnation
of a Mother Goddess.

In contrast to Vivekananda, Bankimchandra Chattopadhya, in his
propagation of national identity, emphasized Hindu valor and blamed
Hindus' excessive otherworldliness for the lack of national unity among
Hindus in India. He also asserted that Hindu history was falsified by alien
historians, including the Muslim scholars, to dampen the Hindu quest for
liberty and unity. Furthermore, Chattopadhya held that, unlike the Euro-
peans, Hindus were not interested in the acquisition of power but, rather,
sought knowledge as a way to personal salvation.[10]

Chattopadhya and other early Indian nationalists became ardent devotees
of Durga, the goddess of power. Early nationalists deified India, and
nationalism became a new religion for them. Thus Chattopadhya and
Bipanchandra Pal, another early protagonist of Hindu nationalism,
established a parallel between ancient Hindu gods and goddesses and the
new god called nation.[11] It should be added, however, that despite the
Hindu national sentiment, the emergence of a national idea in India had
noticeable European characteristics to it.[12]

Such an ideology of nationalism, laced with symbols and myths of
Hindu religion, was further popularized by Lokmanya Bal Gangadhar Tilak
and his associates in the Congress movement and by the writings of a host
of authors in regional languages of India, especially in Maharashtra,
Bengal, Gujarat, and Hindi writings of north India. Such an ideology not
only gave a glorious vision of the past but also visualized a future where
the religious and cultural traditions of the ancient times would serve as
guideposts for the upcoming generations.

Their concept of nation was rooted in the religion and the culture of Hindus, and they sought its manifestation in the unity of Hindus throughout the country. Like that of Indian nationalism, the ideology of Hindu nationalism was pan-Indian in its approach.

Nehruvian Nationalism: The Dominant Post-Independence Ideology

Given the complexity of Indian society, diversity of its religions, multiplicity of its languages, importance of regional identities of its people, and the existence of a host of sub-cultures, it is not surprising that many intellectuals and political leaders of the independence movement sought an alternate version of nationalism, one in which religious identities would play no role.

Influenced by both liberal and Marxist thought, the second group of Indian nationalists, led by Jawaharlal Nehru, after World War I developed an alternate model of Indian nationalism. India, according to this group, needed a nationalist ideology based on rational ideas and norms of behavior which could rise above religious beliefs and practices. At the same time such an ideology should embody a scientific temper so that it could enable a person to override the narrow caste, communal, and regional loyalties which are so deeply embedded in the psyche of the average Indian.

Drawing on the nineteenth-century experiences of western European societies, Nehru and his associates believed that industrialization would erode the influence of religion. With increased economic development through industrialization, ethnic and religious loyalties would be replaced by class identification. Nehru perceived that it was economic factors that aggravated social and religious conflicts in India.[13] He was convinced that if and when traditional societies like that of India based their course of development on science and technology, secularism would become the norm of politics.[14]

Nehru and his associates did not totally reject Hindu cultural ethos, recognizing the synthetic nature of Indian culture to which many other cultures, especially Muslim, had made major contributions. However, according to Hindu nationalists, their goal was to "remake India in the Western image."[15] Under such ideological premises the state would become a powerful agency for the spread of Western values and mores.[16] In reality, Nehru promoted cultural and ideological consensus among the people of India irrespective of their race, religion, and place of birth.

It was the Nehruvian school of Indian nationalism that became the dominant ideology in post-independence India and led to the introduction of liberal democratic institutions, along with the principles of federalism. Such a polity, this school of thought believed, would provide suitable outlets for the utilization of creative energies as well for the satisfaction of the political ambitions of the regional and local elites. The Nehruvians were further convinced that if citizens could participate in the political process, they would rise above religious and ethnic identities. Thus, national unity would be consolidated and the pan-Indian national identity created by the nationalist movement would be strengthened. Furthermore, they believed that this was the most practical approach to the delicate task of nation-building in a culturally and socially plural society.

However, the operation of democracy requires restraint on the part of political elites, especially in a culturally and socially plural society. In plural societies, the successful operation of democracy is possible only when political elites are able to rise above sub-cultural cleavages, recognize the danger inherent in aggravating the existing divisions within the society, and are willing to accommodate the demands of the religious or ethnic minorities.[17] Nehru was aware of these limitations. He not only sought to build consensus among the groups contending for power but strongly disapproved of appealing to sectarian sentiments for political gain. This approach became an integral element of Nehru's version of Indian nationalism.

In practice, however, the post-independence Indian state—constituted on the principle of universal suffrage and equal voting rights—was unable to create a cohesive electorate guided by rational self-interest and above the influence of its religious or caste-based identities. Since Indian politicians and political parties, especially in the post-Nehru era of Indian politics, seem to have adopted C.B. Macpherson's attitude toward democracy as a kind of market mechanism—with voters as consumers with varied demands and politicians as the entrepreneurs out to buy their votes[18]—politicians and party leaders openly appealed to religious or primordial loyalties in their quest for power. Consolidation of religious and caste-based identities thus became inevitable, leading to the formation of vote banks. It is common knowledge that the centrist political parties, whether the Congress or the Janata Dal, before giving the party tickets to their candidates consider their religious and caste affiliations.

Because of these developments, the secularist nature of the Nehruvian nationalism came to be challenged on theoretical and practical grounds. In a society like India's, where religious practices and identities are deeply rooted in the psychology of the common people, operation of a secular state is not easy. A secular state can either act neutral to religious beliefs of the people (*dharm nirpaksh*), provide equal respect and protection for the followers of all religions (*sarvadharm samabhava*), or guarantee the religious and social identities of the followers of all religions.

In an ideal secular state, religious beliefs and practices are to be considered personal and private; the state, as a public institution, neither favors nor intervenes in religious affairs of a person or a community. Given the nature of South Asian political culture, the operation of a genuinely secular state in India is an ideal unlikely to be achieved. It has been observed:

> . . . secularism in South Asia as a generally shared credo of life is impossible, as a basis for state action impracticable, and as a blue-print for the foreseeable future impotent. It is impossible as a credo of life because the great majority of the people of South Asia in their own eyes are active adherents of some religious faith. It is impracticable as a basis for state action either because Buddhism and Islam have been declared state or state-protected religions or because the stance of religious neutrality or equidistance is difficult to maintain since religious minorities do not share the majority's view of what this entails for the state, and it is impractical as a blue-print for the future because, by its very nature, it is incapable of countering fundamentalism and fanaticism.[19]

Reasons for such a theory are not difficult to find. In practice, as has been pointed out by observers of Indian politics, the Indian state has been unable to maintain neutrality in the religious affairs of the majority and the minority communities. From time to time various state and national governments have taken action and passed laws concerning the management and regulation of Hindu temples. Besides abolishing the practice of untouchability, the government of India passed a comprehensive law, the Hindu Code Bill, governing the Hindu family system, marriage, divorce, and inheritance practices, despite the opposition of many prominent Hindu leaders and groups. The state, in this type of situation, seemed to represent Hindu India and acted as if it knew what was in the best interests of Hindus.[20]

On the other hand, the government of India, under the Congress party leadership of Nehru and his grandson, Rajiv Gandhi, would not take any liberties with Muslim personal laws. In the now well-known *Shah Bano vs. Mohammad Ahmed Khan* (1981) case, the Supreme Court upheld the decision of a lower court raising the maintenance allowance of a divorced Muslim woman. Five Supreme Court justices ruled that under section 125 of the Indian Penal Code, a husband must pay reasonable alimony to a woman who does not have any other means of support. The Chief Justice,

Y.V. Chandrachud, criticized the existing Muslim Personal Law by citing the Koran. Also, he asserted that the time had come to introduce a common civil code for all the citizens of the country regardless of their religion.

The Supreme Court verdict and the comments made by the Justice enraged the members of the Muslim Personal Law Board as well as the orthodox Muslim clergy. The judicial body's interpretation of the holy Koran resulted in a massive agitation against the court decision.[21] One of Rajiv Gandhi's Muslim cabinet ministers, Z.R. Ansari, described the judges of India's Supreme Court as "*telis* and *tambolis* [oil-pressers and betel-leaf growers],"[22] and the judgment was labeled a threat to Islam and to Indian Muslims' distinct religious identity. Such efforts were successful in whipping up fundamentalist religious sentiments among the Muslim masses against the government. Many liberal Hindus and other intellectuals were shocked when they found that many educated middle class Muslims, even the progressive Muslim intellectuals, sided with the orthodox clergy and opposed the Supreme Court decision.

Fearing the loss of the Muslim vote as well as the disruption of peace, the Rajiv Gandhi government in 1985 hastily pushed through Parliament the Muslim Women (Protection of Rights on Divorce) bill, making it a law, and exempted the Muslims from the force of section 125 of the Code of Criminal Procedure.

Whatever the motives of the Congress party government or the reasons for leftist and secularist intellectuals' support for the Muslim Personal Law,[23] the Hindus saw obvious inconsistency in the operation of a secular state in India. If religion is to be excluded from politics, there should be uniform standards applicable to both the majority and minority communities. In the words of S. Sahay, "even in criminal law, a discrimination is being made in favor of a particular community."[24] Such inconsistency becomes all the more glaring when it is apparent that for Muslims there is no separation between religion and politics.[25]

Since the Indian state does not operate in isolation, policies of other states, particularly those of its South Asian neighbors, also have an impact on the ideologies espoused by the ruling elites and by the mass political culture. In neighboring Pakistan, for instance, the majority's religion, Islam, has become the state religion and the Hindu-Sikh minorities have been driven out. By law, no non-Muslim can hold a top state position. The state has become an instrument for both the promotion of Islam and the enforcement of Islamic laws. Pakistan's appeal for Islamic solidarity, its support for Muslim causes, and direct or indirect promotion of terroristic activities in India are perceived by Indian Hindus as a threat to their security. On March 17, 1988, Islam became the official religion of another neighboring state, Bangladesh. The Hindu minority there has been reduced to a position of second-class citizenship.

Furthermore, "Islam being a polity as well as one ethical ideal," Muslims believe that "the entire Islamic world may be regarded as one *umma*, or nation, which should, ideally, be constituted as one state."[26] Under this ideological assumption Indian Muslims become part of the larger Islamic world, and according to Hindu nationalists, many of them display extra-territorial loyalties. Indian Muslims' continuous adherence to pan-Islamism would undermine the validity of Nehru's secular version of Indian nationalism.

A more fundamental criticism of the Nehruvian school of Indian nationalism is that it completely ignores the essence of Indian culture and civilization. According to Hindu nationalists, in defining Indian nation-hood it is Hindu culture and civilization which ought to be the central element. Not only did Nehru and his associates ignore it, but they actually seemed to deny it. In fact, many thought that Nehru had nothing but contempt for Hindu religious traditions and that this was the main reason he rejected the ideology of Hindu nationalism since it emphasized the primacy of Hindu religious traditions, culture, and civilization in the development of Indian national identity.[27]

According to Hindu nationalists, the so-called secular nationalist ideology is "a euphemism for irreligion and repudiation of the Hindu ethos."[28] They perceive Indian nationalism as the ideology upheld by Islamized Indians, like Nehru, or westernized and Marxist intellectuals, who are rootless and completely alienated from their own unique and rich cultural heritage.[29]

Gandhi's version of Indian nationalism was closer to the cultural realities of India than Nehru's. Unlike Nehru, Gandhi was not enamored of Western culture. He was not alienated from Hinduism and thus he did not distance himself from Hindu cultural traditions. He used the symbols of Hindu folk culture and traditions to appeal to the national sentiments of Indians.

The encounter of Islam and Hinduism in the Middle Ages led to the development of a devotional (*bhakti*) movement which merged and blended the values of the two religions; it also strongly denounced the inflexible and orthodox ways of Hindu priests and Muslim *maulvis*.

Such movements have left a deep impression on the psyche of Indians, especially in rural areas where syncretic religious worship is practiced and where the majority of Indians live.

Deeply influenced by the devotional movement, Gandhi was able to find common ground between the two religious communities. He favored granting maximum autonomy to state and local communities seeking to safeguard the cultural and social identities of different groups and opposed centralization of political and economic power, which Nehru envisioned for a modern nation-state in India.

Nehru sought to build Indian national identity by emphasizing the virtues of modernization through industrialization and economic development, while Gandhi emphasized the virtues of Hinduism by focusing on its traditions of religious tolerance and social pluralism as the basis of the Indian national issue. However, in post-independence India the Gandhian version of Indian nationalism received only lip service from India's ruling elites since it was not secular enough for them.

For the Hindu nationalists, however, it is Hinduism, not as a religion but as the foundation of Indian civilization and culture, which should be given central place in the ideology of Indian nationalism. While Islam, Christianity, Buddhism, and other religions have contributed to the stream of Indian culture and civilization, its fountainhead has been Hinduism.

Many intellectual critics of the Nehruvian ideology would agree with the assertion:

> Over the centuries the Indian civilization had molded and provided a common underlying bond between different Hindu sects and schools. It had also shaped and indigenised such alien religions as Islam and Christianity. Despite their different origins, belief systems, and social structures, all Indian communities thus share common "ethos" or "spirit" and were bound together by deep civilizational bonds. A common civilizational basis was thus not only available in India but formed the ineliminable substance of its collective life. However secular the Indian state might pretend to be, it could never transcend and avoid being structured by the "spiritual" ethos of the civilization in which it was deeply embedded.[30]

A political doctrine which is out of tune with the culture of the people, which does not conform to their beliefs, values, and shared perceptions, is not likely to become part of their psychological makeup.

The Nehruvian version of Indian nationalism also emphasized certain egalitarian tenets, particularly in relation to the distribution of material goods and services, equality of opportunity for the weaker segments of society, centralized economic planning, and utilization of national resources for the collective good of the community. The Indian state was to play a central role in the achievement of these goals. Elements of the British version of democratic socialism, in this way, became intertwined with the ideology of Indian nationalism.

Reassertion of Hindu Nationalism as an
Alternate Ideology of the Indian State

There are many proponents arguing the cause of Hindu nationalism, yet the various arguments are far from consistent. Despite the internal contradictions, however, there seems to be a broad agreement among them as to the majority's right to set the goals of the Indian state.

First of all, Hindu nationalists argue that the partition of India on the basis of religion and the creation of the Muslim-majority state of Pakistan was itself a testimony to the failure of the Nehruvian ideology of Indian nationalism. If Muslim nationalism was the reason for the creation of Pakistan, logically Hindu nationalism should have become the dominant ideology of the Indian state. They contend:

> Rightly or wrongly, the Congress in fact robbed the Hindu majority of its legal right to succeed the British Raj. With Hinduism as its religion, India could have been a truly secular state. . . . Intentionally or otherwise the move of Nehru's reduced the Hindu majority to an impotent political nonentity, a game that has been played by the successive Congress regimes to perpetuate its rule—and that too on the strength of the Hindu vote.[31]

Hindu nationalists reject the idea that Indian culture is a composite or synthetic culture. While it might have been influenced by other cultures, it is not simply a mixture of those cultures. "India has only one national culture . . . which is known as Hindu culture,"[32] they believe. All others, such as Buddhist, Jain, or Sikh cultures, are really Hindu sub-cultures, since all of them originated in India. They were born out of Hinduism. They are part of Bharatiya culture.[33]

For Hindu nationalists India does not need a European version of a secular state. In dealing with the minorities, the Indian state should be guided by its own cultural heritage. Basically, Hindus consider their religion and culture very flexible and tolerant. According to L.K. Advani, the Bharatiya Janata Party leader:

> Religious tradition in India has been remarkably free of taboos or intolerance. . . .
> In ancient times, this country had Charvaka ridiculing God and religion in a forthright manner. . . . Even such an unabashed protagonist of atheism and materialism has been acknowledged as a *Rishi* [sage]![34]

We agree that Hinduism did not require an institutional system to protect dissent within its fold. Institutionally, Hinduism may be "rigid but interprets its conventions so broadly and allows the individual such a large choice within the orthodoxy that it is impossible to be a dissenter unless one is a dedicated and doctrinaire non-conformist."[35]

However, the way Hinduism is being presently propagated by Hindu revivalist organizations and has been politicized by militant Hindu nationalists, leaves little room for tolerance.

The BJP leaders insist that secularism is natural to Hinduism because it is "impossible for the Hindus to evolve an established church or proclaim a state religion and call upon the state to impose it by force."[36] For the Hindu nationalists, as Advani puts it, "secularism means guarantee of equality and justice to all citizens irrespective of their faith. No discrimination against or in favor of anyone."[37] One can hardly deny, as the Hindu nationalists assert, that Nehru and his associates were able to declare India a secular state only because of India's Hindu majority. Such a step could not have been taken in a Muslim-majority state. According to them, however, the Nehruvian version of secularism ultimately became "a euphemism for Hindu-baiting."[38] There has been strong criticism of secular intellectuals, such as the Marxists and the socialists, who, Hindu nationalists charge, have borrowed their ideologies from the West and have deliberately distorted and misrepresented the Hindu cultural heritage.

Logically, therefore, Hindu nationalists argue that the Indian state needs to take no special action to safeguard the distinct cultural or religious identity of such minorities as the Muslims. History shows that Muslims enjoyed cultural and religious freedom in such Hindu kingdoms as those of the Rajputs, the Jats, the Marathas, and the Sikhs. We should not forget, however, that there was no politicization of religion in those kingdoms.

In contemporary India the politicians have contributed to the misuse of the term *minority* for electoral and political purposes. India has many kinds of minorities. But it is hard to agree with Advani when he says that recognition of religion as the primary basis of a minority, claiming to have a distinct culture of its own, would lead to the endless fragmentation of the society.[39]

Hindu nationalists, however, insist on the Muslims' acceptance of the pre-Islamic cultural heritage of India. They argue that the Bharatiya culture, that is, the ancient civilization of India and its traditions, preserved to the present,[40] is the heritage of all Indians irrespective of their religion. Advani, for example, says that the *Ramayana*, the great Indian epic, is part of Indian cultural heritage, and therefore Muslims should accept Ram, and not Babur, the founder of the Moughal empire in India, as their hero.[41] In short, the aim of the Hindu nationalists is to make "the present and future generations of Muslim Bharatiyas to take pride in their pre-Islamic ancestry."[42]

Insistence on the Muslim minority's identification with the history and culture of the majority may be understandable on the intellectual level, but Islamic teachings and ancient Indian values and norms of behavior may be incompatible, especially for the orthodox Muslim clergy.

More significant, however, is the fact that while the intellectual advocates of Hindu nationalism insist on Muslims' acceptance of the ancient cultural heritage of India, most refuse to recognize the contributions of Muslims to the development of Indian culture. For them Hindu religion and Indian culture have become indistinguishable, while the reality is otherwise.

Any student knows that Ashoka and Akbar, the great emperors, and Tulasidas and Ghalib, the great poets, are integral parts of Indian cultural heritage. If culture, and not religion, is the basis of the Indian state as the Hindu nationalists assert, then how can one exclude the Muslims' contributions to Indian civilization and culture and thus to the development of Indian national identity? It is this exclusionary aspect of Hindu nationalism which raises serious doubts about the Hindus' version of a "secular" India.

In order to assuage the pride of the Hindus, some believe that the Muslims "should disassociate themselves from the medieval invaders and rulers and the glorification of their misdeeds in the name of Islam."[43] For the Muslims to do this, however, the Hindu nationalists would also have to acknowledge the contributions of the Muslim rulers toward building Hindu places of worship. Without making this kind of acknowledgment, the Hindu nationalists' demand would appear to be not only seeking to rewrite history but also insisting on Muslims' acceptance of their version of Indian history.

Revival and Redefinition of Indian
National Identity: Hindu Rashtra

The revival and reassertion of Hindu nationalism in the 1980s not only has led to the rejection of the Nehruvian concept of secularism but also is directed toward actually redefining Indian national identity.

The concept of Hindu *Rashtra* (nation) is considered the logical product of this movement. Historically, the people living in the region east of the river *Sindhu* (Indus) are called Hindus, whatever their religion. Used in this sense, the term *Hindu* does not denote religion. Vasant Sathe, a former member of Indira and Rajiv Gandhi's cabinets, asserted recently that "all the citizens of Hindustan are Hindus. . . . Hindu does not mean religion; rather, it signifies nationality."[44] But it is much more than simply the description of the inhabitants of Hindustan.

Hindu nationalism, according to its proponents, advocates a single homogeneous national identity for the whole country,[45] rejecting the idea that India is a multi-national state. To them, the term "Hindu" has geo-cultural connotations. According to Seshadri, the Hindu nationalist ideo-logue, "It denotes the national way of life here. All those who feel firmly committed to the unity and sanctity of our country and our people, and look upon our great forebears as their national heroes and sublime values of our cultural life as their points of veneration and emulation, are all Hindus."[46] Thus, in practice, the concept of Hindu *rashtra* becomes virtually identical to Hinduism as a religion. The primary task of its proponents is to unify the Hindu society by de-emphasizing the caste and sectarian divisions existing in Hinduism.

For Hindu nationalists the political-cum-territorial concept of nationalism without its Hindu cultural content, as advocated by Nehru and his associates, is incapable of sanctifying the unity of the country. For them the secular concept of Indian national identity, based upon an alien ideology of socialism, is limited to the state and lacks those psychic elements which bind the people as a nation. They argue that it is not common economic interests that give birth to a nation; people's love for their land is based on common traditions and *chiti* (culture). For the Hindu nationalists, Bharat, or India, is not only their motherland; it is also their holy land.

Hindu nationalists believe that the groups that make up a nation come together for a purpose. They represent a community of projects and desires. They have an ideal and a vision for the future. Such essentials for nation-making are provided by the culture based upon peoples' shared experience. Since they believe that India's struggle for freedom was rooted in Hindu spirituality,[47] for them genuine decolonization, and not simple material advancement, was the goal of the independence movement. Therefore, restoring the cultural content of Indian national identity brings it back to its original intent.

Those of different faiths, such as Islam or Christianity, need not fear discrimination, Hindu nationalists insist, because Hindu *rashtra* is not a theocratic concept but is cultural in content. Hindus have no single church and Hinduism does not bestow any religious authority on the state.

The concept of Hindu *rashtra*, as the foundation of Hindu nationalism, does not promote the development of authoritarianism. Rather, it calls for the country to have a democratic system of government, with equal voting rights. The fear of domination of the minority by the majority is "just a phantom propped up by interested politicians and religious fanatics to maintain their separatist grip upon their faithful."[48] Politicians tend to treat the minorities as vote banks; they do not take care of their economic and educational needs.

In their perception of minorities' place in a Hindu-dominated India, Hindu nationalists seem to contradict themselves. While they say that Hinduism "in its pristine form . . . create[s] a climate of plurality which enables all religions to thrive," at the same time they demand that in the interest of national unity minorities respect the wishes of the majority as well as other minorities.[49] Furthermore, democracy is not simply the granting of equal voting rights; it also implies the acceptance of cultural diversity, which Hindu nationalists are unwilling to do.

Hindu ideologues, to stress their political moderation, state that they perceive nationalism only as a stage in human evolution.

> A stage for the self-expansion of the human spirit, it is not for self-aggrandizement. It is a journey toward selflessness; towards sacrifice for the larger whole. . . . But the nation itself does not represent the end of the journey. That is a major stage, from which [a person's spirit] moves on to entire mankind. . . .[50]

In theory such a desire of Hindus for the unity of the universe may be valid. In practice, however, Hindu nationalism, not unlike other ideologies of nationalism, is narrow and seeks unity among those who believe in specific values and norms of behavior. This becomes evident when we look at the *Hindutva*, the key concept of Hindu national ideology.

Hindutva or Indianness is the "sum total of the ever-evolving qualities and attributes, moral and ethical values, and the attitude of mind which all make the inhabitants of this country a distinctive entity by themselves."[51] In theory the term *Hindutva* may not mean identification with the values of the followers of a particular religion. In its practical application, however, it would be hard to deny that dominant attributes of *Hindutva* are found in the people who constitute the overwhelming majority of the population of the country. They also have "the largest and unbroken history of civilizational and cultural evolution of an essentially indigenous nature."[52] In this way *Hindutva* acts as an exclusionary force in Indian society rather than universalistic and open to the values of other cultures.

Integral Humanism: An Alternate to
Nehru's Socialism?

In the areas of economic organization; relations between the individual, state, and society; and limits on state authority, Hindu nationalists have frequently referred to the philosophy of Integral Humanism as developed by Deendayal Upadhyaya. Upadhyaya rejects Nehruvian economic policies and industrialization on the grounds that they were borrowed uncritically from the West, in complete disregard of the cultural and spiritual heritage of the country.

There is a need, according to Upadhyaya, to strike a balance between the Bharatiya (Indian) and Western thinking in view of the dynamic nature of the society and the cultural heritage of the country. India should seek a reconciliation of spiritualism and materialism, he said.

The Nehruvian model of economic development, emphasizing the increase of material wealth through rapid industrialization, has unleashed unbridled consumerism in Indian society. Not only has this ideology of development created social disparities and regional imbalances in economic growth, but it has failed to alleviate poverty in the country. Thus, according to Hindu nationalists, it has also failed to achieve distributive justice, which was its professed objective.

The philosophy of Integral Humanism, like Gandhism, opposes unbridled consumerism, since such an ideology is alien to Indian culture. This traditional culture stresses putting restraints on one's desires and advocates contentment rather than ruthless pursuit of material wealth.[53]

A centralized system of economic planning has led to the growth of a huge bureaucracy in control of the economy, leading to widespread corruption and erosion of traditional norms of behavior. The Congress or the centrist political parties have exercised monopolistic control over state power since independence, practicing amoral politics, in which the goal of social justice was replaced by personal aggrandizement.[54]

The Hindu nationalists argue that recent developments show that all political and economic ideologies, such as capitalism, communism, and socialism, which originated in the West have failed to meet humankind's material and spiritual needs wherever they have been applied. As one critic noted, "Man is a conglomerate of body, intellect and soul. . . . Along with the material development we have to consider the moral and spiritual development also."[55] Western political and economic models which emphasize only material development cannot serve as guideposts for Indian society, say the Hindu nationalists. India needs to develop its own model of industrialization and economic growth suited to its own culture.

Upadhyaya stated:

> Really speaking, every nation should think of its own ethos. Freedom without it has no meaning. Every nation wants to live a happy and prosperous life according to its own nature and that is the motive behind its intense desire for freedom. The nation that tries to follow thought and action discordant with its own nature meets with disaster. This is the reason why our nation has been caught up in a whirlpool of difficulties.[56]

Socialism and communism, according to Hindu nationalists, deny individual freedom, whereas capitalism promotes profit motives and self-aggrandizement. Unchecked, rapid industrialization is also unsuitable for maintaining an ecological balance.

The philosophy of Integral Humanism, following the essentials of Bharatiya *samskriti* (culture), seeks to discover the unity underlying diversity. It takes an integrated view of both the society and the individual and finds that basically there is no conflict between them. Without the individual there is no society, and without society the individual can hardly exist.

In Hinduism an individual's moral and material progress is possible only when he is guided by *Dharma*. *Dharma* is not religion, as the term is frequently translated in English. *Dharma* means "those eternal principles that sustain an entity—individual or corporate—and abiding by which, that entity can achieve material prosperity in this world and spiritual salvation in the next."[57] In the context of society *Dharma* is defined as "the enunciation of all those duties and obligations of everyone, both as an individual and as a member of the society, at different stages in life and different roles for the attainment of the ultimate purpose of human existence."[58]

In the context of politics, *Dharma* sustains the individual, society, state, and the rulers. *Dharma rajya*, which Integral Humanists believe ought to be the goal of the Indian state, is rule of law, in which individuals have both rights and obligations. Such a rule accepts religious diversity, displaying respect for the teachings of all religions.

The philosophy of Integral Humanism recognizes the urge for freedom, on the part of both individuals and the nation, as natural. Democracy (*loktantra*) is a device to uphold people's rights. But it cannot be confined only to political participation to safeguard the people's rights; it needs to be extended to economic and social spheres, too.

The need for state regulation of the economy to achieve certain goals and to protect the national interests is recognized by Hindu nationalists, but centralization of economic and political power is opposed. Centralization of authority, whether in the economy or in the polity, is inimical both to human freedom and to the operation of a democracy. As one writer put it, "Decentralization is highly congenial to the all-round development of human personality."[59] All development plans have to be centered around the welfare of man. It is on these grounds that large-scale industrialization is opposed. Both the Western and Indian experience of industrialization, according to this group, shows that large-scale industries lead to the concentration of wealth and to the development of monopolies.

Economic order, according to the philosophy of Integral Humanism, should be directed toward providing a minimum standard of living. Any surplus created beyond meeting the minimum standard of living should be guided by the culture of the society and directed toward the general welfare of citizens worldwide. Excess production and consumption lead to social and ecological degeneration. Emphasis ought to be on saving rather than spending, and on reconstruction and preservation rather than on excessive consumption of resources. It is the duty of the state or the society to provide meaningful employment to all able-bodied citizens of the country.   As a result, economic development policies ought to be labor—rather than capital—intensive.

In technological development, the emphasis of Integral Humanism is on appropriate technology, self-reliance, and *swadeshi* (indigenousness). India should develop its own technology, which is suitable to its own environment and culture, rather than borrow blindly from other societies. In all areas, from economic thinking to capital formation to management and production, Indians should be guided by the ethos of their own culture.[60]

The philosophy of Integral Humanism, as developed by Deendayal Upadhyaya, is offered by the BJP and Hindu nationalists as an alternative to Nehru's socialism. Nehru's ideology, to them, represented cultural domination of India by the West both economically and politically, whereas Upadhyaya's thinking is closer to the Gandhian world view and thus genuinely Bharatiya (Indian).[61]   The revival and reassertion of Integral Humanism by the Hindu nationalists in recent years may also be considered a reassertion of the Bharatiya cultural identity, as represented in the initial stages of Indian nationalism.

In presenting Integral Humanism as an alternative model of India's economic and technological development, however, Hindu nationalists contradict themselves on both ideological and practical levels. They advocate acceptance of religious diversity and respect for others' teachings yet, as seen earlier, display little tolerance for non-Hindu minorities, especially for the followers of Islam. They advocate extension of political democracy to economic and social spheres without specifying how such ideals could be achieved.

The whole concept of *Dharma*, as drawn from classical Hindu thought, with its emphasis on the performance of an individual's duties in congruence with his status and occupation in the society, seems inapplicable in a society that is undergoing transformation as fast as is Indian society. In fact it is a restatement of the Hindu concept of *varnashram dharma*, wherein an individual is expected to perform his obligations based upon his caste and stage in life.

Despite Upadhyaya's criticism of capitalism, in reality a large majority of Hindu nationalists are ardent advocates of capitalism and free enterprise. The BJP leadership, as we will see in the following chapters, is committed to the building of a strong and powerful Indian state, highly industrialized and capable of manufacturing modern weapons of war. While paying lip service to the goal of developing its own technology, the BJP would allow the multi-nationals to enter India provided they bring the latest technology. In short, the BJP has accepted the Western version of a modern Indian state short of centralized planning and state control.

Communalism Versus Nationalism

Community, whether organized around religion, sect, *jati*, *biradari*, or caste, has been the basic unit of Indian society. Individuals have traditionally perceived themselves first as members of a community and only then as an ethnic group or nation. The development of consciousness of larger identities based on ethnicity or sub-nationality, along with pan-Indian ideologies of nationalism, is of more recent origin. Pan-Indian ideologies are intended to subsume sectarian identities based upon caste, *jati*, *biradari*, or other sub-groups. Modern Indian history, as stated earlier, seems to show two distinct ideologies of pan-Indian nationalism. Both represent the values of the elite political culture, which are expected to be absorbed by the masses.

In both political parlance and academic discussion, however, the term *communal* is used in a derogatory sense representing narrow sectarian interests. In pre-independence India, political leaders as well as scholars committed to Indian nationalism described the Indian Muslim League as a communal organization. However, for many Marxist and European scholars it represented Muslim nationalism. And in the 1946 elections an overwhelming majority of Indian Muslims voted for the Muslim League in the belief that the creation of Pakistan would fulfill Indian Muslims' nationalist aspirations.

Similarly, the Akali Dal party, representing the Sikhs of India, has often been described as a communal organization by Indian scholars and politicians, whereas many Sikh and Western scholars look upon it as representing the Sikh nationalist aspirations.[62] We believe that in the context of Indian politics the use of terms like *national, communal,* and *sub-national* reflects the ideological predisposition of a person, whether a scholar or a politician.

Identity is a set of ideas defining a person's position in relation to others in the context of a social organization. In a psychological sense, nationalism is indicative of self-definition. A person has multiple identities, and in the course of the changing history of a community or society these identities keep changing. Nationalism is a generalized identity in a society like India's. Thus it is possible to suggest that the essence of such an identity may change with the radical transformation of the image of the society. Such a transformation may be caused by political upheaval, by the rise of a charismatic leader, or by catastrophic events.

For example, in the history of the Indian sub-continent the rise of M.A. Jinnah as the charismatic leader of the Muslim League; the division of India on the basis of religion; the June 1984 army attack on the Golden Temple, the most sacred shrine of the Sikhs; and the December 1992 demolition of the Babri mosque in Ayodhya have brought about drastic transformation in the perception of society by such affected groups as Hindus, Sikhs, and Muslims. Such events may result in the rise of different types of nationalist or sub-nationalist movements. Therefore, we believe that the use of the term *communal* hinders rather than helps in an objective analysis of the various versions of nationalism in India as political phenomena.

In post-independence Indian politics, the dominant elite professed adherence to a rational-secular version of nationalism, with an emphasis on state-controlled centralized economic planning. We believe that an alternate ideology of nationalism, which emphasizes the indigenous religious identities and cultural values as well as decentralization of both economy and polity, is an option in the effort to reshape the character and nature of the Indian political culture.

Whether emphasizing rational-secular norms or indigenous religious and cultural identities in their versions of nationalism, both groups employ the "concept of the state that was only a minor variation of the post-seventeenth century European concept of nation state."[63] Both groups utilize certain symbols and slogans to create a sense of cohesion among different groups and seek to mobilize people belonging to different communities for political purposes.

Agreeing with Karl Mannheim, Ainslie T. Embree says that all ideologies are utopian, nonempirical, and lack grounding in reality.[64] A nationalist ideology based upon secular-rational norms intended to create a sense of national identity, along with a scientific temper, among people who have deep-seated religious beliefs can be as utopian as the ideal of seeking *Dharma rajya* (the rule of law) in a culturally plural society.

It is not surprising that for many Indian intellectuals, of all the post-independence leaders Nehru symbolized the best traditions of Indian nationalism.[65] On the other hand, the Gandhian legacy is described as "remote, distant and steeped in Hindu traditions."[66] In their view, most of the Congress leaders, such as Govind Ballabh Pant and Mohan Lal Saxena in states like Uttar Pradesh and Bihar, were virtually communalist, favoring Hindus over Muslims.[67] Subsequently, in the early 1980s the Congress moved to the right and in the 1984 elections, it openly adopted the rhetoric of majoritarian communalism (Hindu nationalists).[68] Thus, it could be argued that Nehru's ideology of Indian nationalism proved to be a short-lived utopia. The basic flaw in this approach is its perception of religious and cultural identities as primitive hurdles to the progress of mankind or as mere symbols used by the ruling classes to ensure their hegemony.[69]

This is a very superficial view of the role of religion. Many people do believe in certain higher values, which may or may not be based upon rational principles. The state can play only a limited role in the secularization of the society. On the other hand, no state, especially the Indian state in its present form, is in a position to teach higher moral values to a citizenry that follows numerous different religions.

Furthermore, group identity, whether based upon culture or religion, in the words of E. Erickson, "points to an individual's link with the unique values, fostered by a unique history, of his people . . . identity of something in the individual's core with an essential aspect of group's inner coherence."[70] Despite an enormous increase in the power of the state, history demonstrates that the state is incapable of destroying identities based upon religion and culture.

At the same time it should be recognized:

It is the great power of religious belief and affiliation for the individual that has underpinned the great power of religion in the social and political history of every society. It has served as both a stabilizing and mobilizing force in the pursuit of mixed religious and non-religious ends by those in power. Indeed, the meshing of religious and political beliefs and institutions is a characteristic common to almost all cultures.[71]

Hindu nationalists seek to develop an ideology that will fit the psychocultural dispositions of the majority of the people. To characterize such a mix of religion and nationalism as communalism, or fundamentalism, and something reactionary and opposed to modernization and social change, is grossly to misunderstand its nature.[72]

National identities can be formed on territorial, cultural, ethnic, or religious bases or on a combination of these, depending upon the emotional intensity that the people attach to a particular aspect of a nation. For Hindus, India is not only their motherland, it is also their sacred land. It is the land of their saints and sages; it is where their sacred rivers flow and where their history was created. Hindu places of pilgrimage located in the four corners of the country help in creating common cultural and religious bonds among the Hindus despite their regional, ethnic, and linguistic differences.[73] Hindu nationalists emphasize this common cultural and religious bond to create an emotional attachment to the territories of India and in turn to produce a cohesive Hindu society. Internal cohesion and national unity are considered preconditions for modernization.

However, such an ideology of nationalism would play a divisive role in a culturally and socially plural society like India's. It tends to generate an anti-minority neurosis, raising doubts about the loyalties of such minorities as the Muslims, Christians, and Jews who do not consider India their sacred land. A more valid argument against Hindu nationalism is that its proponents either make selective use of Hindu religious heritage or distort it to suit their political goals. Gandhi was able to meet the challenge of such divisive ideologies without denouncing religion.

Ideologies, Political Power, and Political Parties

It is political parties that use ideology to gain political power. An ideology provides political parties the glue needed to bind diverse groups of people to the cause of building a base of support. Ideologies promise to create new visions, provide blueprints for a new society, a kind of utopia, and appeal to the emotions of common people. In turn, politicians use ideologies and political parties to gain offices, thus advancing their personal and collective goals. In the real world of politics, therefore, we agree with D.W. Brogan that it is an "erroneous assumption that parties are and must be doctrinal bodies."[74]

Political elites are likely to interpret an ideology from different perspectives. The ideology of Hindu nationalism is no exception. Such diverse interpretations are likely to lead to the formation of different ideological factions.

Furthermore, the experience of political parties in the older as well as in the new democracies shows that parties sometimes tailor their convictions to the demands of the particular political contest,[75] or change their ideological strategies to meet electoral needs. The degree of a political party's ideological flexibility, however, is dependent upon the party's age and on its electoral and administrative experience.

In Indian politics, as implied in the preceding pages, the Congress party has represented the Nehruvian ideology of Indian nationalism. There was among its leaders a degree of commitment to "open discussion, tolerance of diversity, probity, the need for reform to promote greater social justice and so forth."[76] Through its clear acceptance of the cultural plurality and through its socio-economic reform programs it was able to build a widespread support base, effectively preventing the emergence of other major political organizations to challenge it.[77] Starting with the 1970s, however, an amoral pursuit of politics in India not only rendered the Congress party an organization "held together largely by opportunism—by the power, patronage, and money that public office can command"[78] but brought into the public other leadership that was willing to appeal to the sentiments of Hindu nationalism.

The decline and degeneration of the Congress party in the 1980s, in both its organization and ideology, provided an opportunity for the Bharatiya Janata Party, the proponent of Hindu nationalism, to challenge the Congress and its political ideology.

We should recognize, however, that even when accepting the broad premises of the ideology of Hindu nationalism, the BJP leaders differ both in their methods of achieving their goals and in their interpretations of the ideology. The primary goal of parties is political power. Without such power a party is incapable of implementing its program, whatever its ideology. In its quest for political power, therefore, the BJP, like other ideologically oriented political parties, is expected to maintain a degree of ideological cohesion as well as flexibility of strategy.

Notes

1. Alexis de Tocqueville, *Democracy in America* (New York, Alfred A. Knopf, Inc., 1945), Vol. II, p. 12.

2. Robert Lane, *Political Ideology* (New York, The Free Press of Glenco, 1962), p. 15.

3. Rajni Kothari, "Integration and Exclusion in Indian Politics," *Economic and Political Weekly*, October 22, 1988, p. 2223.

4. Charles H. Heimsath, *Indian Nationalism and Hindu Social Reforms* (Princeton, NJ, Princeton University Press, 1964), p. 139.

5. Ashis Nandy, *At the Edge of Psychology* (New Delhi, Oxford University Press, 1980), pp. 57-58.

6. *Ibid.*, p. 60.

7. Quoted in Dennis Dalton, "The Concept of Politics and Power in India's Ideological Traditions," in J.R. Wilson and Dennis Dalton (eds.), *The States of South Asia: Problem of National Integration* (London, C. Hurst and Co., 1982), p. 117.

8. *Ibid.*

9. Sri Aurobindo, *On Nationalism* (Pondicherry, Sri Aurobindo Ashram, 1965), p. 15.

10. Partha Chatterjee, *Nationalist Thought and the Colonial World* (London, Zed Press, 1965), pp. 54-84.

11. Jalaul Haq, *Nation and Nation-Worship in India* (New Delhi, Genuine Publication, 1992), p. 8.

12. *Ibid.*, p. 244.

13. Jawaharlal Nehru, *Discovery of India* (New York, Doubleday, 1946), Chapter 1.

14. Support for this view is found in the writings of such Western theorists as Leonard Binder, Lucian Pye, James Coleman, Sidney Verba, Joseph LaPalombara and Myron Weiner, *Crises and Sequences in Political Development* (Princeton, Princeton University Press, 1971); Cyril E. Black, *The Dynamic of Modernization* (New York, Harper and Row, 1966); Dankwart A. Rostow, *A World of Nations* (Washington, Brookings, 1967); Samuel P. Huntington, *Political Order in Changing Societies* (New Haven, Yale University Press, 1968); Neil J. Smelser, "Process of Social Change," in Neil J. Smelser (ed.), *Sociology* (New York, Wiley and Sons, 1967); and S.N. Eisenstadt, *Modernization, Protest and Change* (Englewood Cliffs, N.J., Prentice Hall, 1966).

15. Girilal Jain, "A Turning Point in History," *Manthan*, Vol. 13, No. 1-2 (May-June 1991), p. 20.

16. *Ibid.*, p. 21.

17. Arend Lejpharl, "Typologies of Democratic Systems," *Comparative Political Studies* 1 (1968), pp. 3-33, and *Democracy in Plural Societies: A Comparative Exploration* (New Haven, Yale University Press, 1977), chapters 1-3.

18. C. B. Macpherson, *The Life and Time of Liberal Democracy* (New York, Oxford University Press, 1977), pp. 79-81.

19. T. N. Madan, "Secularism in Its Place," *Journal of Asian Studies*, 46:4 (November, 1987), pp. 748-49.

20. Bhikhu Parekh, "Nehru and the National Philosophy of India," *Economic and Political Weekly*, January 5-12, 1991, p. 42.

21. Asghar Ali Engineer (ed.), *The Shah Bano Controversy* (New Delhi, Orient Longman, 1987), p. 19.

22. *Hindustan Times*, April 3, 1992, p. 12.

23. Kuldip Nayar, "Separate Personal Law Would Not Dilute Secularism," *Telegraph*, March 15, 1986, p. 6.

24. *Statesman Weekly*, May 17, 1986, p. 12.

25. G. Hossein Razi, "Legitimacy, Religion, and Nationalism in the Middle East," *American Political Science Review*, March 1990, p. 76.

26. Anwar Hussain Syed, *Pakistan: Islam, Politics and National Solidarity* (New York, Praeger Publications, 1982), p. 13. On this issue see also Jerrold D. Green, "Islam, Religiopolitics, and Social Change," *Comparative Studies in Society and History* 27 (1985), pp. 312-322; Daniel Pipes, *In the Path of God: Islam and Political Power* (New York, Basic Books, 1983); Edward Mortimer, *Faith and Power* (New York, Vintage Books, 1983); Edmund Burke III and Ira M. Lapidus (eds.), *Islam, Politics, and Social Movements* (Berkeley, University of California Press, 1988).

27. Chandan Mitra, "Fountainhead of Indian Nationalism," *Manthan*, Vol. 13, No. 1-2 (May-June, 1991), pp. 33-40.

28. Girilal Jain, "A Turning Point," p. 23.

29. *Ibid.* On this point also see Ram Swarup, *Cultural Self-Alienation and Some Problems Hinduism Faces* (New Delhi, Voice of India, 1987), pp. 6-9.

30. Parekh, "Nehru," p. 43.

31. Amar Zutshi, "Politics of Secularism," *Statesman Weekly*, November 22, 1986, p. 12. On this point also see Gurudutt, *Bharat: Gandhi aur Nehru ki chhaya main* (*India in the Shadow of Gandhi and Nehru*) (New Delhi, Bharatiya Sahitya Sadan, 1969), Chapter 1 and *Dharm, samskriti aur rajya (Religion, Culture and the State)* (New Delhi, Bharatiya Sahitya Sadan, 1966), Chapter 4.

32. Harshnarayan, *Sammishra sanskriti aur savradharm-samata pravad* (New Delhi, Bharat-Bharati, 1989), pp. 2-37.

33. *Ibid.*

34. L. K. Advani, "Backward March: The Bane of Minorityism," *Statesman Weekly*, October 29, 1988, p. 12.

35. Ashis Nandy, "Making and Unmaking of Political Cultures in India," in S. N. Eisenstadt, *Post-Colonial Societies* (New York, W.W. Norton, 1972), p. 120.

36. Interview with L. K. Advani, *Sunday Hindustan Times Magazine*, January 19, 1992, pp. 1-22.

37. Interview with L. K. Advani, *Manthan*, Vol.13, No. 1-2 (May-June, 1991), p. 12.

38. Interview with L. K. Advani, *Sunday Hindustan Times Magazine*, January 19, 1992, p. 2.

39. *Ibid.*

40. A. L. Basham, *The Wonder That Was India* (Calcutta, Rupa, 1991), p. 4.

41. Interview with L. K. Advani, *Sunday Hindustan Times Magazine*, January 19, 1992, p. 2.

42. *Manthan*, Vol. 13, No. 1-2 (May-June, 1991), p. 6.

43. *Ibid.*

44. *Organiser*, September 27, 1992, p. 13. Also see A. K. Ray, "Hinduism: A Geo-Cultural Concept," *Manthan*, Vol. 13, No. 1-2 (May-June, 1991), pp. 25-28.

45. H.V. Seshadri, et al. *Why Hindu Rashtra?* (New Delhi, Suruchi Prakashan, 1990), p. 33. Also see C. P. Bhishikar, *Pandit Deendayal: Ideology and Perception: Part V: Concept of Rashtra* (New Delhi, Suruchi Prakashan, 1988), Chapters 1-5.

46. *Ibid.*

47. Ram Swarup, *Cultural Self-Alienation and Some Problems Hinduism Faces* (New Delhi, Voice of India, 1987), p. 3.

48. *Ibid.*

49. Hiranmay Karlekar, "Hinduism and Indian Unity," *Manthan*, Vol. 13, No. 1-2 (May-June, 1991), p. 61.

50. H. V. Seshadri, *Universal Spirit of Hindu Nationalism* (Madras, Vigil, 1991), p. 7.

51. A. K. Ray, "Hinduism: A Geo-Cultural Concept," *Manthan*, Vol. 13, No. 1-2 (May-June, 1991), p. 27.

52. *Ibid.* Also see Prabha Dixit, "The Ideology of Hindu Nationalism," in Thomas Pantham and Kenneth L. Deutsch (eds.), *Political Thought in Modern India* (New Delhi, Sage Publications, 1986), pp. 122-141.

53. Jagdish Shettigarh, "Deendayal ji's Economic Thought and Its Relevance Today," *Organiser*, September 27, 1992, p. 9.

54. James Manor, "Anomie in Indian Politics: Origins and Potential Wider Impact," *Economic and Political Weekly* (Annual Number, 1983), pp. 725-734.

55. V. V. Nene, *Pandit Deendayal Upadhyaya: Ideology and Perception: Part II Integral Humanism* (New Delhi, Suruchi Prakashan, 1988), p. 11. For discussion of Integral Humanism see also Sudhakar Raje (ed.), *Destination* (New Delhi, Deendayal Research Institute, 1978).

56. *Ibid.*, p. 10.

57. *Manthan*, Vol. 12, No. 7-9 (July-September, 1991), p. 10.

58. Bhishikar, *Pandit Deendayal Part V*, p. 32.

59. *Manthan*, Vol. 12, No. 7-9 (July-September, 1991), p. 15.

60. *Ibid.*, pp. 58-59.

61. Richard G. Fox, "Gandhian Socialism and Hindu Nationalism: Cultural Domination in the World System," *Journal of Commonwealth and Comparative Politics*, Vol. 25 (November, 1987), pp. 233-247. Also see P. Parameswaran (ed.), *Gandhi, Lohia and Deendayal* (New Delhi, Deendayal Research Institute, 1978).

62. Joyce Pettigrew, "In Search of New Kingdom of Lahore," *Pacific Affairs* (Spring, 1987), p. 18; "Take Not Arms Against Thy Sovereign," *South Asia Research* (November, 1984); Paul Brass, *Language, Religion and Politics in North India* (London, Cambridge University Press, 1974), p. 277.

63. Ashis Nandy, "The Political Culture of the Indian State," *Daedalus* (Fall, 1989), p. 4.

64. Ainslie T. Embree, *Utopias in Conflict: Religion and Nationalism in Modern India* (Berkeley, University of California Press, 1990), p. 12.

65. Mushirul Hasan, "Adjustment and Accommodation: Muslims After Partition," in K. K. Panikkar (ed.), *Communalism in India: History, Politics and Culture* (New Delhi, Manohar, 1991), p. 75. Also see Rajni Kothari, "Class and Communalism," *Economic and Political Weekly*, December 3, 1988, pp. 2589-2592.

66. Hasan, "Adjustment and Accommodation," p. 75.

67. *Ibid.*, p. 66.

68. Zoya Hasan, "Changing Orientation of the State and the Emergence of Majoritarianism in the 1980s," in Panikkar, *Communalism in India*, pp. 144-45. Also see D. L. Sheth, "Movements, Intellectuals and the State: Social Policy in Nation-Building," *Economic and Political Weekly*, February 22, 1992, pp. 425-432, and Rajni Kothari, "Cultural Context of Communalism in India," *Economic and Political Weekly*, January 14, 1989, pp. 81-85.

69. Randhir Singh, "Communalism and the Struggle Against Communalism: A Marxist View," in Panikkar, *Communalism in India*, p. 119. Also see S. Khan, "Towards a Marxist Understanding of Secularism," *Economic and Political Weekly*, March 7, 1987, pp. 406-408; Romila Thapar, Harbans Mukhia and Bipan Chandra, *Communalism and the Writing*

of Indian History (New Delhi, People's Publishing House, 1984); and Sumanta Banerjee, "Hindutva—Ideology and Social Psychology," *Economic and Political Weekly*, January 19, 1991, pp. 97-101.

70. Quoted in Harold Isaacs, *Idols of the Tribe: Group Identity and Political Change* (Cambridge, MA, Harvard University Press, 1989), p. 32.

71. *Ibid.*, pp. 148-49. On this point also see Daniel Bell, "The Return of the Sacred? The Argument on the Future of Religion," *British Journal Of Sociology*, Vol. 20, No. 4 (December, 1977), pp. 419-448.

72. Embree, *Utopias*, Chapter 1.

73. Surinder Mohan Bhardwaj, *Hindu Places of Pilgrimage: A Study in Cultural Geography* (Berkeley, University of California Press, 1973), Introduction.

74. M. Duverger, *Political Parties* (New York, John Wiley, 1954), p. v.

75. Herbert McClosky, Paul J. Hoffmann, and Rosemary O'Hara, "Issue Conflict and Consensus Among Party Leaders and Followers," *American Political Science Review* (June 1964), p. 406.

76. James Manor, "Anomie in Indian Politics," p. 725.

77. Anil Nauriya, "Indian National Congress: Its Place in Politics," *Economic and Political Weekly*, November 23, 1991, p. 2675.

78. Robert Hardgrave, "India on the Eve of Elections: Congress and the Opposition," *Pacific Affairs* (Fall, 1984), p. 409.

2

The Bharatiya Janata Party: Its Heritage and Leadership

Heritage

In its ideological, organizational, and leadership structure the Bharatiya Janata Party (BJP) is the direct descendant of the Bharatiya Jana Sangh (BJS). The Jana Sangh ideology was based on the traditions of Hindu nationalism, with its emphasis on *Bharatiya samskriti* (Indian culture) and *maryada* (traditions). The Jana Sangh leadership asserted that unlike the Congress, Socialist, and Communist parties, which wished to transform India on the basis of Western economic, philosophical, and political models, their party sought to develop India on the basis of its own vast cultural heritage. However, unlike the Hindu fundamentalist and revivalist parties like the Ram Rajya Parishad, the Jana Sangh believed in the reform-oriented traditions of Bharatiya culture reflected in the reform movements led by such Hindus as Swami Dayanand Sarswati, Swami Vivekananda, and Lokmanya Bal Gangadhar Tilak.

These leaders perceived that to be dynamic, the Bharatiya culture had to adapt itself to face the challenges of modernization, without losing its identity. In the words of Deendayal Upadhyaya:

We find two tendencies working in the society: One accepts the old, which in effect means the existing, as something sacramental, not be questioned and never to be changed; the other denounces everything old and yearns for a change unmindful of the direction and shape it takes. The Jana Sangh disapproves of both these tendencies. Let the past inspire us. But we must be forward looking. Jana Sangh has to become a fit instrument of the Renaissance of our people. We have to lead a movement and not simply build a party.[1]

The Jana Sangh was founded on October 21, 1951, and Dr. Syama Prasad Mookerjee (1901-1953), a distinguished statesman, became its founding president. Even though he was once the president of the Hindu Mahasabha, an organization opposed to the policies of the Congress party, he was invited by prime minister Jawaharlal Nehru to join his cabinet because of his administrative experience and personal integrity.[2] Later on, however, because of policy and ideological differences with Nehru, Dr. Mookerjee resigned from the cabinet and sought to organize an alternative to the Congress party. He felt that the Congress party, under the leadership of Nehru, followed policies designed to appease Pakistan and the Muslim minority in India at the cost of Hindus. In his efforts to organize an alternative to the Congress party he sought the support of the Rashtriya Swayamsevak Sangh (the RSS). Such an organization, he believed, could provide his party a mass base.

The Rashtriya Swayamsevak Sangh, a militant Hindu nationalist organization with a large cadre, was banned by the government of India after the murder of Mahatma Gandhi in 1948. The ban was subsequently lifted when the government could not find any evidence of its linkage with the conspiracy to assassinate Gandhi. The Sangh claimed to be primarily a cultural and social organization. But the ban on its organization and activities, and the treatment of its workers by the government, convinced many of its leaders that, without any influence in politics, the Sangh would be subjected to arbitrary actions in the future by those in power. The top leadership of the RSS was, however, opposed to its conversion into a political party, but it was willing to extend its support to a political party sympathetic to its activities and ideological goals. It provided such support to the new party by permitting its *swayamsevaks* (volunteers) to work for the Jana Sangh in their individual capacities.[3]

Thus, the Jana Sangh and the RSS worked in tandem in various stages of the development of the party. Despite the efforts of many RSS volunteers, the new party was unable to mount a major challenge to the domination of the Congress party, especially in the Hindi-speaking states of north India, where the party initially concentrated its efforts. The party's critics constantly denounced it as a backward-looking communal party with a reactionary political ideology seeking to take India back into the Middle Ages.

The party's electoral performance, though not spectacular, was not disheartening either. In the 1952 elections, when the Jana Sangh entered electoral politics for the first time, it received 3.06 percent of the votes for the Lok Sabha. By the 1967 general elections, it received up to 9.41 percent. In the state legislative elections in 1952, the party secured 2.76 percent of the votes. In 1967, its share went up to 8.77 percent.

The Jana Sangh contested these elections with a major handicap. After the death of Dr. Mookerjee, the BJS did not have nationally known leadership. The party was headed by Mauli Chandra Sharma, who had no national or even regional support base. The party's management was in the hands of Deendayal Upadhyaya, a general secretary of the party. Upadhyaya was a modest person and a dedicated RSS *pracharak* (instructor-propagandist) but had little national exposure.

The steady increase in the percentage of the votes polled by the party was the result of the hard work of its cadre, most of whom came from the ranks of the RSS. Despite these successes, however, the Jana Sangh, because of its strong commitment to the ideology of Hindu nationalism, remained an untouchable of Indian politics; very few political parties were willing to cooperate with it. But, with the 1967 elections, there emerged a multi-party system in India, and "the sheer compulsions of political arithmetic would prompt others to overlook, for the time being, Jana Sangh's untouchability, and have business with it."[4] Consequently, after the 1967 elections, the Jana Sangh joined coalition governments formed in many north Indian states. According to Madhu Limaye:

> In Uttar Pradesh, Bihar and Punjab, *Samyukta Vidhayak Dals* [SVD—United Legislature Parties] were formed, and, in view of the electoral verdict against the Congress, both the Jana Sangh and the Communist Party of India (CPI) agreed to set aside their ideological differences and co-operate in the formation of coalition governments.[5]

Jana Sangh in the Mainstream of Indian Politics

Because of the Jana Sangh's opposition to the Nehruvian model of Indian nationalism, its struggle to enter the mainstream of Indian politics was not easy. Its leadership was, however, willing to adopt a variety of strategies to achieve this goal.

Recognizing the emergence of the multi-party system as the main feature of Indian politics, the Jana Sangh leadership, at first, sought coalition partners. To facilitate the formation of stable governments in states, its working committee invited the opposition parties to join in forming non-Congress governments on the basis of mutually agreed programs.[6] In 1967, therefore, the Jana Sangh participated in united front governments in Bihar, Haryana, Madhya Pradesh, Punjab, and Uttar Pradesh. However, since most of the other non-Congress parties pursued opportunistic policies, its leadership's efforts to create political stability were not very successful, and, as a result, most of the coalition governments in the states were shortlived.

In pursuit of its goal, the party also tried to cultivate social and political relations with prominent leaders of the opposition. The Jana Sangh leaders were candid enough to give credit to socialist leaders, like Ram Manohar Lohia and Jayaprakash Narayan, for helping their party break out of its political isolation.[7] Although both these leaders were aware of the plural-istic nature of Indian society and were committed to religious tolerance, they were realistic enough to recognize the importance of the dedication and discipline of the Jana Sangh and the RSS workers. Probably, they also thought that by bringing the Jana Sangh into the mainstream of Indian politics, they might modify its militant Hindu nationalism. Whatever the reasons, in the early 1960s, Lohia was instrumental in inducting the Jana Sangh into the anti-Congress camp.

Cooperation and collaboration between Jayaprakash Narayan and the leaders of the Jana Sangh and the RSS took shape after the 1971 national and 1972 state electoral sweeps of the Indira Gandhi-led Congress party. The massive electoral victories of the Congress party brought about drastic change in the nature of Indian political culture. A pragmatic pursuit of political power by Congress leaders led to widespread corruption and erosion of moral values and traditional ties based upon community and kinship. Politics became dominated by the so-called political mercenaries, among whom formation of amoral political alliances was common.[8] For this new breed of politicians, in the words of Ashis Nandy:

> Electoral successes and failures and political office are a matter of life and death. Such persons are always willing to go all out in politics. In fact, they enter politics not, as in the case of liberals and the radicals produced by the middle classes, to realize some particular vision of good politics, but to openly use politics to improve their own and their family's social status, mobility and more generally, their life chances.[9]

The Jana Sangh leadership, supported by the RSS, favored value-based politics and was highly critical of the pragmatic politicians of the centrist political parties.

In 1973, middle-class discontent with the growth of this type of political culture led to political agitation in different parts of the country. The Jana Sangh leaders saw an opportunity to enter the mainstream of Indian politics through these movements. The first such agitation was the student-led *Navnirman* (reconstructive) movement in Gujarat, which was joined by the Jana Sangh and the Akhil Bharatiya Vidyarthi Parishad (ABVP). The Jana Sangh members of the legislature resigned their seats and joined the agitation, demanding dissolution of the state assembly[10] and the dismissal of the corrupt state government of Chimanbhai Patel.

Subsequently, the Jana Sangh extended its support to Narayan's agitation for the dismissal of the corrupt Congress government in Bihar and his call for *sampoorn kranti* (total revolution). For the Jana Sangh and the RSS, the Jayaprakash Narayan (JP)-led movement provided an excellent opportunity to prove their credentials for their value-based politics. In the words of Nana Deshmukh, "India's politics saw a resurgence of morality when JP launched his movement. It was the moral force behind the movement which was the real catalyst."[11] Although many opposition parties such as the Socialists and the Congress (O) (Organization: stands for the faction opposed to Indira Gandhi) had joined the JP movement, it was the "Jana Sangh [which] had plunged itself into the movement in full force. It was the RSS which provided much of the cadre for the agitation."[12]

To facilitate its entry into the mainstream of Indian politics, the Jana Sangh leadership suggested creating an "institutionalized arrangement which people can look up to as an alternative instrument for the country's governance."[13] Instead of creating a unified party of all the groups participating in the JP movement, it advocated joint group actions on the basis of common programs. Once a common program was formed, all these groups and the parties participating in the agitation could constitute a joint front inside and outside of the Parliament for policy formulations and for electoral contests.[14] The Jana Sangh was unwilling to dissolve itself; for its leadership the preferred model was the *Jana Morcha* (People's Front) of Gujarat. In May 1975, all the opposition parties participating in the *Navnirman* movement, under the leadership of Morarji Desai, came together, made seat adjustments, contested elections jointly, and defeated the Indira Gandhi-led Congress party in Gujarat.

Gandhi's imposition of Emergency Rule in June 1975 and the arrest of the opposition leaders, including the leaders of the Jana Sangh and the RSS, however, brought an abrupt end to all efforts at forming a joint front or a single united party consisting of all the non-Communist opposition parties.

Perhaps it was the common experience of incarceration during the Emergency (June 1975-February 1977), or the pressure of public opinion, or the moral authority of ailing leader Jayaprakash Narayan and the possibility of defeating the Indira Gandhi-led Congress party in the forthcoming elections, or all of them, which forced the opposition parties to contest elections jointly. The opposition parties' victories in the March 1977 elections resulted in the hasty formation of a single united party called the Janata Party, through the merger of such parties as the Bharatiya

Lok Dal, Socialist party, Congress (O), the Congress for Democracy (CFD), the Jana Sangh, and others.

If the goal of the Jana Sangh leadership was to join the mainstream of Indian politics and to end its political isolation, the party was successful. The Jana Sangh not only had the largest contingent of the Janata Party MPs in the Parliament but also had three cabinet positions. Atal Bihari Vajpayee, L.K. Advani, and Brij Lal Varma, three senior leaders of the Jana Sangh, were given the portfolios of foreign affairs, information and broadcasting, and industry. By all accounts, their performance in their respective departments was highly rated.

Subsequently, in the June 1977 state legislative elections, the Jana Sangh component of the Janata Party secured absolute majorities in Madhya Pradesh and Delhi. It also constituted the single largest group in Rajasthan and Himachal Pradesh. As a result, Jana Sangh members were elected the chief ministers of three states, Madhya Pradesh, Rajasthan, and Himachal Pradesh. The Jana Sangh elements of the Janata Party also played a significant role in such states as the U.P., Bihar, Haryana, and to a lesser extent, Orissa.

The disparate elements which constituted the Janata Party represented different and often contradictory subcultures of Indian politics. The members of the Jana Sangh, however, not only had ideological cohesion but also displayed a high degree of discipline and the ability to subordinate their personal interests and political ambitions for a particular cause or in the interest of party unity. They tended to be more loyal to institutions than to personalities. On the other hand, members of the Lok Dal, Congress (O), or the Socialists had often diffused and ambiguous ideological commitments and also tended to be more opportunistic. They showed less loyalty to the institutions and principles than the Jana Sangh group and depended heavily on powerful factional leaders for their political fortunes. Thus emerged the phenomenon of personality-oriented politics. This group represented the pragmatic and power-oriented political sub-culture which came to dominate Indian politics at that time.

From the beginning, therefore, the Janata Party was plagued by internal conflicts. These conflicts were centered around the political ambitions of the powerful personalities of Charan Singh, Morarji Desai, and Jagjivan Ram, all former Congressmen. All of them aspired to be the prime minister of the country as well as the leader of the party. Since there was constant struggling among these three leaders for the top position, the Jana Sangh contingent of the MPs represented a solid bloc of votes, able to tip the balance in favor of one or the other contestants, and its leaders were dragged into this power struggle.

When the no-holds-barred power struggle degenerated into a conflict of personal political ambitions, the different actors involved tried to disguise their ambitions in ideological terms. The Jana Sangh had first accepted Morarji Desai as the leader of the party and the prime minister of the country. When Charan Singh challenged Desai's leadership, however, the Jana Sangh accepted Jagjivan Ram, rather than Singh, as the leader of the party and potential prime minister. This led the followers of Singh to cause a split within the Janata Party. The political battle brought down the Desai government and raised questions about the "secular" credentials of the Jana Sangh.

Since a large number of the Jana Sangh contingent of MPs came from the ranks of the RSS or were still associated with its activities, the followers of Charan Singh objected to their "dual membership." They branded the RSS a Hindu communal organization and claimed that any association of the Jana Sangh MPs with the RSS compromised the secular character of the Janata Party. Singh's contingent charged that the political activities of the Jana Sangh MPs within the Janata Party were controlled by the RSS leadership. The Jana Sangh MPs countered that the RSS was purely a cultural organization and many Janata Party members also belonged to numerous other cultural organizations as well.

A more important fact, however, was that these issues were never raised either during elections or at the time of the merger of the Jana Sangh into the Janata Party. They were raised only later when the struggle for power within the party became intense. It has been correctly pointed out that "The Jana Sangh cohesiveness, not the RSS manipulation, was the problem. The Jana Sangh group acted as a unit, and this capability enhanced its potential to assert power because other groups were not nearly so united."[15]

The Jana Sangh leadership had a broader agenda than just joining the mainstream of Indian politics. It also sought to change its image and extend its appeal beyond the Hindi-speaking states. The members accepted Morarji Desai as the party leader not just because he was chosen by Jayaprakash Narayan but also because he was looked upon as an elder statesman, had a national reputation, and came from a non-Hindi-speaking state. Charan Singh was recognized as only a regional leader, with a narrow caste-oriented power base in north India.

When Desai resigned, the Jana Sangh accepted Jagjivan Ram, a former untouchable, as their leader. Ram had extensive administrative experience and held several important positions in various post-independence cabinets at the national level. He was also recognized as a shrewd and flexible politician who could provide a stable government at the national level. By accepting an ex-untouchable, the Jana Sangh leadership also wished to demonstrate that it was not restricted to upper-caste leaders but could also work with the political elites originating from the lower castes.

The efforts of the Jana Sangh leadership to stay in the mainstream of Indian politics and to establish its secular credentials did not pay many dividends, however. Even after the split of the Janata Party and the revival of the Bharatiya Lok Dal (BLD) by Charan Singh, the Jana Sangh continued to be part of the Janata Party, which was then headed by Chandra Shekhar. In January 1980, when India held its seventh general elections, the Jana Sangh group contested the elections as part of the Janata Party. That party was humiliated at the polls by the Congress (I), winning only thirty-one seats compared to the 203 it held when the party split in 1979. In 1977, the Jana Sangh contingent had won ninety-three seats in the general elections; in 1980 it captured only sixteen. Such a pathetic electoral performance forced the different groups within the Janata Party to rethink their strategies. It was public disgust with the performance of the different factions of the Janata Party that led to its defeat.

Nevertheless, led by Ram, the many former Congressmen who dominated the Janata Party leadership were not hesitant to find scapegoats. These leaders blamed their party's association with the Jana Sangh and the RSS groups for diluting its secular image, resulting in the loss of Muslim and lower caste votes and leading to the massive defeat of the party. Apparently building a permanent political alliance of diverse groups into a viable political party could not be achieved without ideological cohesion or an agreement based on a minimum common program. But the people who came together to form this alliance had diametrically opposite personalities, goals, and motivations, and they were products of different cultures. Therefore, it was not surprising that the Jana Sangh group bolted the Janata Party and founded a party of its own.

Founding of the Bharatiya Janata Party

The fall of the Janata Party was not unexpected, and its failure did not terminate the Hindu nationalists' quest for a broader base in Indian politics. The revival of the Jana Sangh would have been a step backward because its support base was confined to the high caste, urban middle class of the Hindi-speaking states of north and central India. Therefore, to emphasize the continuation of real Janata traditions, both in ideology and political aspirations, the new party was named the Bharatiya Janata Party. A deliberate effort was made by the leadership of the new party to distance itself from the legacy of the Jana Sangh. In order to capture political power, the

Hindu nationalists needed to broaden their electoral reach on both a geographic and demographic basis.

The new party sought to build a new image through its ideological rhetoric. This change, in both its ideology and strategy, was prompted by its recent political experience. Leaders like Jayaprakash Narayan and Morarji Desai had considerable impact on the thinking of its leadership. In his inaugural address delivered in December 1980 in Bombay, for instance, Atal Bihari Vajpayee, the founding president of the party, stressed that the Bharatiya Janata Party was not simply a new name for the former Jana Sangh and added that it represented the inspirations of Narayan.[16]

In addition, to distance the new party from the behavior of former Janata Party leaders like Charan Singh and Raj Narain, Vajpayee stressed the need for value-based politics. He said, "I believe that the country's crisis is essentially a moral crisis. The biggest curse of our life is that moral values have given way to self-seeking and power-lust, and politics has become a pure power game."[17] He held that this moral decay had also permeated the Indian society. In order to rebuild both the society and the polity, they needed to resurrect the programs and policies advocated by Mahatma Gandhi, Jayaprakash Narayan, and Pandit Deendayal Upadhyaya. These men had sought to focus the nation's development strategy to benefit the weakest sections of the society by removing social inequality. To achieve such a goal, Vajpayee called upon the new party to mobilize the "poor peasantry, workers, the Harijans, the tribals, and other exploited sections of the population."[18]

In a bold attempt to depart from the chauvinistic Hindu nationalism of the Jana Sangh and to present itself in more moderate and humanistic guise, the BJP leadership adopted Gandhian socialism as the cornerstone of its new political ideology. Unlike socialism based upon Marxism, which uses a materialistic interpretation of history foreign to Indian cultural traditions, many believe Gandhian socialism fits the Indian cultural milieu better because it is based upon the spiritual heritage of India. A scheme of economic distribution to prevent exploitation of human by human should not be value-neutral or scientific as Marxism claims; rather, it should be based upon ethical and moral principles. The leadership rejected Marxism because it condoned violence and unchecked concentration of power in the state. Since independence, under the Nehruvian plan for political and economic development, wealth and productivity had increased; nevertheless, Vajpayee pointed out that increased productivity had not led to an equitable distribution of wealth.

During this period, there had been an enormous increase in the power of the Indian state and an unprecedented extension of bureaucratic control over various aspects of civil society. The leaders of the new party asserted that both Marxism and capitalism are based upon the exploitation of human by human. If capitalism creates inequality in society, Marxism denies individual freedom. The Gandhian concept of trusteeship provides an alternative model of economic and political democracy that can lead to an end of the exploitation. Reconciliation of freedom and equality, according to the BJP, are possible only under Gandhian socialism. Gandhism advocates decentralization of economic and political powers, revitalization of the representative institutions, especially at the local level, participatory democracy, and reduction in the size of the state bureaucracy.

To further modify the radical thrust of militant Hindu nationalism, the BJP leadership also committed itself to nationalism and national integration, democracy, positive secularism, and value-based politics. These five commitments were stressed as the striking features of the new party, distinguishing it from the Congress.[19]

According to the BJP leadership, the Congress party represented the denial of democracy, as demonstrated by its imposition of Emergency Rule in India in 1975, its policy of appeasement of the minorities and thus distortion of secularism, its debasement of Indian politics by tolerating corruption in public life, its unprincipled pursuit of power, and the introduction of consumerism in disregard of India's cultural traditions. The BJP asserted that "Secularism of the Congress has been totally immoral and opportunistic and a fraud played on the people of this country because it increasingly communalized the Indian politics."[20]

Reflecting these five commitments, the party leadership expressed its willingness to cooperate with all political parties to help the poor masses of India. In this way the leaders indicated that even though the BJP was ready to be flexible on specific policy issues, it was not ready to compromise on such fundamental issues as the territorial integrity of the country and its opposition to authoritarianism and political corruption.

Since the primary goal of parties is to win political power, however, it is not unusual for party leadership to keep modifying its ideological rhetoric with the changing political environment. It is in the leadership structure and recruitment patterns that we find the continuation of its linkages with its Jana Sangh and RSS heritage.

Leadership and Recruitment Patterns

To understand the nature of the BJP, its links with the past, its inner workings, and the depth of its commitment to old or new ideological rhetoric, it is necessary to give brief biographical descriptions of its top national leaders.

Atal Bihari Vajpayee is one of the best known national leaders of the BJP. A powerful orator, a versatile and enduring politician, and a charismatic personality, Vajpayee was able to convince his reluctant party members, in the Bombay session of the BJP, to accept his Gandhian socialism and humanistic liberalism as the new political creed of the party in order to broaden the base of the BJP.

A founding member of the Bharatiya Jana Sangh, he never gave the impression of being a spokesman for Hindu fundamentalists or Hindu chauvinism despite his long and close association with the RSS. Vajpayee was the president of the Jana Sangh from 1968 to 1973; earlier he had held the position of general secretary. From 1957 to 1977 he was also the leader of the Jana Sangh parliamentary party.

Born in 1926, in a Brahmin family from Gwalior (Madhya Pradesh), Vajpayee was educated in Victoria (now Laxmibai) College of Gwalior and D.A.V. (Dayanand Anglo Vedic) College of Kanpur, where he earned a Master of Arts. He started his political career as a journalist and served as editor of various Hindi language fortnightly and monthly magazines or newspapers, including *Rashtra-Dharma*, *Panchajanya*, and *Veer Arjun*, all of them associated with Hindu nationalist organizations. His first real encounter with politics came when he served as private secretary to Dr. Syama Prasad Mookerjee, the founder of the Jana Sangh.

Vajpayee was first elected to the Lok Sabha, the lower house of the Indian Parliament, in 1957. After he was defeated in 1984 for a seat in the lower house, he was elected to the upper house of the Parliament, Rajaya Sabha, in 1986. A skilled parliamentarian gifted with a sense of humor, a rare quality for an Indian politician, Vajpayee has earned the respect of his colleagues, in both his own party and the opposition. It was during his term as the Janata government minister for external affairs that he displayed his flexibility, diplomatic sophistication, and administrative abilities. Vajpayee was frequently mentioned as a potential prime minister, who, on the basis of his personality and mass appeal, could challenge even a popular prime minister like Indira Gandhi.

Vajpayee's ideological liberalism and political flexibility have often been misunderstood by both his own party members and his opponents. Subramanian Swamy, a Harvard-educated economist and a former colleague of Vajpayee, has commented that "Vajpayee is as wishy-washy as Nehru was. I don't think he has any ideology."[21] Many political observers, however, find Vajpayee neither deceitful nor underhanded.[22] He is a simple and straightforward person who has grown into an astute and mature observer of Indian politics and thus is able to make realistic adjustments in his political strategy. In this process he has not, however, given up his strong commitment to Hindu nationalism. In a recent interview, he stated that *Hindutva* is the essence of Indian nationhood, and he believes that "there is no difference between *Hindutva* and being Indians . . . [as the very] basis of Bharatiyata [Indianness] is *Hindutva*."[23]

In June 1993 Vajpayee became the leader of the opposition in the Lok Sabha, replacing L. K. Advani.

Lal Krishan Advani is a close associate of Vajpayee and a skillful political strategist who, though lacking the charisma of Vajpayee, has demonstrated a remarkable ability to mobilize the masses. Advani also came from the ranks of the RSS and held key positions in the Jana Sangh, general secretary and president of the party, before joining the Janata Party, holding a cabinet position in the Janata government of 1977. Janardan Thakur observed:

> The man who has really helped gain a greater respectability for the Jana Sangh constituent of the Janata party without ever projecting himself is Lal Krishan Advani, by far the cleanest and straightest leader in Indian politics. Clean, sophisticated, business-like, mild-looking, but firm when needed, the Minister for Information and Broadcasting is almost a freak in today's political world.[24]

Vajpayee is considered to be a poet and, as some of his younger colleagues describe him, a visionary and romantic liberal. Advani, on the other hand, is described as blessed with an analytical mind, endowed with enormous powers of logic, and possessing killer instincts, which Vajpayee lacks.[25] Nanaji Deshmukh, an elder statesman of the former Jana Sangh and now a respected social worker, says that Advani "has never been a self-promoter. He studies problems in great depth. His expression is precise, exact, and never ambivalent. He does not know how to deceive or dodge. And once he is convinced of the path to take, he can never be deflected."[26]

Like Vajpayee, Advani has extensive organizational and administrative experience. Besides being the Minister for Information and Broadcasting, he was also the chairman of the Delhi Metropolitan Council between 1967 and 1970. He was a member of the Rajya Sabha for nineteen years before he was elected to the Lok Sabha in 1989.

In 1986, Advani took over the presidency of the party from Vajpayee and seriously set about the task of reorganizing and revitalizing it. His goal became to project the BJP as an alternative to the Congress (I) in both ideology and numbers. Vajpayee believed that "an ideologically based party like ours . . . cannot stoop . . . to electoral calculations,"[27] and the party ended up with an electoral disaster in the 1984 elections, capturing only two seats in the Lok Sabha. However, Advani pursued the cause of Hindu nationalism with a clever electoral strategy. He realized that without broad-based electoral support and a majority in Parliament, the BJP could never displace the Congress (I) from the position of power. With brilliant mass mobilization techniques, Advani fired the imagination of the people, especially in the Hindi-speaking states of north India. He was able to marginalize the influence of the centrist parties and reap rich electoral dividends for his party in the 1989 and 1991 elections.

More significant was Advani's assault on the Nehruvian concepts of the Indian state and its political culture. Although Advani's approach to the redefinition of Indian nationalism was characterized as communal by his political opponents, he never attacked any religious minority. He declared that "Nehru's thinking made Indian nationalism an amorphous thing" and added that "Democracy and liberalism as preached by Nehru were denuded of their Indianness. So, Hindu-bashing became synonymous with secularism. I believe that India is what it is, because of its ancient heritage. Call it Hindu or call it Bharatiya. If nationalism is stripped of its Hinduness, it will lose dynamism."[28]

It is to Advani's credit that he raised the intellectual level of discussion, focusing the debate on the nature of the Indian state and political culture as it had developed during the dominance by the Nehru-Gandhi dynasty. Advani insisted that the Nehruvian brand of thinking, supported by the Marxists and the liberals alike, had no roots in the culture of Indian society. Furthermore, he asserted that such Indian nationalism had led to Indira and Rajiv Gandhi's pragmatic and unprincipled manipulation of national symbols and slogans for electoral success. It bred what he called "minorityism," i.e., exploitation of the minority religious communities by creating the fear of majority domination. In this process, the ruling classes, under the Congress leadership, pampered the religious minorities by making symbolic concessions, and this kept them isolated from the mainstream of Indian politics. The reaction to this treatment was the assertion of Hindu identity. Advani declared that "Majority consciousness has been built up by this minorityism. Otherwise, the Hindu is never conscious of being Hindu. And therefore, the political parties tend to take him for granted."[29]

James Manor has observed that, in Indian politics, "Congress occupied not only the broad center of the political spectrum, but most of the left and right as well. This relegated the opposition parties not only to the margins of Congress, but to the margins of the political and party system as well."[30] Vajpayee had earlier diluted the party's ideology by incorporating

Gandhism and liberalism in the party plank. Advani's task was to establish a distinct political and ideological identity for the BJP. By attacking the Nehruvian concepts of secularism and centralized, state-controlled, planned economy of the country, Advani reestablished the distinctive role of his party in Indian politics.

Advani, who started his political career as a journalist (associated for a long time with the RSS *Organiser*), used a noticeably intellectual approach to tackle fundamental issues of the Indian state. As a result, he earned respect for the BJP and for Hindu nationalism among the middle classes and professionals. These people had tended to distance themselves from such an ideology, looking upon it as a sign of reaction and backwardness. Advani also provided many of the young and older intellectuals encouragement to ridicule the Nehruvian and Marxist intellectuals, characterizing them as a rootless group of people living on borrowed ideas.

Born in 1927 in Hyderabad City of Sindh, now a province of Pakistan, Advani came from a family of businessmen. He was brought up in a cosmopolitan environment and educated at St. Patrick's School, an English-medium school run by Irish missionaries in the City of Karachi. His parents, while not particularly religious, like many other Sindh Hindus read *Granth Sahib*, the sacred book of the Sikhs, while celebrating many Hindu festivals. It was his entry into the RSS at age fifteen that brought about his identification with the Hindu nationalist cause.

In 1947, his family migrated to India after the formation of Pakistan and settled in Bombay, where he completed his education in law at the Government Law College. Subsequently, he became actively involved in the work of the RSS in Rajasthan. His membership in the Jana Sangh in 1953 brought him into active politics. Until June 1993, Advani served as the leader of the parliamentary wing of the BJP as well as the leader of the opposition in Parliament.

According to Khushwant Singh, a well known Sikh historian and journalist and no admirer of the BJP, Advani is "really one of the most able, cool headed, courteous and clean politicians left today. That breed of politicians has practically disappeared from the country. I am pretty certain that he will never be unfair to Muslims if he becomes minister."[31]

However, while Advani may be a polite and clean politician and no religious fanatic, his technique of mass mobilization and his brand of nationalism have created fear among the religious minorities, especially the Muslims. His critics have described him as a pseudo-nationalist, trying to appeal to the chauvinism of Hindu middle classes.[32] His opponents have called him a political demagogue who is bent upon creating a permanent division among Hindus and Muslims in order to achieve his political goals.

Nevertheless, even his strong critics concede that Advani is not off the mark when he says that minority communalism is responsible for undermining the basis of pluralistic democracy in India.[33]

Given the volatile nature of electoral politics in India, it is difficult to predict the strategy the politicians will adopt in the future. However, since his assumption of the party presidency in June 1993, it appears that Advani is trying to steer his party close to the center of Indian politics, as evidenced by his recent address to the party's national executive.[34] Given the rhetoric of Hindu militants and the actions of some of his supporters, however, Advani will have to work hard to convince the minorities of their security if the Hindu nationalists led by the BJP ever come to power.

Murli Manohar Joshi succeeded Advani as the president of the party in 1991. A Ph.D. and a professor of physics at Allahabad University, he is one of the younger (born in 1934) leaders of the party. Although a brilliant intellectual and a powerful speaker, Joshi lacks the political sophistication of Vajpayee and Advani. Joshi rose through the RSS/BJP ranks and held the position of general secretary of the party during the period when Advani was the president.

Earlier, Joshi was active in the Akhil Bharatiya Vidyarthi Parishad, the student wing of the BJP, and was also one of the general secretaries of the Janata Party (1977-79). Thus he is no stranger to national politics, but his close association with Nanaji Deshmukh, a strongman of the former Jana Sangh and not a great admirer of the Vajpayee contingent, causes some unease among the party moderates. He is considered a party hardliner, close to the Vishwa Hindu Parishad (VHP-World Hindu Council), a Hindu revivalist organization, and favors adopting a militant and unambiguous Hindu stand on political and social issues. Originating from U.P., India's largest and most populous state, Joshi is trying hard to build a secure political base for himself.

Perhaps Joshi was installed as the president by the party elders to provide greater exposure to the younger generation of party workers. However, he does not seem to have lived up to the expectations of the party elders and has failed to serve as a role model for the younger workers. His level of political thinking has not been innovative nor his political strategies very inspiring. But Joshi is popular with the rank and file of both the RSS and VHP.

Some press observers of BJP politics have accused Joshi of using "machiavellian maneuvers and coercive tactics"[35] to consolidate his position within the party. The BJP leadership has been known for encouraging team spirit and it is against building a personality cult. Despite this, some journalists charged Joshi with creating factional fights. Whether such a charge is accurate or not, it is true that during Joshi's term of office, factional fights within the party became public. Given Joshi's dismal record as the president of the party and his combative public posture, the party elders denied him a second term despite his strong efforts to retain the position.

Rajmata Vijaya Raje Scindia is one of the most distinguished senior leaders of the party and, according to party insiders, plays a key role in the party's inner workings. Born in 1926, originating from the royal family of Gwalior, a former maharani, she is enormously influential in her home state of Madhya Pradesh, where she has helped her party in gaining power. Like many of her senior colleagues, Scindia was also imprisoned in 1975, when Indira Gandhi imposed Emergency Rule. Scindia has been elected to the Lok Sabha several times from her home state.

Scindia has served as a senior vice-president of the BJP and is presently a member of the party's National Executive. Ideologically, Scindia is closer to Joshi, the party hardliner, than to Vajpayee or Advani. It was Scindia who led the opposition to Vajpayee's line of ideology, declaring that adopting Gandhian socialism as the party's ideology would make the BJP look like a "photocopy" of Indira Gandhi's Congress party.[36] Scindia is often referred to as the *shakti* (goddess of power) of Hindu womanhood. However, despite her ideological toughness, in strategy and public posture Scindia stands closer to Vajpayee and Advani. She keeps working to broaden the base of her party inside and outside of her home state.

Sundar Singh Bhandari, a senior vice-president of the party, is known for his strong ideological commitment, discipline, and indefatigable organizational abilities. Born in 1920, the former RSS *pracharak* (instructor-propagandist) hails from Udaipur city of Rajasthan. The son of a medical practitioner, Bhandari is a lawyer-turned-politician, who held the position of the deputy leader of the Janata Party in the Rajya Sabha when the Jana Sangh was a constituent element of the Janata Party in 1977. Basically an organization man, Bhandari joined the RSS at the age of seventeen. Subsequently, he became a founding member of the Rajasthan unit of the Jana Sangh and the All India General Secretary of the Bharatiya Jana Sangh (1976-77). Deeply influenced by the personalities of Syama Prasad Mookerjee and Deendayal Upadhyaya, Bhandari considers politics more a mission than an occupation. In his personal appearance and behavior he still shows the dedication and austerity of an RSS *pracharak*. He still has unrestricted access to the inner recesses of the RSS.

Bhandari has asserted:

It is my sense of responsibility to my country which brings me into politics. Our country faces numerous problems, they need solutions, I believe that our party can provide solutions for these problems. But we need to capture political power in order to implement our platform. Without dedicated party workers a party cannot capture political power.[37]

For this reason Bhandari has turned his attention to the party organization and personnel. He is also known as the "Ambedkar of the BJP" due to his contributions to the formulation of the party constitution.[38] In 1992, because of his experience, public service, and seniority, Bhandari's name was mentioned as a possible candidate for vice-president of India. He was recently reelected as a member of the Rajya Sabha.

K. R. Malkani is another senior member and one of the vice-presidents of the BJP. A sophisticated and polished gentleman, Malkani is considered a part of the BJP intellectual establishment. With an excellent command of English and several publications to his credit, Malkani served for many years as the editor of the RSS mouthpiece, *Organiser*. He has been very close to Advani, a fellow Sindhi, who was his assistant while Malkani edited the RSS paper.

Born in 1921 in the city of Hyderabad of Sindh, now in Pakistan, and the son of a lawyer, Malkani became interested in politics at the urging of his elder brother, who was a Congress activist and who was twice nominated to the Indian Parliament. However, Malkani's political views have been deeply influenced by the RSS and the personality of Guruji M.S. Golwalkar, the late RSS chief. As a serious student of history, Malkani is a great admirer of the writings of Arnold Toynbee and Will Durant. But it is the RSS and the Guruji that provided him with the incentive and the motivation to join politics. He is candid enough to admit that politics is the essence of his life.[39]

Malkani started his political career as a journalist. He maintains close relations with the New Delhi press establishment and continues to write articles and columns in newspapers. Since Malkani holds M.A. degrees in political science and economics, he serves as an official spokesperson on the party's stance on political and economic issues in the English language. He is an accomplished publicist and one of the important members of the BJP inner circle. Malkani has been instrumental in recruiting many intellectuals, civil servants, writers, and former high-ranking officials of the Indian armed forces to the BJP cause.

Malkani is a skillful defender of the BJP and believes that "the day the Congress acquiesced in Partition [the possibility of] its exit and emergence of a party such as the BJP was inevitable."[40] Like many other Hindu nationalist intellectuals, he is a strong critic of the Nehru heritage. He argues that criticism of Hindu organizations like the RSS and the labeling of them as communal are the legacy of the Nehru-Indira Gandhi families; true nationalists like Subhash Bose or Sardar Vallabhbhai Patel had only praise for what the RSS represented or what it contributed to Indian society.[41]

In recent years he has frequently engaged in intellectual/ideological dialogue with his secular/Muslim counterparts through his writings. He tries to project a moderate image of his party although in the power struggle within the party, Malkani has often sided with the party hardliners against the activist "young Turks."

Krishan Lal Sharma is another vice-president of the party, who, despite maintaining a low profile, plays a key role in the policy formulation of the BJP. It was under his chairmanship that a sub-committee, appointed by Advani, recommended modifying the Vajpayee line of the party's ideology. Sharma was responsible for reinstituting the Deendayal Upadhyaya philosophy of Integral Humanism as the central creed of the party to restore its distinct political identity. Under his chairmanship, the BJP sub-committee called for the revival of the Jana Sangh traditions, with an emphasis on unadulterated Hindu nationalism. He has worked closely with the party president, Advani, in changing the public image of the party.

Born in 1925, in a Brahmin family of a police officer in Multan district (now in Punjab province of Pakistan), Krishan Lal Sharma was educated in D.A.V. School and Emerson College of Multan, where he earned a B.A. degree. He joined the RSS at the age of twenty-one. After the partition of India he went to Jullundur, where he became the RSS *pracharak*. In 1964, he joined active politics. Sharma held various positions in the Jana Sangh in Punjab before moving to New Delhi as the general secretary of the party.

Like many other former RSS *pracharak*-turned-politicians, for Sharma politics is instrumental in achieving ideological goals. Therefore it becomes a mission, not just an occupation. He says, "Some people feel that a person who has ambitions for elective office joins politics and seeks office. I did not have any such ambition. I joined politics in the spirit of selfless service in the cause of national unity and welfare."[42] He holds politicians responsible for the decline of standards of behavior in India. Critical of the behavior of contemporary politicians, who, he says, use all kinds of methods to attain their selfish ends, he believes that only politicians, by exemplary behavior, can help restore social and political morality. Sharma expects very high standards of behavior from the members of the BJP. His assertion is that there should be virtually no vulgar display of wealth by the members of the BJP, which is common among the Congress party members.

Like many other RSS *pracharaks*, Sharma is a bachelor. Since he is a member of the Rajya Sabha, he lives modestly in official accommodations provided for the MPs.

Jagdish Prasad Mathur, All India secretary of the BJP and a party spokesman, is an old-time RSS *pracharak* and Jana Sangh activist and officeholder. Born in 1921 in Bijnor district of U.P., the son of a small landholder, Mathur joined the RSS before he could finish college. Because of his Kayasth family background, he is well read in both Urdu and Hindi literature and loves music, although now, with his various political preoccupations, he finds little time for these hobbies.

Deeply influenced by the personality and writings of Deendayal Upadhyaya, Mathur is very concerned about the increasing anomic tendencies within Indian society. He is highly critical of the role of the new rich class, in general, and politicians, in particular, in eroding the moral values which have traditionally guided the behavior of the people in north India. He is also deeply disturbed by the divisive tactics used by the centrist parties to win political power without considering how such tactics affect the society.[43]

A member of the Rajya Sabha, Mathur, even at the age of seventy-one, plays a very active role in both the parliamentary and mass wings of the party.

Govindacharya, until recently one of the most influential general secretaries of the BJP and an emerging party ideologue, was brought to national party headquarters by the then-party president, L.K. Advani. K. Govindan (his given name) was born in 1943 into a poor Tamil Brahmin family of south India. A young intellectual with a M.S. in physics, Govindacharya, as he is now popularly known, rose to national fame within a short time as an astute young BJP strategist. He has been working as an RSS *pracharak* since 1960 but joined the BJP in 1980.

Govindacharya had gained considerable organizational experience before he was made the general secretary of the BJP. At first, he was closely associated with the Akhil Bharatiya Vidyarthi Parishad (ABVP) and is credited with the expansion of its activities in both north and south Indian states. Subsequently, he worked to organize the mass movement led by Jayaprakash Narayan in Bihar.

Because of his strong background in mathematics and statistics, Govindacharya has minute and intimate knowledge about the BJP strength in different parliamentary constituencies as well as about the party candidates. His intelligence and sharp memory led party members to nickname

him the "human computer."[44]   He has been able to provide the party
leaders with detailed electoral analysis.

During his term as the general secretary of the party, Govindacharya has
been credited with establishing friendly relations with the media,
bureaucrats, and leaders of other political parties. According to Chawala,
a well-known journalist, "even on important policy matters, like the party's
relationships with the Congress and other opposition parties, Mr.
Govindacharya's views found a ready audience as they had a certain clarity
which the views of the old guard lacked."[45]

Govindacharya, fluent in English and in many Indian languages
including Hindi, Marathi, and Tamil, has led a simple and austere life,
living in one-room quarters provided on the premises of the party
headquarters in New Delhi. Whether because of his relationship with Uma
Bharati, a fiery young woman MP from Madhya Pradesh, or the power
struggle between the young Turks and the party old guards, in April 1992
Govindacharya was suddenly shifted from New Delhi to Madras in Tamil
Nadu.[46] *Indian Express*, a newspaper sympathetic to the BJP, commented
that the "Govindacharya-Uma Bharati episode has nothing to do with
ideology and is linked to purely personal ambitions. It is aimed at
suppressing debate rather than opening the party to free and frank exchange of opinion."[47]

A faithful and disciplined party worker, Govindacharya accepted his
banishment to Tamil Nadu as ordered by the party president, M. M. Joshi.
However, men like Govindacharya, who constitute the young and credible
leadership core of the party, are not kept in political exile for long.
Recently the party leadership brought him back to New Delhi and made
him the general secretary.

Promod Mahajan is another rising young star of the party. Like
Govindacharya, Mahajan was also brought to the forefront of the party by
Advani. Possessing oratorical skills of Vajpayee's caliber and the organ-
izational efficiency of Advani, Mahajan seems to have potential to become
a BJP leader of national stature. A former RSS *pracharak*, he served in
leadership positions in both the ABVP and the Bharatiya Janata Party Yuva
Morcha (Youth Front). Earlier, he was active in the BJP's predecessor, the
Jana Sangh.

A son of a Maharashtrian Brahmin high school teacher, Promod
Mahajan was born in 1950 in Andhra Pradesh. After earning his B.S. in
physics, at the urging of RSS leaders Mahajan started his political career
as a Jana Sangh activist. He successfully organized the youth wing of the
Jana Sangh in Maharashtra. During Indira Gandhi's Emergency Rule,
Mahajan was detained for fifteen months. While in jail he earned an M.A.

in political science through correspondence courses. He assumed the position of national secretary of the BJP in 1983, the youngest politician to hold such an important post in a major national party.

In 1986, Mahajan was elected a member of the Rajya Sabha from Maharashtra. During his term in the Indian Parliament, he earned a reputation as an alert and active MP and one of the most eloquent speakers of Parliament. He is counted among the few young politicians of the country who practice value-based politics and are willing to devote their time to political, social, and cultural causes.

Brajesh Mishra is an example of the new breed of politicians recently brought into the ranks of the BJP: one who has never been through the discipline and harsh training provided by the RSS. He is a retired member of the prestigious Indian Foreign Service and served as India's permanent representative in the U.N. He held many other important diplomatic positions before he joined the BJP.

A son of Dwarka Prasad Mishra, a former Congress chief minister of Madhya Pradesh, Brajesh did not find the Congress party as attractive an organization for starting his political career as many of his former colleagues did. Whether it was the *durbar* (court)-like milieu of the Rajiv-dominated Congress or the more open and democratic environment of the BJP, his entry into the latter party helped both the BJP and its new entrants.

In order to change its image, the party leadership has been actively recruiting intelligent bureaucrats or former government officials. These recruits provide enough talent for the party to think through its policy positions on different issues. For experienced and ambitious men like Mishra, the BJP provides both an opportunity to influence the foreign policy options of the party and a forum where he is likely to have few competitors. Besides being a member of the BJP's National Executive, Mishra is closely associated with its foreign policy cell.

For a man like Mishra, the BJP may also be a more suitable ideological choice since his father, a staunch Hindu, was a follower of Sardar Patel, a well known sympathizer with Hindu nationalists, rather than Nehru. Mishra finds the BJP's nationalism, discipline, and the dedication of its cadre to the party ideology more appealing than the pragmatism of Congress members. He is deeply concerned about the decline of moral values in public life and feels that the true spirit of service must be restored if the country is to make real progress. The leadership of the BJP, in its dedication to public service, he strongly believes, can provide a role model for other parties.

Jay Dubashi, a member of the BJP's National Executive, may not be counted among the nationally known leaders of the party. However, because of his long association with the top party leadership and his academic background, he is frequently called upon to advise the leaders on policy matters, especially economic and industrial issues.

With a Ph.D. in economics from London University, Dubashi has worked with various organizations on economic policy matters, including the Council for Applied Economics and the Economic and Scientific Research Foundation, both funded by private business groups. However, he entered politics via journalism. Though not an RSS man, Dubashi became associated with Jana Sangh and RSS publications in English, sometimes as editor and other times as a writer. During this period he became a staunch critic of the Nehruvian model of Indian economic planning. He still writes a regular column in the RSS organ, *Organiser,* and serves as a regular member of the BJP's study group on economic policies. He is the author of several books and a contributor to various newspapers and periodicals.

Not a political activist, Dubashi, a Goan Brahmin, was born in 1927 and brought up and educated in the cosmopolitan city of Bombay. He served as an advisor to Brijlal Varma when he was a Minister for Industries in the Morarji Desai government of the Janata Party.

It was in January 1985 that he was invited to serve on the BJP's National Executive, and since then he has been serving on that body regularly. A great admirer of L.K. Advani, Dubashi gives Advani credit for changing the vocabulary of Indian politics. Dubashi is presently part of an informal group which meets daily in the party's national headquarters to take stock of the party's political affairs.

T. N. Chaturvedi is another highly respected former civil servant. Chaturvedi, another non-RSS entrant to the party, was recently invited to become a member of the National Executive of the BJP. Chaturvedi has held various key positions at the national level of Indian bureaucracy, including Secretary of the Ministry of Home Affairs and Comptroller and Auditor General of India. He has had vast administrative experience.

Basically a nonpolitical person, born into a Brahmin family of U.P. in 1928, Chaturvedi earned his M.A. and L.L.B. degrees from Allahabad University, a premier institute of higher learning in the country. He spent all his life as a bureaucrat, with little or no political involvement. This does not mean, however, that Chaturvedi did not have any social or political consciousness. He gives credit to one of his uncles and to the Arya Samaj movement for the formulation of his social and political attitudes.

It was not surprising that, after his retirement from government service, he was invited by the leaders of different political parties, including the Congress and the Janata Dal, to join their ranks. Chaturvedi, however, decided to join the BJP because of its RSS culture, dedication of its members, and their strong commitment to the cause of nationalism. He never felt enamored of the Congress brand of secularism.[48]

Even though the ideology of the RSS, especially its militant pro-Hindu stance, has been criticized by the westernized Hindus, the RSS' projects, especially the recent educational and vocational training by the Seva Bharati of the tribals, slum-dwelling untouchables, backward castes, and the rural poor, have impressed even its critics.[49] It is not surprising, therefore, that men like Chaturvedi, motivated to join politics for altruistic reasons, are attracted to the BJP, since its top leadership comes from the ranks of the RSS.

The recruitment of members of Chaturvedi's caliber to the party is indicative of the top party leadership's efforts to broaden the base of the otherwise closely knit organization. Already, Chaturvedi has been on the lecture circuit, explaining to the party rank and file the complexities of the administrative process in the government. Also, he is frequently consulted by the party leaders on policy matters related to the restructuring of the Indian economy and administration.

Besides these key national leaders there are several old and young leaders working at the state level who exercise considerable influence within both the BJP and the RSS. From among the old guard, leaders like Kushabhau Thakre of Madhya Pradesh, Bhairon Singh Shekhawat of Rajasthan, Baldev Prakash of Punjab, and Kedarnath Sahni of Delhi state deserve special mention.

Thakre, one of the general secretaries of the party and an RSS veteran, is a Maharashtrian Brahmin well known for his ascetic lifestyle and iron discipline. He is in charge of organizational affairs of the party in Madhya Pradesh. Along with Sunderlal Patwa, the chief minister of the BJP-ruled state, Thakre has tried to quell the rebellion within the party led by Uma Bharati, the young MP from Madhya Pradesh.

Shekhawat, a consummate politician and a non-RSS man, is a strong proponent of Hindu nationalism. A close ideological associate of Vajpayee, Shekhawat has been very successful in increasing pro-Hindu credibility in Rajasthan. Shekhawat came into state power with the support of V.P. Singh's Janata Dal. When in October 1990, the Janata Dal tried to topple his government, Shekhawat won the support of a section of the Janata Dal by his shrewd political moves and saved the BJP government.

In the last two years, Shekhawat has tried to extend the BJP support base in the state by pursuing pro-rural and pro-poor policies.

Prakash and Sahni, both in their late sixties, have their power base among the Hindus of Punjab and Delhi, respectively. Both are national BJP officeholders supporting militant Hindu nationalism and fighting the weakening of the party's Jana Sangh line of political thinking.

From among the younger members, Arun Jaitly from Delhi, Sushil Modi from Bihar, and Narendra Modi from Gujarat are being groomed by the party's national leadership. Jaitly, a lawyer, is frequently consulted on legal matters. Sushil Modi, a former general secretary of the ABVP, gained prominence for his role in organizing the JP movement in Bihar. He is presently serving as party whip in the Bihar legislative assembly. Narendra Modi has been put in charge of party activities in West Bengal. All of them are in their early forties and come from the ranks of the RSS.

At the national level, these senior and young leaders project a sophisticated image of the party and advance intellectual arguments for Hindu nationalism on the basis of India's ancient cultural heritage. While they do not directly appeal to anti-Muslim sentiments, the lesser known party leaders like Uma Bharati, Vinay Katiyar, Mahant Avaidyanath, and Ashok Singhal, all BJP MPs, openly appeal to the latent Hindu religious hatred and bigotry and create anti-Muslim hysteria. They seem unwilling to engage in rational dialogue and are motivated by religious revivalism. Often they flout the authority of courts and the established norms of political behavior.

This group is especially popular with the lumpen element of Hindu society. Such behavior of the BJP leadership, unless controlled by the senior leaders, could lead to disaster for both the party and the country. Vajpayee, after assuming the BJP leadership in the Lok Sabha, impressed upon the members of his party the need to maintain decorum in their behavior inside and outside of Parliament.

The BJP Activists: Some Empirical Observations

The biographical sketches of members of the BJP leadership presented in the preceding pages, besides showing its upper caste/middle class background, also demonstrate its close association with the Jana Sangh and the RSS, which should not come as a surprise for any close observer of Indian politics.

A comparative study of the party officeholders at the district levels, conducted in 1987 in four states of north India (Delhi, U.P., Rajasthan, and

Haryana), can also provide us with insight into the socioeconomic background, education, occupation, and motivations which bring people into the political arena. This study specifically looks at the political functionaries, referred to as the middle-level political elites, who run the party organization at the local level, recruit volunteers to mobilize voters, organize party rallies and conduct day-to-day affairs of the party.

Findings reported in Table 2.1 show that almost sixty percent of the BJP party functionaries whose fathers were active in politics had affiliation with the former Jana Sangh. This finding is not surprising, given the ancestry of the BJP. However, the table shows that the BJP also draws functionaries whose fathers were active in the Congress or the Socialist parties. Thus, it appears that the BJP has been able to broaden its base at the local level.

When we look at Table 2.2, we find that, although almost all the major political parties of India draw a large number of their functionaries from the educated classes, the BJP seems to have the largest percentage with post-graduate degrees. Juxtaposing these findings with the figures in Table 2.3 confirms the common assumption in India that the BJP's cadre as well as its officeholders are dominated by people from the business world.

Despite the leaders' claims that there has been a significant increase in the number of Muslims in the party's national executive,[50] the findings in Table 2.4 clearly indicate that the BJP has a long way to go in recruiting non-Hindu functionaries at the local level.

TABLE 2.1 Respondents' Current Affiliation by Father's Affiliation

Variable	Congress	Lok Dal	Janata	BJP	CPI
Congress	40.78	23.30	22.33	11.65	1.94
Hindu Mahas	.00	.00	.00	100.00	.00
Jana Sangh	.00	35.29	5.88	58.82	.00
Socialist	.00	42.86	14.29	14.29	28.57
None	19.72	19.72	21.13	22.54	16.90
Other	.00	57.14	28.57	14.29	.00

Cramers V = .2920   p = .00000
Source: Yogendra K. Malik and Jesse F. Marquette, *Political Mercenaries and Citizen Soldiers: A Profile of North Indian Party Activists* (Delhi, Chanakya Publications, 1990), p. 89.

TABLE 2.2 Respondent Level of Education by Party

Education	Congress	Lok Dal	Janata	BJP	CPI
Some primary	1.72	1.92	2.17	.00	.00
Completed primary	.00	5.77	4.35	4.55	23.53
Some secondary	13.79	21.15	21.74	25.00	35.29
Completed secondary	17.24	17.31	25.09	4.55	11.76
Some college	13.79	.00	4.35	15.91	.00
Completed college	34.48	34.62	23.91	22.73	5.88
Post graduate	18.97	19.23	17.39	27.27	23.53

Cramers V = .23   p = .01000
Source: Yogendra K. Malik and Jesse Marquette, *Political Mercenaries*, p. 113.

TABLE 2.3 Respondent Occupation by Party

Occupation	Congress	Lok Dal	Janata	BJP	CPI
Law	25.86	15.38	10.87	18.18	11.76
Business	39.66	42.31	60.87	52.27	23.53
White collar	13.79	7.69	6.52	22.73	17.65
Agriculture	12.07	15.38	15.22	6.82	5.88
Miscellaneous	5.17	7.69	4.35	.00	17.65
Full-time politician	3.45	11.54	2.17	.00	23.52

Cramers V = .22   p = .00382
Source: Yogendra K. Malik and Jesse F. Marquette, *Political Mercenaries*, p. 113.

TABLE 2.4 Respondent Religious Preference by Party

Religion	Congress	Lok Dal	Janata	BJP	CPI
Hindu	86.21	90.38	91.30	97.73	70.59
Muslim	10.24	3.85	6.52	2.27	5.88
Sikh	3.45	1.92	2.17	.00	5.88
None	.00	3.85	.00	.00	17.65

Cramers V = .21   p .01
Source: Yogendra K. Malik and Jesse F. Marquette, *Political Mercenaries*, p. 116.

Findings reported in Table 2.5 show that the largest percentage of the BJP functionaries enter politics to serve people and to remove corruption from public and political life. Such a commitment is reinforced by the fact that when they were asked, "what is least appealing about politics?" more than fifty percent of the BJP functionaries named political corruption.

TABLE 2.5 What Is Most Appealing About Politics by Respondent Party

Variable	Congress	Lok Dal	Janata	BJP	CPI
National service	44.83	3.85	15.22	18.18	17.65
Serving people	22.41	48.08	41.30	29.55	52.94
Personal goals	18.97	23.08	21.74	6.82	.00
Anti-corruption	8.62	19.23	17.39	27.27	.00
Miscellaneous	5.17	5.77	4.35	18.18	29.41

Cramers V = .2642   p = .00000
Source: Yogendra K. Malik and Jesse F. Marquette, *Political Mercenaries*, p. 95.

Conclusions

The continuation of the party's linkage with its ideological and organizational ancestry is natural. At the same time, it appears that the party's efforts to broaden its base and to enter the mainstream of Indian politics will continue and its leadership will keep adjusting its strategies to capture political power.

The BJP, then, possesses a leadership with national recognition but with little administrative experience. Since the party has been mainly in opposition, its leaders have spent most of their time organizing protests, rallies, and demonstrations. Their administrative skills have yet to be tested.

The party leadership has a narrow social base. They do not reflect the great cultural diversity which India represents. The significant absence of minorities or persons of lower class origin from their leadership ranks is the result of their exclusionary tendencies, despite their assertion to the contrary.

Unlike the Congress (I), the BJP does not have regional leaders who have strong roots in their communities or castes. Since the party held power for only a short period of time, it has not been able to build stable linkages with the local or regional elites through a system of political patronage as the Congress (I) did. Thus the BJP is heavily dependent on party cadre, political symbols, slogans, and ideology to mobilize the voters.

Notes

1. Quoted in Geeta Puri, *Bharatiya Jana Sangh: Organization and Ideology* (New Delhi, Sterling Publishers, 1980), p. 7.

2. S.R. Bakshi, *Syama Prasad Mookerjee: Founder of the Jana Sangh* (New Delhi, Anmol Publications, 1992), p. 7.

3. Dina Nath Mishra, *RSS: Myth and Reality* (Sahibabad, Vikas Publishing House, 1980), pp. 29-30, and Craig Baxter, *The Jana Sangh: A Biography of a Political Party* (Philadelphia, University of Pennsylvania Press, 1969), p. 69.

4. L.K. Advani, *The People Betrayed* (New Delhi, Vision Books, 1979), p. 74.

5. Madhu Limaye, *Decline of a Political System: Indian Politics at Crossroads* (Allahabad, Wheeler Publishing, 1992), p. 24.

6. Advani, *The People Betrayed*, pp. 74-75.

7. *Ibid.*, pp. 64-65.

8. Yogendra K. Malik and Jesse F. Marquette, *Political Mercenaries and Citizen Soldiers: A Profile of North Indian Party Activists* (Delhi, Chanakya Publications, 1990), p. 3.

9. Ashis Nandy, "Political Consciousness," a paper presented at the seminar held at the India International Centre, New Delhi, December 16, 1979, p. 19. Also, see his "Myths, Persons and Politics," *Seminar* (October, 1979), pp. 242-46.

10. Ghanshyam Shah, "Tenth Lok Sabha Elections: The BJP's Victory in Gujarat," *Economic and Political Weekly* (December 21, 1991), p. 3921.

11. Nana Deshmukh, *RSS: Victim of Slander* (New Delhi, Vision Books, 1979), p. 3.

12. Janardan Thakur, *All the Janata Men* (New Delhi, Vikas, 1978), p. 14.

13. Advani, *The People Betrayed*, p. 65.

14. Advani, *The People Betrayed*, p. 66.

15. Walter Andersen and Shridhar D. Damle, *The Brotherhood in Saffron: The Rashtriya Swayamsevak Sangh and Hindu Revivalism* (Boulder, CO., Westview Press, 1987), p. 221.

16. Atal Bihari Vajpayee, *India at the Crossroads* (New Delhi, Bharatiya Janata Party Publications, 1980), p. 2.

17. *Ibid.*, p. 4.

18. Bharatiya Janata Party, *Our Five Commitments* (Delhi, Asiatic Printers, n.d.), pp. 1-20.

19. *Ibid.*, p. 4.

20. *Ibid.*

21. Quoted in Janardan Thakur, *Janata Men*, p. 137.

22. *Probe India*, May 1988, p. 4.

23. *Panchjanya*, March 29, 1992, p. 1.

24. Thakur, *Janata Men*, p. 143.

25. Interview with Promod Mahajan, February 27, 1992.

26. *India Today*, March 31, 1990, p. 24.

27. *Probe India*, May, 1988, p. 5.

28. *Sunday Observer*, January 7, 1991, p. 5.

29. "The New Avtar," *Telegraph*, December 31, 1989, p. 11.

30. James Manor, "Parties and the Party System in India," in Atul Kohli (ed.), *India's Democracy: An Analysis of State-Society Relations* (Princeton, Princeton University Press, 1988), p. 65.

31. *Telegraph*, December 31, 1989, p. 15.

32. Rajni Kothari, "Pluralism and Secularism: Lessons of Ayodhya," *Economic and Political Weekly*, December 19-26, 1992, p. 2695.

33. *Ibid.*

34. Bharatiya Janata Party, *Lal Krishan Advani ka adhyaksheeya bhashan June 18-20, 1993* (New Delhi, Bharatiya Janata Party Publications, 1993), p. 16

35. Prabhu Chawla, "Power Corrodes BJP: Factional Feuds and Machiavellian Maneuvers," *Indian Express*, April 25, 1992, p. 8.

36. Andersen, et al, *Brotherhood*, p. 228.

37. Interview with Sundar Singh Bhandari, March 12, 1992.

38. *Onlooker*, July 31, 1990, p. 17.

39. Interview with K.R. Malkani, February 13, 1992.

40. *Hindu*, August 9, 1991, p. 5.

41. *Ibid.*

42. Interview with K.L. Sharma, February 25, 1992.

43. Interview with J.P. Mathur, March 4, 1992.

44. *Onlooker*, July 31, 1990, p. 14.

45. Prabhu Chawla, "Power Corrodes BJP," p. 8.

46. *Sunday*, May 10-16, 1992, pp. 28-36.

47. *Indian Express*, April 29, 1992, p. 8.

48. Interview with T.N. Chaturvedi, April 24, 1992.

49. *India Today*, July 31, 1992, p. 27.

50. K. R. Malkani, "The Well-Oiled BJP Machine," *The Daily Bombay*, February 24, 1991, p. 10.

3

Strategies: Collaboration, Alliances, Cooperation, and Confrontation

Political parties adopt a variety of strategies in order to gain power and to implement their programs and policies. Ideologies provide a broad framework within which policies and issues are sorted out and political platforms adopted. If political power is the primary goal of the party leadership, strategy becomes the key in understanding the dynamics of a political party. The BJP is an ideologically oriented party; nevertheless, ideology has little value in a power vacuum.

Given the fact that electoral politics in India is a major determinant in the power equation, it is clear that political parties formulate their political strategies to influence the electoral outcome. While the imperative of organizational self-preservation encourages leaders to follow a strategy of adaptation to the existing political environment, ideological and power orientations may encourage the leadership to develop strategies to dominate the political environment. Therefore, we expect that political parties are likely to pursue strategies designed to achieve two goals: self-preservation and control of government.

Strategy of the Mainstream Ideology

In the first stage, soon after the founding the new BJP party in 1980, the political ideology itself became a part of the BJP's strategy for both self-preservation and attaining power. It appears that the lessons of the electoral performance of the BJP's predecessor, the Jana Sangh, and the success of the Janata Party in the 1977 elections encouraged the party leadership to reformulate its ideology so that it could broaden its electoral base. Many believed that India needed an alternative to the Congress party and, since the Janata Party was not in a position to offer such an alternative, the BJP, with a new political ideology, might be able to take the place of the former Janata Party.

The leadership recognized the historic role of the Congress party in the freedom struggle, in the establishment of a viable institutional structure, in the formulation of the basis of India's foreign policy, and in laying the foundation of India's economic development in post-independence India. However, the BJP leaders correctly observed that over the previous two decades, at the hands of the Congress party leaders, political institutions had been either eroded or corrupted to retain power.[1] Following Indira Gandhi's accumulation of enormous power within both the Congress party and the government and the resulting distortion of political institutions, it was asserted that "A single individual has appropriated the entire power of the executive, the cabinet formation has become a mere formality."[2] The BJP lamented that Congressism had led to the decline of the powers and prestige of the Parliament and posed a threat to the independence of both the press and the judiciary, the cornerstones of a liberal democracy.

The BJP committed itself to defend democratic institutions and norms and to "fight ceaselessly against emerging fascist trends."[3] More significant, however, was its leaders' willingness to cooperate with other democratic parties to defend democracy and fundamental rights.[4] The party sought to build a distinct libertarian image for itself, and, therefore, it declared that people adhering to different ideologies and faiths should be able to coexist.

To position itself on the center stage of Indian politics, the BJP leadership adopted Gandhian socialism as its central creed. "Bread, Freedom and Employment are the Gandhian first principles. BJP would make these principles the central core of development strategy and try to build a national consensus around them."[5] Since Gandhian socialism had been criticized for its anti-technology stance and for its opposition to large-scale industrialization, the BJP took pains to point out that Gandhism was broad enough to accept large, medium, and small industries as long as industrialization did not dehumanize society.

To distinguish itself from the Nehruvian tradition of a western model of science and technology development, the BJP leadership found no contradiction between India's spiritual heritage and science and technology development. This was because "Indian civilization has always progressed on the basis of a combination of moral values and positive approach to science. Science and religion will have to be harmonized."[6] In their view, Gandhian socialism was capable of achieving such harmony.

Not only does Gandhian socialism eschew violence, which is an essential part of Marxist traditions, but it is also against exploitation of humans by humans. In the words of Atal Bihari Vajpayee, "Gandhian socialism insists that, if economic exploitation of man by man is to be ended, it cannot be ended within any value neutral and so-called scientific social system. It can be stopped only through a value system on which the changes in the social system are to be structured as well as tested."[7] Gandhian socialism, according to the BJP, provides for the blending of humankind's quest to satisfy both material and spiritual needs.

Its proponents argue that the Western concept of socialism leads to the monopolistic control of political and economic power by the state, while capitalism, as practiced in the West, breeds greed and selfishness. However, Gandhi's concept of trusteeship avoids the pitfalls of both the systems. Trusteeship is envisioned as a post-capitalist arrangement. Under such a system, say its advocates, the present property-owning class man- ages the property and the system of production on behalf of the society and for the welfare of the society.

The BJP leadership's incorporation of Gandhian ideals into its political ideology was both a tactical move and an effort to seek an indigenous basis for its economic and industrial development model. Vajpayee, the president of the BJP in 1980, declared:

> If we had evolved an indigenous pattern of development in conformity with our genius and requirements and having regard to our human and material resources, we [India] would not have been in our present plight. As it is, we are having to suffer the worst features of both western capitalism and Soviet planning.[8]

Gandhi offered an alternative road to economic and political development for India. However, because of Nehru's domination of both the Congress party and post-independence national politics in India, Gandhi's political thinking was relegated to a peripheral role. The BJP, under the leadership of Vajpayee, attempted to bring it to the center of Indian politics.

Gandhi also sought spiritualization of politics by reintegrating morality into the process.[9] Gandhi was secular, yet "he thought poorly of those who wanted to keep religion and politics separate. Those who believe in such separation, he said, understood neither religion nor politics."[10] Gandhi held that competitive individualism, as advocated by the doctrine of liberal democracy, needs to be restrained by ethical principles; otherwise it will lead to the development of amoral politics.

Following this line of argument, the BJP leadership advocates the adoption of the concept of "positive secularism." Such a concept seems to

have two dimensions. Besides implying religious tolerance of the followers of different faiths, "it also means distillation of common moral
values whether derived from different religions or from other historical and
civilizational experiences and approaches, which always remained integral
to the Indian civilization."[11] On the other hand, it also implies that the
Indian state would never discriminate among the followers of different
faiths, that it is committed to *Sarva dharma samabhava* (all religions are
equal). According to these principles, members of the majority and the
minority religions would be treated equally. A more significant fact is,
however, that to distinguish itself from the Janata and the Congress parties
and to satisfy hard core Hindu nationalists, the Indian state under the BJP
would not offer any special protection or privileges for the followers of
any minority religion, because such a practice leads to the development of
two classes of citizenship.[12] In reality, however, Gandhian socialism could
hardly find widespread acceptance among militant Hindu nationalists, who
have looked upon Gandhi as one of the national leaders out to appease the
Muslim minority.

Collaboration, Alliance Formation, and Electoral Adjustment

Another dimension of the BJP's strategy, under the leadership of
Vajpayee, was to seek collaboration with the opposition parties. The
Congress party (which since 1977 has come to be known as the Indira
Congress or Congress (I) because of the domination of the party by Indira
Gandhi and her family) in 1980 was in power at the national level and in
a large number of Indian states. The BJP and the other opposition parties
were in a political wilderness. After the 1980 defeat of the opposition
leaders, India's multi-party system was adjusting to the return of the
Congress (I) to the dominant position in Indian politics.

The BJP leadership's goal was to present the party as an alternative to
the Congress (I). The BJP had both organization and an ideology, but it
lacked a nationwide electoral base. In 1983, the party increased its membership from 2.2 million to 3 million[13] and held its local and state-level
elections. Its national council, the highest policy-making agency of the
party, had a representative from each Indian state.

Despite these achievements, the party leadership was quite aware of the
limitations under which the BJP had to work. In 1983, Advani, then the
BJP general secretary, was realistic enough to admit that "we are not yet
a national alternative to the Congress (I), but we have the potential of
becoming that alternative."[14] At the same time he added that "politics, like

nature, abhors a vacuum, and to that extent, if genuine opposition parties cannot fill this developing vacuum, it is bound to be filled by regional parties and the breakaway groups of the Congress (I)."[15] The party needed to join forces with other opposition parties and, therefore, it issued a call for the formation of an anti-Congress democratic front.

At that time there were many political parties with regional support bases, most of them dominated by powerful personalities or factional leaders. Among the major players were the Bharatiya Lok Dal, led by Charan Singh; the Janata Party, headed by Chandra Shekhar; and the Congress (S, Socialist) led by Sharad Pawar.

The Lok Dal and Charan Singh were influential in U.P, especially in the Jat-dominated rural areas in the western districts of the state, while the BJP enjoyed considerable electoral support in the urban areas of north India. Any electoral alliance between the Lok Dal and the BJP could pose a major threat to the Congress (I) in the Hindi-speaking states of north India. The Congress (S), in 1982, had Pawar with considerable regional appeal in Maharashtra. The Janata Party had many leaders but did not have much of an electoral base.

In the four 1982 state elections and in elections for the Lok Sabha seats, the BJP made selective seat adjustment with various opposition parties. In Haryana it made an electoral alliance with the Lok Dal and virtually defeated the Congress (I). In Himachal Pradesh the BJP showed that it could take on the Congress (I) on its own, and "The Congress (I) and the BJP . . . emerged as well matched adversaries."[16] Furthermore, in Maharashtra, the BJP's alliance with the Congress (S) yielded dividends to both: the BJP retained Thane Lok Sabha seat and Congress (S) retained Omerga.

However, the BJP was not entirely satisfied with its electoral alliance with the highly factionalized Lok Dal. One faction worked for the alliance and the other against it, so it was unable to deliver its side of the bargain. The Janata Party, on the other hand, refused to ally with the BJP and went on to lose many seats to the Congress (I), which it might have won if it had been in alliance with the BJP.

The sweeping 1980 electoral victories of Indira Gandhi led the Congress party, and the returns of the 1982 mini general elections made it evident that a divided opposition would not be able to dislodge the Congress party from power at the national level. Despite its past unhappy experience of working with the opposition for electoral purposes, the BJP leadership showed greater interest in opposition unity than others. Vajpayee, the president of the BJP, observed that the attitude of some of the other parties "seemed to suggest that they were fighting not against the Congress (I), but against the BJP."[17]

The BJP's desire for a broad-based alliance of the opposition parties increased after its electoral reverses, first in the January 1983 local elections of Delhi and then in state assembly elections in June in Jammu and Kashmir. In Delhi the elections were held for the Metropolitan Council and Municipal Corporation of Delhi. Delhi was considered the stronghold of the BJP. However, in the January elections the Congress (I) captured thirty-four of the fifty-six Council seats and fifty-seven of the 100 Corporation seats. The BJP could win only nineteen Council and thirty-eight Corporation seats. It had an electoral alliance with the Lok Dal, which won only two Council and three Corporation seats. The party's final humiliation came in the defeat of V.K. Malhotra, the president of the Delhi unit of the BJP and the state campaign chief.[18] Vajpayee, accepting the responsibility for the electoral debacle, resigned the party presidency, although he was later persuaded to withdraw his resignation.

In the Jammu state assembly elections, Indira Gandhi openly appealed to the Hindu nationalist sentiments and captured the majority of seats, which traditionally went to the BJP. As a result, the BJP leadership moved to create a united front consisting of the non-Communist parties. At the same time many opposition leaders also came to the conclusion that without the support of the BJP, no united opposition party had any realistic chance of defeating the Congress (I). Only the BJP, with its organization and cadre, had the ability to mobilize the voters. The BJP also had a solid electoral support base in states like Madhya Pradesh, U.P., Bihar, Rajasthan, and Gujarat, and the recent extension of its electoral successes in southern states, like Karnataka and even Andhra Pradesh, demonstrated that the BJP was a political force to reckon with.

To pursue its goal of national political power, the BJP leadership had various options: merger with the non-Communist opposition parties, electoral alliance and seat adjustment, and the lone wolf approach.

Adoption of any of these options depended not only on the likely response from the opposition parties but also on the attitude of different factions within the BJP. Despite its appearance as an organizational mono-lith, the party was divided into factions. Broadly speaking, they may be categorized as the ideological hardliners, moderates, and pragmatists.

Most of the ideological hardliners came from the ranks of the RSS; they judged issues primarily on the basis of ideological correctness. The moderates were those who came from the ranks of the former Jana Sangh. Some of them might have been former RSS *pracharaks* (instructors-propagandists), but political realities had made them more practical in their politics. The pragmatists consisted of those who had experienced the realities of electoral and party politics in India and had held offices in the government at various levels. This group included the former Jana Sangh members as well as the new entrants from the Janata Party. It must be added, however, that these factions keep changing in leadership structure and membership. J.P. Mathur, Sundar Singh Bhandari and K.R. Malkani, at one stage of the party's development, constituted the hardliners. The moderates were led by Advani and supported by K.L. Sharma. Vajpayee led the pragmatists with the support of such people as Bhairon Singh Shekhawat of Rajasthan, Kalyan Singh of U.P., K.N. Sahni, V.K. Malhotra, M.L. Khurana of Delhi, and Ram Jethmalani of the former Janata Party. All of them had some administrative or legislative experience.

Vajpayee opposed the isolationist, "going-it-alone" stance advocated by the hardliners. The latter, who had not fully accepted the new ideological line adopted at the behest of Vajpayee, became concerned about the dilution of the BJP support base, which was the urban Hindus. In the Delhi local elections, although the BJP gained some Muslim support, it lost the votes of the Hindu traders, who had traditionally constituted its vote bank in the state. The loss of the Hindu vote to the Congress (I) in Jammu confirmed the hardliners' doubts about the wisdom of Vajpayee's line.

They were also not sure about the dependability of the opposition leaders in electoral alliances. Their argument was that the opposition parties still had the same group of leaders who had earlier undermined the unity of the Janata Party. For instance, Charan Singh and Madhu Limaye, the president and the general secretary of the Lok Dal respectively, were the prime forces in undermining the Janata Party. They pointed out that, despite the BJP's adoption of Gandhian socialism as its new ideology, the leaders of the non-Communist parties still looked upon the new party as basically a communal organization dominated by the RSS. Under these conditions, the hardliners argued, how could the BJP have any link with these groups?

It was further pointed out that many of the Janata Party leaders, like Surinder Mohan and Subramaniam Swami, and Madhu Limaye of the Lok Dal, were RSS baiters and had, in the past, questioned the secular credentials of the party. Having no support base of their own, the hardliners asked, how could these people help expand the BJP's support base?

The pragmatists, led by Vajpayee, thought in terms of the larger picture. With an increase in political and communal violence, sluggish economic growth, increased inflation, and allegations of widespread corruption, they held that the Congress (I) was unlikely to win a majority of the seats in the Lok Sabha in the 1984 elections.

Given the nature of the multi-party system in India, with no party having an absolute majority in Parliament, Vajpayee thought that only a coalition was likely to emerge. In order to have a share in the power at the national level, as well as capture majorities in such crucial states as U.P., Madhya Pradesh, and Gujarat, the pragmatists favored some kind of alliance with the opposition parties. While the party's hardliners might have had reservations about the alliances, they were strongly opposed to merging with the opposition to form a new party. They did not want to give up their own party's identity.

In August 1983, Vajpayee was finally successful in forming the National Democratic Front with the Lok Dal, led by Charan Singh. This coalition appeared to be pure political opportunism, which was not likely to enhance the stature of Vajpayee. It was Singh, who had previously questioned the secular credentials of the BJP and wrecked the Janata Party because of the BJP's close associations with the RSS, who now asserted that "there is nothing wrong with the BJP leaders' RSS connections so long as the RSS continues to be a cultural organization."[19]

Singh's turnabout was based upon his cold electoral calculations. Seeing Indira Gandhi courting Hindu votes, he figured that an alliance with the BJP would help the Lok Dal win the urban Hindu vote, where the Lok Dal did not have any base. And he was also sure that he would be elected chairman of the joint steering committee of the front, which would enable him to control the distribution of party tickets for elections.

For the BJP leadership, association with the Lok Dal of Charan Singh meant an end to its political isolation. It would no longer be considered the political untouchable. The merger would also enable the party to extend its rural base. With the Lok Dal as its partner, the BJP would be able to share power in U.P. and Bihar, the two crucial states of north India, where an alliance of the two parties was considered unbeatable. Furthermore, Vajpayee and his associates hoped that their alliance might serve as the nucleus to attract other non-Communist parties to the United Democratic Front. The party's national executive endorsed the policy of expanding its political base through strategic alliances with other parties. There was, however, not much enthusiasm for the strategy in the party's rank and file.

The BJP's courting of the Lok Dal's leadership might have been a useful electoral strategy, but it was politically unwise. Charan Singh and his associates provided only limited electoral help to the BJP in small states. In Haryana, the Jat leader, Devilal, was a very unreliable political ally. In large states like U.P. and Bihar, where Singh and his Lok Dal could help the BJP, Singh himself could have demanded the lion's share in the distribution of the seats and marginalized the BJP. Singh and the Lok Dal were of little help to the BJP in Gujarat, Maharashtra, Madhya Pradesh, Rajasthan, and some of the southern states, where the BJP had built its independent support base.

Furthermore, Singh, being an opportunist, offered no political reliability. In October 1984, without consulting the BJP leadership, Singh announced the formation of a new party, the Dalit Mazdoor Kisan Party (DMKP), consisting of various splinter groups, which resulted in the dissolution of the United Democratic Front. Meanwhile, the centrist parties like the Janata Party led by Chandra Shekhar and the leftists like the Communist Party of India (CPI) and the Communist Party of India (Marxist-CPI [M]) all decided not to have any electoral alliances or seat adjustment with the BJP.

The BJP's 1984 Electoral Strategy

Its strategy of electoral alliance and seat adjustments with the non-Communist parties having failed, the BJP entered the 1984 electoral race on its own. Without such adjustments and alliance, the BJP had to rely basically on its new image and ideology, playing down its commitment to Hindu nationalism. The October 31, 1984, assassination of Indira Gandhi by her two Sikh security guards caused widespread Hindu backlash in north India and made the BJP's electoral plans all the more confused.

The BJP entered the 1984 race with a rededication to value-based politics, democracy, positive secularism, and Gandhian economics.[20] Its electoral manifesto expressed grave concern about the decay and decline in the state of Indian polity. It declared that "the state of the nation is exemplified by the breakdown of law and order, an absence of purpose and direction in the governance, deep divisions within society marked by deliberately engineered communal and castiest passions, and a serious erosion of institutions."[21] In order to save the territorial integrity of the country, the BJP pledged to reestablish national consensus and undertake new initiatives to solve the national problems.

To maintain national unity, the BJP election manifesto stressed the need to restore a balance between the Center and the states. It deplored the way the Congress party leadership over the years had reduced the states to a position of glorified municipalities. Such a development, the BJP believed, was against the spirit of the Constitution and was likely to undermine the unity of the country.

The BJP pledged to introduce several reforms, based on observations made over the years by intellectuals and academics, into India's electoral process. These included using voting machines, lowering the voting age to eighteen, and issuing identity cards to the voters. Without extensive electoral reforms, the BJP believed, it would be impossible to remove corruption from public life.

The party found that during previous few years:

> Corruption has not only become a way of life, but has, in fact, been institutionalized and legitimized. An unholy nexus has developed between the corrupt politicians, the corrupt bureaucrats and the corrupt businessmen. The volume of black-money has grown phenomenally and is now estimated at around fifty percent of the total money in circulation.[22]

Besides the electoral reforms, the BJP proposed creating an office of Ombudsman-*Lokpal* and *Lokayukt* to look into cases of corruption, to require ministers to make an annual declaration of their assets, to streamline procedures and rules for awarding of government contracts, and to undertake extensive tax reforms.

The BJP promised to deal with the political unrest in the northeastern states and in Punjab by resuming political dialogue. It blamed the Congress party for converting basically political agitation into separatist movements and mishandling the genuine demands of the people of Assam and Punjab for partisan gains.

During Indira Gandhi's domination of Indian politics, efforts were made to politicize the Indian judiciary and law enforcement agencies. In addition to working to stop the deterioration of law and order in the country through judicial reforms and implementation of the Police Commission's recommendations to modernize the police force and to raise its morale, the BJP also proposed deregulating the economy.

The BJP was not in favor of increasing taxes; rather it sought rationalization of the tax structure. At the same time, it promised to introduce a pension system for the aged poor, without spelling out how it would meet the cost. Like other political parties in India, the BJP also appealed to various groups like the laborers, farmers, women, and the scheduled castes and tribes, promising to improve their lots. The party also spelled out its stand on energy, national security, foreign policy, public housing, health, science and technology development, and a host of other issues.

The 1984 Electoral Failures and Search
for a New Strategy

Despite its elaborate electoral platform, ideological changes, and the projection of a new image, the 1984 election results spelled disaster for the BJP. It won only two out of 224 Lok Sabha seats which it contested. Even its president, Vajpayee, was defeated in his Gawalior constituency of the state of Madhya Pradesh, a stronghold of the BJP. "We failed to gauge the tide that was building up. The assassination [of Indira Gandhi] made things so different,"[23] he observed. Most observers agree that the assassination profoundly shocked the people of India and generated sympathy votes for the Rajiv Gandhi-led Congress (I), resulting in a landslide victory for the party, the main rival of the BJP.

However, there were much deeper reasons for the BJP's failure than the sympathy vote for the Congress (I).

Hindu Revivalism

In the 1980s India's Hindus, the dominant majority community of the country, were going through a militant transformation. Hindu militancy has taken several distinct forms. Religious revival, with emphasis on ritualism and organization of *poojas* and processions for Hindu gods and goddesses, and flocking to Hindu places of pilgrimages were expressions of this transformation.

This Hindu revivalism brought different, and even antagonistic, sectors of the Hindu society together. As strange and diverse bedfellows as Brahmins and members of the scheduled castes—even the supposedly godless cadre of the Dravida Munnetra Kazhagam and the All India Anna Dravida Munnetra Kazhagam—united to organize rituals such as the three *rathas* (chariots) named *Shakti* (power), *Gyanam* (knowledge), and *Deep* (light). The *rathas* started from villages in Tamil Nadu, crisscrossed south India each day carrying Hindu deities and swamis from various *maths* (monasteries), and passed through villages and Harijan *bsastis* (settlements) offering the lower castes the opportunity to perform certain *abhishekas* (rituals) which they are not allowed to do in the temples. Such rituals and ceremonies were designed to mobilize the Hindus into a united political force irrespective of caste and sectarian differences.

One very politically significant event was the *Ekamata Yagna* or integration rites. In this yagna, *Bharat Mata* (Mother India) joined the ranks of Hindu deities and was taken in procession and worshipped by hundreds of thousands of people on a *yatra* (pilgrimage) from one part of India to another. The pilgrimage was designed to express the Hindus' commitment to the territorial integrity of the country.

This *yagna* was conceived by the leaders of 85 sects comprised of more than 600 million Hindus. Its goal was to stress the fact that "India cannot be kept united without uniting the Hindus."[24] Even Indira Gandhi participated in this *yagna*. Earlier in 1982 she had spoken of the threat to Hindu *Dharma* at a meeting held in Ajmer. In the same year she had inaugurated the VHP-built *Bharat Mata* temple at Hardwar.[25]

Such a revival was puzzling to many intellectuals. One writer observed, "dogmas and rites, words and symbols and empty ceremonies have come to supplant the philosophy that was to help us to unveil the deepest layers of being. To most Hindus today these external trappings of religion have become the substance."[26] Another wrote that although there had been a flurry of religious activity in all areas, "I have never seen the kind of religious fervor that exists today. It is the response of a people who are not at peace."[27]

Such religious revival has deep psychological implications; it symbolized the assertion of Hindu identity, especially in north India where such rites and ceremonies are an integral part of Hindu folk culture. It was also their way of expressing their disapproval of the westernized Hindus, who had nothing but contempt for the Hindu folk culture.

Along with the Hindu middle class's granting of respectability to and the increased popularity of such existing militant Hindu organizations as the Rashtriya Swayamsevak Sangh (RSS) and Hindu Vishwa Parishad (World Hindu Council), several new cultural organizations and Hindu *senas* (armies) and *raksha dals* (defense organizations) emerged. Not only did Hindus express pride in their religious identity, but they also increased in militancy. Many towns and cities in north India resounded with new slogans like *Jo ham se takarye ga choor choor ho jaye ga* (Whosoever confronts us will be crushed) and *Hindu ki pahichan, trishul ka nishan* (Recognize Hindus by the sign of trident).[28] While seeking the conversion of Christians and Muslims to Hinduism, the Hindu revivalists expressed the determination to "liberate" more than two dozen Hindu temples that had been converted into mosques by Muslim rulers of India.

More significantly, many came to the realization that unless the Hindus close their ranks and assert their identity as the majority community, "they will be treated like dirt in their own homeland."[29] A large number of Hindus feared being overwhelmed by aggressive minorities and resented the assertion by politicians that Muslims were underrepresented in the services or suppressed. Amar Zutshi, for instance, considered this view on suppression of minorities a "perversion of historical facts. In fact, it was the Hindus who were subjected to centuries of repressive Mughal rule, culminating in the rise of Aurangzeb and followed by the British raj. But the Hindu spirit, culture and thought survived in spite of this long history of desecration, destruction and oppression."[30]

This revival and reassertion of Hindu militancy in the 1980s resulted from various other factors, too. Incidents like the conversion of scheduled caste Hindus to Islam in Meenakshipuram in Tamil Nadu and elsewhere, the increasing self-assertion of Muslims born in post-independence India, the fear of Islamic fundamentalism seen increasing on the strength of petro dollars, Khomeini religious fervor, and Zia's Islamization in Pakistan also contributed to the increase in Hindu militancy.

The growing militancy and terrorism of Sikhs in Punjab was another disturbing factor leading to the militant Hindu reaction. Sikhs are not one of India's underprivileged minorities; they are one of the most affluent communities of India, with the highest per capita income in the country. They represent almost fifteen percent of the country's armed forces and far more of India's elite civil services than any other minority. They have always been treated with kid gloves and respect, by Hindus and successive governments since independence. As Ashis Nandy points out:

The Sikhs had been traditionally seen by the Hindus as well as by the Sikhs themselves not as alien community but as part of the Hindu social order. After all, the principle of endogamy was never observed in Hindu-Sikh relations and the traditional social ties which bound the two communities were deep. That is, by conventional criteria, the Sikhs were not a minority nor did they see themselves as such.[31]

The leadership of Sant Jarnail Singh Bhindranwale changed this situation. Hindus were outraged when Bhindranwale branded them a community of "spindle-legged cowards" and when his hit squads systematically killed Hindus in Punjab. They noticed, in anger and frustration, that the majority of the Sikh leaders and intelligentsia did not raise their voices to condemn the fundamentalist preacher's hate campaign against Hindus, and their tolerance stretched to the breaking point when Sikhs complained of a Hindu conspiracy to deny Sikhs their due place in the political and economic structure of the country.

Many of the middle class Hindus attributed the aggressiveness of the minorities to the liberalism of Hindu elites and their tendency to appease these minorities. They held that the policies of the liberal-dominated government whetted the appetites of the minorities and encouraged them to make unreasonable demands on the system. To protect and ensure the survival of India's political system, an anxious Hindu middle class concluded that such minority assertions must be restrained.

Indira Gandhi and the Congress (I) party were quick to capitalize on the changing mood of the country. The Congress party took several major steps to win the Hindu vote. The first was to refuse to negotiate with the moderate Sikh leaders of Punjab's Akali party on their demands for greater state autonomy. This addressed the Hindus' concerns about the minorities' demands for preferential treatment.

Second, in June 1984, Indira Gandhi ordered the Indian army to flush out the Sikh militants hiding in the Golden Temple in the city of Amritsar. With this, she endeared herself to the Punjabi Hindus, and she won widespread acclaim among the Hindus of north India for maintaining India's territorial integrity. After her assassination in October 1984, her son, Rajiv Gandhi, won a landslide victory by projecting the Congress (I) as the only party capable of maintaining the territorial integrity of the country, the most cherished goal of the Hindus.

Meanwhile, the BJP, led by Vajpayee, was lost in confusion. While the party opposed the secessionist demands of the Akali Dal party, it sought a political solution to the moderate Sikh leaders' demand for greater autonomy for Punjab. It opposed and criticized the slaughter of the innocent Sikhs in Delhi and other parts of north India, which is believed to have been encouraged by functionaries of the Congress (I). Such an expression of sympathy for the Sikhs was a strategic blunder for the BJP, however, given the increasing Hindu militancy. As late as August 1985, Vajpayee was still insisting that there was no Hindu vote bank and that "the Hindu is liberal, secular and he wants a party whose doors will be open to all."[32]

Vajpayee and his liberal associates, like Jaswant Singh, Shanti Bhushan, Sikandar Bakht, and Ram Jethmalani, all non-Jana Sangh and non-RSS politicians, obviously did not accurately gauge the changes which had taken place in the mood and the concerns of the majority community. Their strategy of inclusion to gain a national political platform had become outdated. Unlike the Congress (I) party, the BJP did not make any strategic concessions to the coalescing Hindu population. As a result, they paid a political price for their insensitivity to the electoral climate, especially in Delhi, where the party lost all its Lok Sabha seats.

Rethinking Strategy and Ideology

The strategy pursued by the liberal-pragmatist group in the BJP had caused considerable confusion in the rank and file of the party. From the beginning, Vajpayee's ideological line, his efforts to make the party a broad-based organization representative of the multi-ethnic society, and the strategic alliance with the non-Communist parties did not get much support from various sectors of the party.

Vajpayee's goal was especially unpopular with the RSS leadership. By 1982, Professor Rajender Singh, the general secretary of the RSS, had declared that all parties, including the Congress (I), were equal for them. In fact, by the mid-eighties, the Congress (I) had become so openly identified with the Hindu cause that some of the key leaders of the RSS declared that no party could be an alternative to the Congress (I). They looked upon it as the guarantor of national unity.

The RSS leadership also no longer perceived the Congress (I) as a threat to Indian democracy. In fact, the RSS workers' disenchantment with the new BJP strategy was evident as early as 1983 when they showed little enthusiasm for the BJP candidates in the Delhi local elections, leading to the party's defeat.[33] Both the moderates and the hardliners within the BJP became alarmed with the RSS' drift away from the party.

The Vajpayee line was not even popular among some of the senior members of the party. For instance, Vijaya Raje Scindia, a senior leader and a formidable political force in Madhya Pradesh, had earlier opposed the Vajpayee line as alien both to Indian culture and to the party's ideological heritage. According to her, socialism was not only Marxist in origin—in whatever disguise it was presented—but it was also designed to create conflict within Hindu society. She believed that by adopting such an ideology, the BJP was likely to lose its distinct identity.[34] Both the party workers and the press expressed concern that the BJP had become a "B team" of the Congress (I).

In a March 1985 meeting of the National Executive Committee held in Calcutta, Vajpayee accepted the moral responsibility for the party's electoral debacle yet defended his strategy of forming alliances for electoral purposes and expressed his reluctance to revive the Bharatiya Jana Sangh ideology. But Vajpayee and his associates were aware of the discontent within the party with their ideological and electoral strategies. To rethink the party's direction,[35] he appointed a working group consisting of twelve members, headed by Krishanlal Sharma, a senior vice-president of the party.

The group went into extensive introspection. This self-analysis was considered imperative because the BJP had suffered a humiliating defeat and also because it had just completed five years of its existence. The National Executive Committee had given the group a broad mandate to assess the party's organizational, agitational, and ideological strategies as well as its electoral performances.

The group focused on establishing a distinct identity as well as self-preservation. A clear-cut ideological stance would give the party a distinct identity which would help mobilize voters and lead to its survival. Considering the increasing Hindu militancy, the Sharma Working Group was also charged with deciding whether the BJP should resurrect the Bharatiya Jana Sangh in place of the Bharatiya Janata Party.

The Sharma Working Group submitted its report on July 20, 1985 at the meeting of the National Executive Committee held in Bhopal. It gave a fairly positive verdict on the party's electoral performance. After an extensive study of Jana Sangh and Bharatiya Janata Party votes since 1952, the group observed that the BJP, in the 1984 elections, was able to maintain its electoral base, losing only one percent of the popular votes. It concluded that "but for the creation of an extraordinary situation and sympathy vote generated by Indira Gandhi's murder, and on the basis of the analysis of the votes polled by the party in the subsequent by-elections, [we believe that] the votes polled [by the BJP] in the 1984 elections would have gone up to ten to fifteen percent."[36] It recommended that over the next five years the party direct its efforts to capturing twenty to twenty-five percent of the votes in the national elections.[37]

Even though the report endorsed the leadership's decision not to resurrect the Jana Sangh, it suggested certain modifications in the party's ideological and organizational strategies in order to become an alternative to the Congress (I). It observed that "it is ideology alone which sparks enthusiasm in the party workers and reinforces their commitment to idealism. Also, an ideology is needed to establish a political party's distinct individuality."[38] Such a reassertion of the central role of ideology was essential to remove the confusion from the minds of the party rank and file.

Furthermore, while paying lip service to Gandhian socialism, the party reinstituted Deendayal Upadhyaya's Integral Humanism as the core of its ideology. It declared that the BJP "believes in the establishment of a society based upon the principles of Integral Humanism. Politics becomes a game of self-interest without commitments to values and principles."[39] The party reaffirmed its commitment to such ideals as integrity and unity of the country, democracy, value-based politics, positive secularism, and

Gandhian socialism. However, it declared, in no uncertain terms, that the BJP was dedicated to building a polity in India which conformed to Indian culture and traditions (*Bharatiya samskrit avam parmpara*).[40] To assure the party cadre for the future, it prohibited its leadership from entering into any negotiations with other political parties which could compromise the BJP's identity. Thus the BJP returned to its Jana Sangh legacy.

The party also sought to strengthen its organizational base. To expand the party support base, the Sharma Working Group suggested the BJP pay attention to the needs of the lower strata of the society, especially the workers, the slum dwellers, the women, the unemployed, the youth, the farmers, and other groups. It recognized that the party's cadre-based organization gave the BJP an edge over other parties, even if it was not enough.

The group also stated that the BJP needed to mobilize the minorities and the depressed sections of the society. The party should engage in not only electoral politics but also activities to penetrate such organizations as the cooperatives and the business, occupational, and labor movements. Diversifying its activities would enable the party to become influential in other sectors of public life.

In the October 1985 National Executive Committee meeting held in Gandhinagar, in the state of Gujarat, Integral Humanism was formally adopted as the basic philosophy of the party.[41] And the party pledged "to build up India as a strong and prosperous nation, which is modern, progressive and enlightened in outlook and *which proudly draws inspiration from India's age-old culture and values . . .* "[42] (emphasis added).

Although the Sharma Working Group adroitly avoided blaming Vajpayee and his moderate associates for the BJP's disastrous performance in the 1984 elections, it was evident that without a drastic change of strategy and reorientation of its ideology the BJP could not survive as a political force. The failure of the moderate wing of the BJP was not the only cause of the rise of hardliners within the party, however. The leaders of non-Congress democratic parties also contributed to the failure of the Vajpayee strategy by refusing to form an electoral alliance with the BJP and by ignoring Indira and Rajiv Gandhi's exploitation of Hindu nationalist sentiments.

Change in the Leadership and New Directions in Strategy

In 1986, the charismatic and liberal Vajpayee stepped down and Lal Krishan Advani became the president of the party. Both had worked closely over a long period of time in the Jana Sangh and Janata Party, and both were instrumental in founding the Bharatiya Janata Party. During their cooperation and close association, one could hardly discern much difference of opinion or of approach in the two. However, with Advani at the helm, the BJP entered a new and dynamic era.

With this change of leadership, the BJP became much more acceptable to the RSS and the old Jana Sangh hard core. The change in the leadership also rejuvenated the rank and file party members who were motivated by the basic tenets of Hindu nationalism rather than Gandhian socialism. By adopting the Sharma Working Group Report, the National Executive had given the signal for a change in the party's ideological stance. It was left to the new president to provide new strategic direction in conformity with the party's ideology.

In his presidential address Advani gave some idea of his strategy, emphasizing issues which were important to the majority of the Hindus. He denounced the cow slaughter in many states of India and the destruction of Hindu temples in Jammu and Kashmir. He declared that "for many politicians, and political parties, the secularism has become only a euphemism for political appeasement of minority sections which tend to vote *en bloc*. These politicians unabashedly propound the thesis that there is no such thing as minority communalism." And he added, "When two months back more than forty-five Hindu temples were destroyed in the Kashmir Valley, and large scale destruction of property took place, not a single party in the country, except the BJP, raised its voice of protest."[43]

Hindu militancy in 1986 no longer remained on the periphery of Indian politics but became a distinct force with enormous political potential. Vajpayee was cautious and avoided appealing directly to Hindu sentiment, recognizing that, for a politically stable India, it was unwise to alienate a religious minority like the Muslims. Advani, being more astute, sought to focus Hindu resentment against the Muslim communalism.

Advani had a better feel for the growing awareness among the Hindus, even the Hindu intellectuals, that many Muslims are communal in the sense that "they possess the necessary degree of community feeling; they are convinced that they have a religious-cultural-linguistic heritage which is worth defending whatever the price . . ."[44] Some Hindu intellectuals feared that if Muslims, in alliance with westernized Hindus, ever came to power, "the consequences would almost certainly be too horrendous to contemplate."[45]

Whether guided by their liberal orientations or by a real concern for the cultural autonomy of the minorities, many westernized Hindu intellectuals refused to criticize the rise of Muslim sectarian leadership in India. They left the Muslim community to deal with its own problems. Even though such a position may be reasonable, especially since Muslims are likely to resent any criticism coming from non-Muslims, this belief of westernized Hindu intellectuals would make them suspect in the eyes of the Hindu middle class, increasing their desire for a state based upon the concept of Hindu *rashtra*.[46]

Tapping into these sentiments, Advani declared that "at the head of the BJP's tally of basic commitments stand Nationalism and National Unity . . . the BJP is the voice of unalloyed nationalism. Ours is a 'Nation-First Party.'"[47] These assertions were designed to position the BJP to regain the votes it had lost to the Congress (I) in the 1984 elections.

Advani was also close to the top RSS leadership. Thus, he was able to bridge the communication gap between the two organizations. In fact, Advani was no longer concerned if the BJP was considered the political arm of the RSS. If Vajpayee was eager to project a secular image of the party, Advani had no such plan. Advani eagerly cultivated his party's relations with the RSS. The party's earlier strategy of distancing from the RSS and of political moderation did not endear it to the secularist parties, and they could not make much headway among the Muslims.

The leaders of the BJP and the RSS, having cadre-based organizations, agreed that they would no longer be tools for others to use for their political ends. After initial hesitation, the RSS chief, Balasaheb Deoras, publicly declared that "my sympathies are with the BJP and I need not be apologetic about it."[48] Although he did not direct the RSS workers to work for the BJP, he declared that the RSS would "support the parties which safeguard Hindu interests."[49]

Widespread discontentment among the Hindus had placed the RSS leadership in such a position that they had leverage even with other political parties. Harish Khare, a well known intellectual, writing in the *Times of India*, had even pleaded with the RSS leadership to consider Rajiv Gandhi as their political partner.[50] The increasing importance of the RSS leadership prompted the BJP to toe the RSS line in politics. The leadership of the two organizations agreed that the BJP and the RSS should work in tandem. They no longer needed disgruntled Congressmen to provide them respectability. The party leadership thought that former

Congressmen had ridden on their shoulders to political power and dumped them after achieving their goals.[51]

This was a period when electoral calculations were uppermost in the minds of the party leaders. It had become evident that the Congress (I) had become vulnerable. Rajiv Gandhi, with his clean political image, was elected with a massive electoral mandate in the 1984 elections. He aroused high expectations in the masses. He had promised to clean up Indian politics and usher India into the twenty-first century by revitalizing Indian polity and society.

The young and handsome grandson of Jawaharlal Nehru, who had entered politics reluctantly, was idolized by the media and Indian masses. However, by early 1987 Rajiv had lost much of his personal luster; he was no longer "Mr. Clean." Instead of eradicating corruption from the Indian body politic and distancing himself from the Congress (I) party's manipulators, power brokers, and influence peddlers, Rajiv's administration became identified even further with amoral politics and corrupt politicians.

His government and the Congress party officials were alleged to have received millions of dollars in kickbacks from foreign companies for huge government purchases for public sector projects.[52] *The Hindustan Times*, a respectable and pro-Congress (I) newspaper, declared, "the Congress has been repeatedly accused, in the press, of loading 'front-end' commission on defense contracts to raise funds for the elections and to meet other party expenses."[53]

A multi-million-dollar deal with Germany for a submarine confirmed the charge. In another important defense contract, with the Bofors company for artillery for the Indian army, it was alleged that Rs. 80 crores went to the coffers of the ruling party headed by Rajiv Gandhi.[54]

Rajiv also developed what many considered an imperial and arrogant style of governance, becoming inaccessible not only to the people but also to high government and party officials. He lacked consistency and stability in his administrative organization. For instance, Rajiv reshuffled his cabinet twenty-seven times during his five-year term of office, and between 1985 and 1989 he changed Congress (I) party chief ministers in the states twenty times. In addition, he surrounded himself with a small number of advisors, primarily civil servants, media experts, and foreign-trained technocrats who did not have roots in traditional Indian society.

Widespread disenchantment with Rajiv and the Congress (I) improved the chances of the opposition parties to dislodge them from power. There could not be a more ominous omen for the Congress (I) than the June 1988 victory of Vishwanath Pratap Singh in a special election held to fill a vacancy in the Lok Sabha from Allahabad. Allahabad, the birthplace of

Jawaharlal Nehru, was considered a Congress (I) stronghold. Furthermore, this election carried a special significance, since Singh, a former defense minister in the Rajiv government and close advisor to the prime minister, was fired in 1987 for raising questions about corruption in high places, especially about commissions received on the purchase of defense equipment from foreign companies. He defeated his Congress (I) party rival, supported by Rajiv, by more than a hundred thousand votes.[55]

Sensing its opponent's weakness, the BJP, under the leadership of Advani, denounced Rajiv and declared that "He is surrounded by a coterie of corrupt sycophants. Serious charges have been levelled against his ministerial colleagues and party functionaries whose probity is in question."[56] In a blistering attack, it added:

> Rajiv Gandhi has compromised, and continues to compromise, on every issue—political, social and economic—that affects national unity and security. The regime has turned out to be even more corrupt, and more incompetent than that of Mrs. Gandhi. Today, the country is a rudderless ship, drifting amidst a sea of sharks and rocks. Today, the unity, integrity, security and honor of India are more in danger than any time since Independence.[57]

At the same time India faced many serious internal problems, including secessionist movements in Punjab, Assam, the northeastern regions, and Darjeeling district of West Bengal. Political upheaval was also brewing in the critical states of Jammu and Kashmir, where, in July 1984, Rajiv Gandhi dismissed the state government of the Kashmir National Conference led by Dr. Farooq Abdullha. Subsequently, an alliance of the Congress (I) and the Kashmir National Conference rigged the state elections, causing widespread discontentment that led to a state of insurgency.[58]

India has also been plagued with frequent outbreaks of violence involving Hindus and Muslims. The number of riots dramatically increased in the 1980s, resulting in thousands of deaths and destruction of property worth millions of dollars. For instance, in the infamous 1987 Meerut riots, 150 people lost their lives while more than a thousand were injured. It is estimated that nearly 4,000 people were killed in communal riots during the 1980s, almost four times the number for the 1970s.[59]

The long-standing Ramjanambhoomi-Babri mosque dispute, an issue of intense emotional confrontation between Hindus and Muslims, resurfaced in the 1980s. In recent years, the VHP (Vishwa Hindu Parishad, World Hindu Council) had launched a campaign to construct a Hindu temple at the purported birthplace of Lord Rama in Ayodhya, where a Muslim mosque built by Babur, the Mughal emperor, stood. In October 1984, the

Ramjanambhoomi Action Committee was formed and demanded access to the birthplace of Lord Ram, the sacred shrine for the Hindus. To counter-act Hindu demands and to protect the mosque, the Muslims organized the Babri Masjid Action Committee. The Rajiv government, fearing a Hindu backlash, directed the officials to provide Hindus access to the shrine. On February 1, 1986, on the orders of a district judge, Hindus were allowed to worship at the shrine. Soon after, the VHP came up with a blueprint for the construction of a Ramjanambhoomi temple at the site where the Babri Mosque stood.[60] Wittingly or unwittingly, the Rajiv government had created a highly emotional issue which would ultimately become a com-munal flashpoint as well as an electoral issue.

Elections were due in 1989. In the absence of intra-party democracy, the Congress (I) organization was in disarray. Rajiv had lost his clean image and was no longer in a position to guarantee electoral majority for his party.

Opposition parties, however, were still unable to devise a strategy which would enable them to defeat Rajiv. V.P. Singh, the former defense min-ister of Rajiv Gandhi, was known for his personal integrity and discipline. He was also a skillful communicator, who demonstrated his ability to establish rapport with the common man in the Hindi-speaking states of north India in the Allahabad election. He could have posed a challenge to Rajiv and his Congress (I). But his Jan Morcha (People's Front), a collection of disgruntled Congress men, was not even a political party and thus had no grass-roots organization. However, there were many old players, representing the Lok Dal (now divided into two factions), Janata Party, the leftist parties like the Communist Party of India (CPI) and the Communist Party of India (Marxists), and a host of regional parties, like DMK of Tamil Nadu, Telugu Desam of Andhra Pradesh, Congress (S) of Kerala, and the Asom Gana Party (AGP) of Assam.

Besides these, the rest of the centrist or secular parties represented various versions of the Congress culture. They were also headed mostly by former Congress men, who had left the Congress (I) because of personality conflicts or ideological differences or were expelled from the party for various reasons. They were mostly men with very limited vision. The BJP, in dealing with these political obstacles, still was unable to challenge the Congress (I) on its own, despite the increase in Hindu militancy.

In 1989, however, the Bharatiya Janata Party and its leadership had set up clear and realistic goals. Advani declared that "Our objective is the ouster of the Rajiv government and to acquire a sizable strength in the [Ninth] Lok Sabha in 1990 . . . sizable enough to be able to give direction to the policy."[61] Again the BJP rejected forming a united single party by the merger of non-communist opposition, as was proposed by some of the opposition leaders. From the history of the working of Indian political parties, Advani concluded that "it is multi-polarity which should be accepted as the rule, and that bipolarity can only be a rare exception, almost a freak." He added that "almost all attempts at fusion have invariably been followed by fission."[62] Thus, the BJP would strictly limit its strategic alliances for electoral seat adjustment.

The electoral strategies of the BJP and the non-Communist opposition parties were also influenced by the leftist and Communist parties of India. Both the BJP and the Communists are cadre-based and ideologically-oriented parties. Both wanted to be the core of the opposition's united front against the Congress (I). As partners in any non-Congress (I) central government, because of their cohesiveness and discipline, whichever became a coalition partner would have to share political power. For the Communists the BJP was a political and ideological untouchable.

Furthermore, the Communists and the leftists, having only a regional base, mainly in West Bengal and Kerala, would not compete for votes with the non-Communist parties opposed to the Congress (I). The BJP was their main competitor in the Hindi-speaking states of north India. The BJP could, however, provide them with the cadre and the organizations which the centrist parties needed to mobilize the voters.

The Communists and the BJP had cooperated with each other in the past, and there was some indication that the BJP leadership, for the sake of the opposition unity, was willing to deal with them. K.R. Malkani, for instance, observed:

> Neither the Right nor the Left can impose itself on the country. The Left will have to move Right, and Right will have to move Left, if either of them hopes to widen its base and become the mainstream. The eventual choice is not going to be between Right and Left, but between a little Right of Center and a little Left of Center."[63]

The BJP leadership was prepared to be flexible in order to oust the Congress (I) from power. But the Communists refused to participate in any alliance which would include the BJP.

By August 1988, through the efforts of N.T. Rama Rao, the chief minister of Andhra Pradesh, a seven-party alliance called the National Front was launched. Its objective was to provide a viable alternative to the Congress (I). V.P. Singh was appointed the convener of the National Front. It was a loose collection of centrist political parties, all of which were allowed to maintain their organizational identities. In the north, various opposition parties and groups, like the factions of the Lok Dal, Janata Party, Smajwadi Janata Party, and Jan Morcha, merged and formed a new party called Janata Dal. Singh was its star attraction and Devilal its president.

The BJP leadership, once again, was faced with a dilemma not entirely of its own creation. The BJP's leadership clearly sought to join the mainstream of Indian politics. Jaswant Singh, presently the deputy leader of the BJP parliamentary wing, observed that the BJP "leaders are committed secularists and humanists who display remarkable restraint in public utterance and behavior. They have true *bhadralok* [middle class] values."[64] While he conceded that the BJP's rank and file inherited a political culture of extreme Hindu nationalism like that of Hindu Mahasabha and Jana Sangh, ". . . its cadre are given to more vocal bigotry than those of other parties who may be no less communal."[65] As a result, "Whenever its national leaders try and usher the party into mainstream politics, two things happen: the cadre gets restive and the other national parties—seeing the emergence of a possible alternative—get nervous and begin wholesale attacks on the BJP."[66]

The BJP leadership extended its support to V.P. Singh, when he was heading the Jan Morcha. It provided him workers to organize his meetings and helped him win the crucial election of Allahabad. However, in 1989, with elections forthcoming and the possibility an electoral alliance with the left parties, he turned his back on the BJP. Singh asked the party leadership to prove its secular credentials. As a result, when shunned by the opposition parties, the BJP returned to its roots.

This time around, however, the BJP leadership displayed considerable confidence. The BJP's performance in the 1988 local elections in the crucial state of U.P. was impressive. In the 1987 elections, the BJP had won only thirty-three block *pramukh* (head) seats. In 1988, the party was able to capture seventy-four seats. Likewise, in 1987, the BJP in the Zila Parishad (district board) elections captured only twenty-eight seats, but in 1988 the number went up to 110. The BJP was equally successful in municipal elections.[67] The BJP was on the march; its leadership could afford to enter into hard bargaining with the leaders of the non-Communist opposition parties.

With increased polarization between Hindus and Muslims, especially due to the Ramjanambhoomi-Babri Masjid issue, there were for the first time clear indications that to counter the Muslims a Hindu vote bank might be emerging. Vishwa Hindu Parishad was successfully mobilizing Hindu masses in the crucial states of U.P., Bihar, Rajasthan, and other Hindi-speaking states of north India. B.L. Sharma, the general secretary of the

VHP, had declared the group's intention to create a Hindu vote bank, and only those who supported their demands would get their votes.[68]

Since 1986 the Congress (I) has been maintaining a balancing act between the two communities. It conceded to the Muslim sentiment on the Shah Bano case and tried to appease them by passing the Muslim Women Protection and Divorce Law. Meanwhile, it tried to please the Hindus by opening the Babri mosque to Hindu worship. But the VHP was not satisfied; it renewed its claim to Krishna Janamboomi (the birthplace of Lord Krishna) at Mathura and Kashi-Vishwanath temple at Varanasi, two Hindu sacred places which were earlier converted to mosques during the period of Muslim rule in India. Hindu revivalism was on the rise.

In the BJP, Advani skillfully used the Ramjanambhoomi-Babri conflict to force the issue of the Congress (I) policy of minority appeasement. The Ayodhya issue, Advani argued, was not simply a dispute, but since "it has become a symbol of pseudo secularism and appeasement of the minorities, the BJP has taken a clear stand [that it is the birthplace of Lord Ram and should be a temple]." At the same time he added that they would not make it an electoral issue.[69] It was a clever ploy. Since the BJP was on the side of the Hindu revivalists, it had already written off the Muslim votes. It clearly put the Congress (I) on the spot. Now, the latter had to come out with a clear stand on the issue. The BJP was determined not to let the Congress (I) play the Hindu card.

The BJP's 1989 Electoral Strategy: The Mobilization of the Hindu Vote Through Electoral Alliance

In 1989, the BJP entered the election campaign after making an electoral alliance with seat adjustments with different components of the National Front, mainly the Janata Dal of V.P. Singh. The Janata Dal's power base was in the countryside of the Hindi-speaking states of north India. The BJP intended to mobilize the Hindu upper caste vote without letting the Congress (I) take advantage of a divided opposition. The BJP leadership seemed to have considered the Janata Dal only a passing phase in the party politics of India, with the Congress (I) its main rival.

The BJP's electoral manifesto sharply attacked the record of the Rajiv-led Congress (I) government. It held the government responsible for the steady deterioration in public morality and added that "people feel sad that through an accident of history this country should have been saddled with a coterie of small men who are not only incompetent and corrupt, but who lack a sense of commitment to the nation, its democratic institutions and cultural traditions."[70] It expressed doubts about Rajiv Gandhi's personal probity on the Bofors issue and accused him of "unabashedly misleading the Parliament and the Nation even on crucial issues of national defense and security."[71]

Commenting on the various accords signed with the regional parties and Sri Lanka to end disputes, the manifesto asserted that "Accords have ended up in discords. The Rajiv regime is bathed in blood and muck from head to foot, from Punjab to Assam and from Kashmir to Sri Lanka."[72]

It was generally agreed that the Congress (I) government had mismanaged the demands for regional autonomy made by the leaders of Punjab, Assam, and Kashmir for partisan purposes. Its intervention in Sri Lanka's internal affairs, after the Sri Lanka government sought India's help in suppressing Tamil insurgency in the northeastern provinces of the island country, proved to be a political disaster.

A majority of the Hindus of India, especially the urban middle class, were at this stage of the country's political development deeply apprehensive about increasing lawlessness as well as the territorial integrity of the country. Capitalizing on these sentiments, the BJP's election manifesto asserted that "the Bharatiya Janata Party is wedded to the Unity and Integrity of India. It stands for Law and Order—for Justice, Social and Economic and for Security, Internal and External."[73] And, it asked, "How can men who lack integrity themselves, and are not above looting the country, defend the country and protect its integrity and honor?"[74]

Appealing further to Hindu sentiments, it criticized the government's mishandling of the Shah Bano case, its banning of Salaman Rushdie's novel, *The Satanic Verses*, without even reading the book, and its hasty recognition of Urdu as the second official language in U.P. on the eve of the elections in order to win Muslim votes. In addition, the BJP charged that "by not allowing the rebuilding of Ram Janam Mandir in Ayodhya, on the lines of Somnath Mandir built by the Government of India in 1948, it has allowed tension to rise, and gravely strained social harmony."[75] The BJP reaffirmed its commitment to "positive secularism which stands for *'Justice for All and Appeasement for None.'*"[76]

The forty-page election manifesto covered a variety of subjects, including the extensive election and campaign finance reforms, removal of corruption from public life, limiting the size of the cabinets, increasing the financial powers of the states, reforming the judicial system in India, and others.

Advani's aggressive embracing of Hindu nationalism and his strategy of electoral alliance and seat adjustment proved to be enormously successful. The BJP was able to capture eighty-six seats in the Lok Sabha, a dramatic increase from the two seats which it had won in the 1984 elections. It became the third largest party in Parliament, after the Rajiv-led Congress (I) with 193 seats and the Janata Dal, headed by V.P. Singh, with 141 seats.

It was evident that Hindu nationalism, with the support of Hindu revivalists, had become a major political force in the country. Balraj Puri wrote that "The major issues in the 1989 elections were [a] concern for the stability and the integrity of the country, [b] consciousness of community, caste and ethnic identities, [c] resentment against corruption and scandals and [d] an urge for socio-economic equality."[77] He added, "however, the election results show that *Hindutva*, Hindu consciousness, Hindu backlash, anti-minorityism, or whatever name might be given to the phenomenon, has emerged as the most significant new force in the politics of India."[78]

Strategy of Selective Cooperation

Following its strategy of trying to get the Congress (I) out of power, the BJP leadership extended its support to the V.P Singh-led National Front, with the Janata Dal being the main component, in the formation of the new government. Singh became the prime minister of India in December 1989.

For the first time in post-independence politics, a minority government at the national level assumed office supported by two parties which belonged to two diametrically opposed ideological camps. The right wing Hindu nationalists and the BJP joined with the Communist parties of the Marxist left. They were guided by different motives in this new experiment.

For the Communists, it was a unique opportunity to influence the decision making in the allocation of resources at the national level. During the Congress (I) regime, they felt that states ruled by the Communist and Left Fronts were denied their fair share in the allocation of development funds. For decades, the Communist parties, though powers to reckon with in West Bengal and Kerala, had failed to extend their influence into the Hindi-speaking states of north India. They were expecting to extend their power base in the north by riding on the shoulders of the Janata Dal.

The BJP allied with the Janata Dal and the National Front for different reasons. The BJP needed time to consolidate its gains. It also needed to demonstrate its ability to act responsibly by supporting a national alternative to the Congress (I). Furthermore, Singh was a very popular leader. The BJP calculated, however, that the Janata Dal, being highly factionalized, internally divided, and dominated by politically ambitious personalities, was unlikely to maintain its internal cohesion and thus its government the full five years. BJP leaders thought that by supporting the government from outside and thus not having a share in the political power when the National Front government fell under its own weight, the party could emerge as the people's sole alternative to the Congress (I). The BJP also needed an electoral alliance with the Janata Dal in the forthcoming state legislative elections to win power in some of the crucial north Indian states.

The BJP's calculations were proven correct when, in the February 1990 state legislative elections, the Janata Dal-BJP alliance made impressive gains in such critical north Indian states as Madhya Pradesh, Rajasthan, and Himachal Pradesh. The BJP formed the governments either on its own or with the help of the Janata Dal and ousted the Congress (I) from power. It also improved its electoral performance in the western states of Maharashtra and Gujarat. In Gujarat, it shared power with the Janata Dal by defeating the Congress (I). Although it did not share power with the Janata Dal in U.P. or in Bihar, in the 1990 state elections it captured more than twice the seats that it had won in the 1985 state elections. Thus, in cooperation with the Janata Dal, the BJP was able to eliminate its main rival, the Congress (I), from the Hindi-speaking states of north India.

Confrontation and Mass Mobilization

The eleven months of the V.P. Singh-led National Front government were not enough for the BJP to consolidate its gains and to mount a challenge to its centrist political ideology in its quest for political power. Nevertheless, driven by the internal power struggle within the Janata Dal, Singh threw a challenge to the BJP, which it could ignore only at its own peril.

On August 7, 1990, following the recommendations of the Mandal Commission, Singh announced a twenty-seven percent reservation of jobs in the central government and public undertaking for the socially and educationally backward castes. This was in addition to around twenty-three percent of such jobs for the scheduled castes and scheduled tribes already provided. This job quota system was undertaken to improve the lot of the underprivileged sectors of Indian society. Whether such a decision was motivated by the government's desire to seek distributive justice in a rapidly changing society or by electoral considerations may be debatable. Many Indians believed that the Singh government's decision to implement the recommendations of the Commission was guided primarily by its goal to build a solid vote bank of lower and backward castes in the countryside, where a majority of this group lived.

The BJP rank and file were already unhappy with many policies of the Singh government. Many of them believed that Singh and his associates were making desperate efforts to consolidate their hold on the Muslim votes. Singh's constant consultation with Abdullah Bukhari, Shahi Imam of Jama Masjid of Delhi, and his declaration of the prophet Mohammad's birthday as a public holiday were cited as examples of the government's appeasement of the minorities. They could not understand the BJP leadership's support of such a government, which many believed was inimical to the interests of Hindus.

The BJP leadership, however, did disapprove of the Singh government's handling of the Muslim fundamentalism in Kashmir and the consequent flight of thousands of Kashmiri pundits from the Valley; its dismissal of a tough governor of the state, Jagmohan; its failure to take a forceful stand against Pakistan's interference in the affairs of Jammu and Kashmir as well as Punjab; its denial of statehood to Delhi as promised in the platform of the National Front; and its failure to waive farmers' loans as promised. The BJP believed that the Singh government was using their party's support to promote its own agenda without even consulting them.[79]

Enforcing of the recommendations of the Mandal Commission was perceived as a direct threat to the BJP's strategy of consolidating the Hindu vote bank by bringing the Hindus of the country, irrespective of their caste affiliations, under the BJP's flag. It was also contrary to the ideological premises of Hindu nationalism which emphasized the political unification of Hindus. The BJP leadership feared that such a move not only would strengthen caste loyalties but might also lead to hostilities between the lower and upper caste Hindus, especially in the rural areas. This would destroy the party's hope of mobilizing the Hindu majority vote in the Hindi-speaking states of north India.

The BJP's traditional support base has been urban upper caste Hindus, who constitute India's rapidly growing middle class. It is the members of this class who exercise control over industry, finance, administration, and even the machinery responsible for maintaining law and order in the country. This class opposed job reservation on a caste basis.

The BJP leaders concluded that only a purely religious issue could unite Hindus, regardless of caste/class divisions. They therefore decided to mobilize the Hindus on the basis of the highly emotional issue of reestablishing their control over the sacred place in Ayodhya, the birthplace of Lord Ram.

This strategy resulted in Advani's *rath yatra*, a journey in an air-conditioned Toyota converted into a chariot through hundreds of miles of Hindu-majority states in September 1990. The massive movement resulted in the fall of the V.P. Singh government in November 1990 and extensive Hindu-Muslim riots involving loss of lives and property. It also prompted the Mulayam Singh Yadav-led Janata Dal government of U.P., in its eagerness to consolidate the Muslim vote bank, to use excessive police force against BJP workers and *karsevaks* (Hindu devotees and volunteers), resulting in the alienation of the Hindu community in India's most populous state. When his party decided to withdraw BJP support from the Singh government, Advani declared in Parliament that "Ayodhya was not the only reason but Ayodhya was certainly the last straw" in bringing the V.P. Singh government down.[80]

The 1991 Elections: The BJP on Its Own

Through its various maneuvers and strategies, the BJP was now successful in projecting the Nehruvian secularism of the centrist parties like the Congress (I), Janata Dal of V.P. Singh, and the Samajwadi Janata Dal of Chandra Shekhar, a breakaway faction of the Janata Dal, as basically an anti-Hindu doctrine which was designed to satisfy minorities, especially the Muslims at the cost of Hindus.

Also, by this time, public disgust with the centrist parties was increasing. The unprincipled public behavior of some of the leaders like Devilal and Chandra Shekhar, the constant factional bickering within their organizations, the complete disregard for the democratic process by the Haryana state Janata Dal leadership, and the formation of opportunistic alliances to capture political power made it evident that these parties represented the same old Congress culture disdained by the people, especially the urban middle class.

The BJP's election platform was directed first toward winning the support of the Hindu middle classes, but it also sought the support of the farmers and socially and economically backward castes among Hindus. This was evident from the fact that despite its opposition to the Singh government's decision to implement recommendations of the Mandal Commission, the 1991 election platform of the BJP declared that "Reservation [of jobs] should be made for the backward classes broadly on the basis of the Mandal Commission Report," but it added that preference should be given to the poor among those classes.[81] To satisfy its middle class supporters, however, the BJP recommended the adoption of economic criteria for the poor upper castes.

The BJP's election platform carried the title "Mid-Term Poll to Lok Sabha, May 1991: Our Commitments Towards Ramrajya." In an open appeal to Hindu sentiments, the platform pledged to construct the Shri Ram temple at Ayodhya and to relocate the Babri structure "with due respect."[82]

Its platform also incorporated a free market-oriented economic program, with a promise to relax bureaucratic control over the Indian economy, decentralize government control over industries, and replace the Industrial Development and Regulation Act by the Industrial Development Act so that the government would not have a commanding role in determining industrial policies. Following its conservative economic and political philosophies, it stated that the state should shift its attention from commercial activities to basic functions like maintaining law and order, justice, welfare programs, the infrastructure, etc.[83]

The more than thirty-seven-page election manifesto of the BJP covered such subjects as election and judicial reforms, removal of corruption from public life, *panchayati raj*, cow protection and cattle wealth, agriculture, handicrafts and village industries, fiscal reforms, and many others. However, the BJP ran its electoral campaign primarily on the issue of the construction of the Ramjanambhoomi temple at the site of the Babri mosque, while strongly denouncing the "pseudo-secular" policies of the centrist political parties and thus exploiting the rising Hindu religious militancy to mobilize votes. This time, the BJP did not hesitate to project itself as the party wholly dedicated to the cause of Hindus and their religious and nationalistic aspirations and, thus, went on its own into the election fray.

The strategy paid rich dividends in the May-June parliamentary elections when it doubled its percentage of votes nationwide. The BJP also made gains in states like Karnataka and Andhra Pradesh in the south and Assam and West Bengal in the northeast. It emerged as the second largest party in the Lok Sabha, after the Congress (I), although it did suffer some setbacks in the BJP-ruled states of Madhya Pradesh, Rajasthan, and Himachal Pradesh and did not win any seats in West Bengal. But the BJP captured a majority of the Lok Sabha seats in Uttar Pradesh, where it also won a majority in the state legislative assembly and formed the government.

The BJP's performance showed that the party had the potential to emerge as an alternative to the Congress (I). The indications were that the sympathy vote generated by the assassination of Rajiv Gandhi helped the Congress (I) at the expense of the BJP in the second round of elections, especially in states like Rajasthan and to a lesser extent, Bihar. Further-more, the BJP, for the first time, fielded candidates in as many as 477 Lok Sabha constituencies and won 120, and its candidates came in second in about 130 districts without making any seat adjustment with any other party. An exit poll conducted by *India Today/MARG* showed that the BJP vote was not confined to the upper castes but gained substantial support among the backward castes, young voters and men.[84]

A Strategy of Cooperation and Responsible Opposition

After the May-June 1991 elections, the BJP controlled four state govern-ments in north India, including U.P, India's most populous state, and Madhya Pradesh, Rajasthan, and Himachal Pradesh. For the first time in its history, the BJP constituted the second largest party in the Lok Sabha and the main opposition, no mean achievement for a party that in 1984 was only on the periphery of Indian politics.

To win the confidence of the people and to emerge as a creditable alternative to the Congress (I) party, the BJP now had to demonstrate to the people that it could act responsibly in the Lok Sabha and that its governments in the states could govern effectively and impartially despite its public espousal of militant Hindu nationalism. It especially had to allay the fears of the Muslims in U.P., where they constituted 15.5 percent of the population and where, in recent years, frequent outbreaks of Hindu-Muslim riots and the ineffectiveness of civil administration had shaken their confidence in the law enforcement agencies.

At the national level, the BJP also had an opportunity to influence the policies of the new government headed by P.V. Narasimha Rao, who, in June 1991, became the leader of the Congress (I) after Rajiv Gandhi's assassination in Tamil Nadu. Even though Rao led a minority government, the uncertain conditions created by Rajiv's assassination and frequent outbreaks of political violence in the country demanded responsible behavior on the part of both the opposition and the new government.

During this critical period, the country also faced a serious economic crisis created by the severe shortage of foreign exchange and the grim possibility of default. Whether under the pressure of the World Bank and the International Monetary Fund or on its own, the Rao government, immediately after assuming power in June 1991, introduced a far-reaching liberalization of the economy, reversing the Nehruvian model of command economy, and brought about drastic changes oriented towards a market economy, all of which were advocated by the BJP election platform. The BJP thus supported the new economic policies of the government. Advani and Rao developed a close personal relationship, leading to frequent consultation and cooperation of the leaders of the two parties.

Rao and the BJP needed each other, since the Rao-led Congress (I) government did not have a majority in the Lok Sabha and many of its economic policies were strongly opposed by the V.P. Singh-led Janata Dal and the Communists and even by a section of his own party. The Rao government depended upon the BJP's cooperation for its approval by Parliament. In turn, the BJP sought Rao's support for the BJP governments in four states.

In this way the mutual interests forced the leaders of the two parties to work in cooperation resulting in the election of the Speaker (a Congress [I] candidate) and Deputy Speaker (a BJP candidate) of the Lok Sabhas and approval of the economic program of the new government in 1991 and also the national budget in 1992, which was again opposed by the centrist and the leftist parties. Such cooperation also reflected the statesmanship qualities of Advani, the leader of the opposition in the Lok Sabha. Advani called Rao the best prime minister India had had since Lal Bahadur Shastri.

However, cooperation between the leadership of the Congress (I) and the BJP was likely to be influenced by the power struggle between the factional leaders of the two parties. Within the Congress (I), Rao was under pressure from two of his main rivals, Arjun Singh and Sharad Pawar, who had adopted a militant anti-BJP posture in public. Singh, in particular, put Rao in a difficult position when he demanded the dismissal of the BJP government in his home state, Madhya Pradesh. Singh also sought to build an independent support base by mobilizing defeated and demoralized Congressmen in the Hindi-speaking states of north India, where Rao had little support.

Advani was also under pressure from his party's hardliners. The BJP had used the Ramjanambhoomi-Babri mosque issue to mobilize the Hindu vote. The militant Hindu organizations, like the Vishwa Hindu Parishad (World Hindu Council) and its paramilitary wing, the Bajarang Dal, were eager to demolish the mosque and demanded action on building the temple.[85] Furthermore, the party hardliners, led by the party president, Murli Manohar Joshi, were bent upon undertaking *Ekta yatra* (a unity march) to highlight the government's failure to protect Hindus and suppress the Muslim militant-led insurgency in Kashmir and other secessionist movements in India. The *Ekta yatra*, it was claimed by some of its supporters, was intended to highlight the outside threats to the geopolitical unity of India and to underscore the seriousness of the situation.[86] However, it was feared that such an undertaking might cause Hindu-Muslim riots. Other observers, both inside and outside of the BJP, looked upon the *Ekta yatra* as a political gimmick employed by Joshi to enhance his personal political stature. By this time, it was evident that the BJP was not free from political infighting. Whatever the motives of these factions, given the volatile situation existing in India, the BJP moderates, led by Vajpayee and Jaswant Singh, sought a cooling off period to sort out complex issues through negotiation, mediation, and legal action.

Finally, this cooperation between the BJP and the Rao-led Congress (I) suffered a sharp setback when Arjun Singh denounced the BJP in the plenary session of the All India Congress Committee held in April 1992 in Tirupati. Singh called upon the Congressmen "to rise and fight the BJP so that the country could be liberated from its communal tentacles."[87] Echoing Singh's line of argument, Rao asserted that non-secular parties (implying the BJP) had no place in a secular state and that "these militate against the spirit of the constitution,"[88] and he called for a legal ban on such parties. While commending Rao for his bold stand, the *Times of India* commented that ". . . Mr. Rao is mentally and politically preparing himself to do, if need be, without the BJP's support in Parliament."[89]

Although Rao's denunciation of the exploitation of religious issues for political purposes, especially for electoral mobilization, was clear and unequivocal, his stand on the nature of the activities of political parties was not. According to the *Hindustan Times*, his call for "legislation to bar so-called communal parties could bring most parties under its mischief. They are all naked under the shirt when it comes to vote-seeking."[90] Whether Rao was vague by design or not, it was evident that he had yielded to the pressure within his party to break the working relationship with the BJP leadership.

These developments within the Congress party put the BJP leadership, especially its moderate sections, in a quandary. The factional lines had become clear: the hardliners, led by Joshi, were no longer willing to wait to strike against the Rao government. They wanted to exploit the issue of the construction of the Ram temple in Ayodhya to whip up Hindu sentiment against the Congress (I). While the moderate section of the BJP believed that the temple issue had outlived its political utility, it could not deliver any more votes.

The reality was, however, that the temple issue could no longer embarrass the Rao government. The issue was already in Allahabad High Court, and the hands of the BJP-led U.P. government were tied by the litigation. The U.P. government could not defy the court. Kalyan Singh, the BJP chief minister of the state, for both political and legal reasons could not demolish the Babri mosque, which the Hindu militants demanded. Therefore, the Rao government did not need to take any drastic action against a popularly elected state government and bid for time. It correctly perceived that it was the BJP leadership which needed to face the challenge to solve the issue.[91]

The BJP hardliners, however, felt that "if the Congress goes out of the way to attack the BJP we are not going to sit back and listen."[92] It was the RSS mouthpiece, *Organiser*, which, while reacting to the Congress (I) attack on the BJP, expressed the hardliners' anger when it declared:

> Suffering from double-talk and double-think, the Indian National Congress, the mother of all terrorist outfits in the country which is ever sacrificing national interests at the altar of vote-banks of Secular Fundamentalists, has . . . launched a frontal attack on the nationalist Bharatiya Janata Party maligning it as a 'communal party' of Hindu majorityism and ruling out any understanding and cooperation with it.[93]

In the May 1992 National Council meeting held in Gandhinagar, Gujarat, the BJP leadership strongly denounced the Rao government not only for its failure to solve the Punjab problem, to complete its enquiry on the Bofors, and to control inflation but also for its economic program. The BJP leaders thought the program would mortgage the future of the country to the international financial agencies. Furthermore, the BJP reaffirmed its

> passionate plank of *Hindutva* but also reiterated its firm and clear commitment to construct or 'reconstruct' the Ram temple at Ayodhya. The Gandhinagar session thus transformed the BJP from a 'consensus-conscious friendly' opponent of the Congress into a self-righteous dogged, if not bitter, opponent of the latter.[94]

Despite all the public posturing, indications were that the moderate BJP leaders were not yet ready to terminate their understanding with Prime Minister Rao. The BJP was still keen to prove itself in the four states where it held power and to play an opposition role at the Center.[95] It did not want to rock the boat. However, at this stage in this power play, the BJP was at a disadvantage. With the start of 1992, the power equation in the Lok Sabha had changed. In the February 1992 elections held in Punjab, the Congress won all the Lok Sabha seats from that state and was also assured of the support of the smaller groups, independent MPs and the breakaway Telugu Desam faction. Consequently the Rao government no longer needed the support of the BJP for its survival.

Back to Confrontation and Mass Mobilization

According to Krishanlal Sharma, the vice-president of the BJP, the developments at the Tirupati Congress (I) session and the Gandhinagar BJP meeting held in early 1992 laid bare the ideological polarization between the two parties. He added that "The Congress has realized we are its main rivals and we will not stop short of replacing it at the Center."[96] Given this kind of attitude on the part of some of its leaders, it is difficult to speculate whether it was the BJP's electoral calculations or the pressure from the hardliners led by the VHP and the RSS, or both, which forced the BJP, by the end of 1992, to adopt a strategy of confrontation and mass mobilization. The focus was again the construction of the Ram temple in Ayodhya, a highly emotional and politically explosive issue. The leaders of all political parties, including the BJP, were aware of the likely consequences of its exploitation for political purposes.

Many were shocked when the leadership of a major political party, seeking to prove its ability to provide a stable government and ignoring the legal implications involved, declared that construction of the Ram temple in Ayodhya was an issue of faith and not of law. In this way the BJP came out, at least indirectly, supporting the VHP's stance on the Babri mosque. Joshi, the party president, and Advani, the leader of the BJP-led opposition in the Parliament, helped the VHP mobilize around a quarter of a million volunteers (*karsevaks*). On December 6, 1992 thousands of these volunteers, ignoring the Supreme Court order, demolished the disputed mosque, while the BJP's nationally known leaders like Joshi and Advani and the Kalayan Singh-led government of U.P. watched helplessly.

The demolition of the Babri mosque led to widespread Hindu-Muslim riots, resulting in the loss of more than 1,700 lives, property damage worth millions of rupees, and deployment of the army on a national basis to maintain order.

As a result, many of the BJP's leaders, including Joshi and Advani, were arrested (they were released within a short time), and the BJP-run state governments in U.P., Madhya Pradesh, Rajasthan, and Himachal Pradesh either were forced to resigned or were dismissed by the Rao government. Bearing the moral responsibility for the demolition of the Babri mosque in Ayodhya, Advani resigned as the leader of the opposition in the Lok Sabha. Shaken by these developments, some of its moderate leaders, especially the group led by Vajpayee, conceded the political miscalculations made by the party and the need to redesign the party strategy to recover the ground lost. This defensive posture of the BJP leadership soon changed, however, when the Rao government—after arresting 5,000 senior and middle-ranking party functionaires and imposing a ban on the RSS and the VHP—determined to rebuild the mosque. When the Rao government's actions did not evoke a favorable response among Hindus, who were especially opposed to rebuilding the mosque, the BJP leadership no longer needed to be on the defensive.

In this contest for power the secularists, the main proponents of Indian nationalism, displayed not only a political and administrative ineptitude and a lack of moral courage but also a lack of imagination. Both the Congress (I) and the Janata Dal leadership were put on the defensive by the political strategy of the BJP and the Hindu nationalists. By pitting Ram against Babur, the BJP changed the context of Indian politics. For the majority of Hindus Ram represents the traditions (*maryada*) of Hindu culture; now he became a national symbol. Babur, on the other hand, was an invader and conqueror who expressed dislike for both the people and the country which he had conquered.

Unable to understand the contextual change of Hindu nationalism and the deep psychological appeal of subtle symbols for the Hindus, the secularists like V.P. Singh, Rao, and Arjun Singh have failed to maintain a balance between different religious communities and are unable to take a stand on principles. Rather, they adopt an opportunistic pro-minority stance by making symbolic concessions to Muslims to consolidate their vote bank. They have occasionally played one community against the other. In this game of politics the actions of the proponents of secularism and the Nehruvian version of Indian nationalism carried little conviction, and they played into the hands of the BJP.

On the other hand, while the BJP and the Hindu nationalists were able to carry their message beyond the north Indian states and gain a foothold in some of the critical states like Karnataka of south India, they created a deep divide within Indian society. Their actions have led to a sense of insecurity among the members of the minorities, especially the Muslims. To maintain political stability in a culturally and religiously divided society, the majority community needs to show a sense of responsibility. No party in India can govern effectively without winning the trust of the minorities, no matter how massive its support base may be. The BJP cannot force the members of the minority communities into submission. For the Hindu nationalists, political flexibility and a change of strategy could be the keys to political success as well as survival.

Notes

1. Bharatiya Janata Party, *Our Five Commitments* (New Delhi, Bharatiya Janata Party Publications, n.d.), p. 7.

2. *Ibid.*

3. *Ibid.*, p. 4.

4. *Ibid.*

5. *Ibid.*, p. 5.

6. *Ibid.*

7. Atal Bihari Vajpayee, *India at the Crossroads* (New Delhi, Bharatiya Janata Party Publications, 1980), p. 6.

8. *Ibid.*, p. 9.

9. Thomas Pantham, "Beyond Liberal Democracy: Thinking with Mahatma Gandhi" in Thomas Pantham and Kenneth L. Deutsch (eds.), *Political Thought in Modern India* (New Delhi, Sage Publications, 1986), p. 336.

10. Ashis Nandy, "An Anti-Secularist Manifesto," *Seminar*, October 1985, p. 14.

11. *Our Five Commitments*, p. 4.

12. Vajpayee, *India at the Crossroads*, p. 11.

13. *India Today*, May 15, 1983, p. 24.

14. *Ibid.*

15. Bharatiya Janata Party, *A Report on the Mini General Election of May, 1982* (New Delhi, Bharatiya Janata Party, 1982), p. 4.

16. *Ibid.*, p. 8.

17. Bharatiya Janata Party, *Presidential Address by Shri Atal Bihari Vajpayee* (New Delhi, Bharatiya Janata Party, 1982), p. 5.

18. *India Today*, February 28, 1983, p. 24.

19. *India Today*, August 31, 1982, p. 21.

20. *Bharatiya Janata Party: Towards A New Polity; Election Manifesto* (New Delhi, Printed by Navchatan Press [P] Ltd., 1984), p. 1.

21. *Ibid.*

22. *Ibid.*, p. 4.

23. *India Today*, January 31, 1985, p. 23.

24. *India Today*, November 30, 1983, p. 34.

25. *Economic and Political Weekly*, April 19, 1989, p. 658.

26. Mohan Guruswami, "Who Will Bell the Hindu Cat?" *Hindustan Times*, April 6, 1987, p. 12.

27. K.C. Kulish, *Rajasthan Patrika,* March, 1986, p. 5.

28. *India Today*, May 31, 1986, p. 32.

29. *Statesman Weekly*, September 30, 1986, p. 12.

30. *Statesman Weekly*, November 22, 1986, p. 12.

31. Ashis Nandy, "Anti Secularist Manifesto," p. 23.

32. *India Today*, August 15, 1985, p. 21.

33. *India Today*, February 28, 1983, p. 27.

34. Walter Andersen and Sridhar D. Damle, *Brotherhood in Saffron: Rashtriya Swayamsevak Sangh and Hindu Revivalism* (Boulder, CO, Westview Press, 1987), p. 228.

35. Bharatiya Janata Party, *National Executive, 15, 16, and 17 March, 1985, Calcutta* (New Delhi, Bharatiya Janata Party Publications, 1985), pp. 3 and 12.

36. Bharatiya Janata Party, *Bharatiya Janata Party: Karyakari dal ke Report* (New Delhi, Bharatiya Janata Party Publications, 1985), p. 14.

37. *Ibid.*, p. 15.

38. *Ibid.*, p. 22.

39. *Ibid.*, p. 23.

40. *Ibid.*, p. 24.

41. Bharatiya Janata Party, *National Executive Meeting October 8 and 9, 1985, National Council Meeting, October 10, 1985, National Study Group Meeting October 11, 12, and 13, 1985* (New Delhi, Bharatiya Janata Party, 1985), p. 1.

42. *Ibid.*, p. 2.

43. Bharatiya Janata Party, *Bharatiya Janata Party Presidential Address by L.K. Advani* (New Delhi, Bharatiya Janata Party Publications, 1986), p. 7.

44. Girilal Jain, "Intra-Hindu Conflict," *Times of India*, July, 17, 1986, p. 8.

45. Girilal Jain, "The Hindu Backlash," *Times of India*, September 10, 1986, p. 8.

46. *Ibid.*

47. *Bharatiya Janata Party Presidential Address by L.K. Advani*, p. 6.

48. S. Nihal Singh, "The BJP: Wanting Its Share, and More," *Telegraph*, February 25, 1989, p. 8.

49. *Ibid.*

50. Harish Khare, "RSS Can Jettison BJP: Choice Between Rajiv and V.P. Singh," *Times of India*, April 25, 1988, p. 5, and *Probe India,* January, 1989, p. 26.

51. *Times of India*, September 8, 1988, p. 5.

52. Nikhil Chakravarty, "The Colour of Money," *Times of India*, April 19, 1987, p. 6.

53. *Hindustan Times*, April 20, 1987, p. 12.

54. *Prem Shankar Jha,* "Cutting One's Own Throat," *Hindustan Times*, April 17, 1987, p. 10. For details, see Yogendra K. Malik, "Political Finance in India," *Political Quarterly,* January, 1989, pp. 75-94; Prem Shankar Jha, *India: Political Economy of Stagnation* (New Delhi, Oxford University Press, 1980); Stanley Kochanek, "Briefcase Politics in India: The Congress Party and the Business Elite," *Asian Survey,* December, 1987, p. 1280; and Bharatiya Janata Party, *The Tip of the Iceberg: The Story of Three Scandals* (New Delhi, Bharatiya Janata Party Publications, 1987), pp. 1-10.

55. *India Today*, July 15, 1988, p. 14.

56. Bharatiya Janata Party, *Two Years of Congress Misrule: A Charge Sheet* (New Delhi, Bharatiya Janata Party, 1986), p. 11.

57. *Ibid.*, p. 1.

58. Jagmohan, *My Frozen Turbulence in Kashmir* (New Delhi, Allied Publishers, 1991), Chapter VII.

59. *India Today*, June 15, 1987, p. 18.

60. *Sunday Observer*, November 6, 1989, p. 5. Also, see A.G. Noorani, "Ayodhya Tangle," *Statesman Weekly*, October 24, 1992, p. 12; Koenraad Elst, *Ramjanambhoomi Vs. Babri Masjid: A Case Study in Hindu-Muslim Conflict* (New Delhi, Voice of India, 1990); Sarvepalli Gopal (ed.), *Anatomy of a Confrontation: The Babri Masjid-Ramjanambhoomi Issue* (New Delhi, Penguin Books India, 1990); and *VHP: History Versus Casuistry: Evidence of the Ramjanambhoomi Mandir Presented by the Vishwa Hindu Parishad to the Government of India in December-January 1990-91* (New Delhi, Voice of India, 1991).

61. *The Economic Times*, October 25, 1989, pp. 5-6.

62. L.K. Advani, "An Alliance is a Better Bet than Merger," *Times of India*, May 4, 1988, p. 6.

63. K.R. Malkani, "EMS Versus BJP: Why is the CPI (M) Leader Angry?" *Statesman Weekly*, March 25, 1989, p. 12.

64. *India Today*, February 15, 1989, p. 37.

65. *Ibid.*

66. *Ibid.*

67. *Ibid.*

68. *India Today*, November 30, 1988, p. 35.

69. *Telegraph*, May 4, 1989, p. 5.

70. Bharatiya Janata Party, *Bharatiya Janata Party: Election Manifesto; Lok Sabha Elections, 1989* (New Delhi, Bharatiya Janata Party Publications, 1989), p. 5.

71. *Ibid.*

72. *Ibid.*

73. *Ibid.*

74. *Ibid.*, p. 4.

75. *Ibid.* Also, see L.K. Advani, *Ramjanama Bhoomi: Honor People's Sentiments* (New Delhi, Bharatiya Janata Party Publications, 1989).

76. *Bharatiya Janata Party Election Manifesto: Lok Sabha Elections*, 1989, p. 6.

77. Balraj Puri, "Can Caste, Region and Ideology Stem Hindu Wave?" *Economic and Political Weekly*, January 6, 1990, p. 15.

78. *Ibid.*

79. Bharatiya Janata Party, *Why B.J.P. Withdrew Support from Shri V.P. Singh Government*. Speech Delivered by Shri L.K. Advani in Parliament on 7-11-1990 (New Delhi, Bharatiya Janata Party Publications, 1990).

80. S.S. Gil, "The Challenge Before the BJP," *Indian Express,* June 28, 1991, p. 8.

81. Bharatiya Janata Party, *Mid-Term Poll to Lok Sabha, May 1991: Our Commitments Towards Ramrajya* (New Delhi, Bharatiya Janata Party, 1991), p. 27.

82. *Ibid.*, p. 5.

83. *Ibid.*, p. 11.

84. *India Today*, July 15, 1991, p. 35.

85. *Organiser*, March 15, 1992, p. 1.

86. Saradendu Mukherjee, "BJP's Ekta Yatra: Confounding the Shrill Chorus of Criticism," *Indian Express,* January 31, 1992, p. 8.

87. *Times of India*, April 15, 1992, p. 1.

88. *Times of India*, April 17, 1992, p. 6.

89. *Ibid.*

90. *Hindustan Times*, April 20, 1992, p. 13.

91. Girilal Jain, "The BJP is Struck with Sterile, Old Slogans," *The Pioneer*, May 11, 1992, p. 8.

92. *The Pioneer,* May 10, 1992, p. 8.

93. *Organiser,* April 26, 1992, p. 1.

94. *Indian Express,* May 10, 1992, p. 8.

95. Jain, "The BJP is Struck," p. 8.

96. *The Pioneer,* May 10, 1992, p. 6.

4

Policies and Issue Orientations

Political parties develop public policies, platforms, and distinct approaches to solve the problems which a society faces and offer them as electoral choices to the voters. The BJP has often been described as India's only right-wing conservative party. The BJP has a distinct agenda in terms of not only India's national identity but also its economy, the nature and pace of its industrialization and technology development, the role of the state governments and the nature of center-state relations, the role of the educational system in the development of the society and polity, and a host of other political, constitutional, and social issues.

The BJP seems ambivalent, however, toward the role of the state and the government in society. Theoretically, it seeks only a limited role for the government in the functioning of the society. It supports an environment "which provides full play to individual initiative and dignity."[1] It accepts the four-fold objectives of life as provided by ancient Hindu traditions, which say the actions of an individual are to be guided by *dharma* (righteousness), *artha* (wealth), *kama* (enjoyment), and *moksha* (emancipation). In pursuit of these objectives, an individual is expected to create a balance between his personal and societal needs.[2] Man does not seek to satisfy only his material needs; he seeks psychic and spiritual satisfaction, too. The state and government can play only a limited role in the achievement of these goals.

The party's leaders believe that to develop sound public policies for post-independence India, it needs to draw on its ancient history and cultural heritage. In ancient India the focus of the development was the individual's inner self, and cultural traditions constantly sought ways to improve the self. As a result, "the emphasis was on integrated development of body, mind, intellect and soul and living in harmony with Nature."[3] According to this view, such a process led to the development of a host of decentralized, self-regulated systems in India in all areas of life including politics, economy, and society.[4]

Within such a philosophical view, the state is looked upon as an artificial entity, one produced by a type of social contract with people to safeguard their nation and satisfy their basic needs.[5] According to this view the primary functions of the state are national security and maintaining order within the society. However, by analyzing its positions we can discern contradictions in the BJP's perception of the role of the state and the government.

Economic and Industrial Policies and Programs

We should understand that the BJP's economic development strategy has been influenced by the policies adopted by the Congress party government and by its own constituent elements such as the RSS, the traders, and the caste/class groups which provide it with campaign contributions and votes. The BJP is opposed to a state-controlled command economy.

In its 1980 Economic Policy Statement, the BJP criticized the Congress party government's economic policies for a "low rate of economic growth, a high and rising volume of unemployment, the vast and growing number of people below the poverty line, and continuing gross inequalities in the distribution of income and wealth." And, it added, "the whole framework of planning and income policy has failed to tackle these problems in the last thirty years."[6]

The reasons for such development, according to the party leaders, are not difficult to find. The Congress party's plan for economic development was borrowed from abroad, and so it has no cultural relevance to the country. From the BJP's point of view, in the planning process of the country "we did not assess properly our specialties, our resource potential, our work force. We were enamored by the glitter and Stalinist state apparatus of the USSR."[7]

This type of state control, according to the BJP, has resulted in a distorted economy which has led to corruption and a black market. Consequently, the BJP declared that "With massive corruption, no desirable national economic policy is possible. The main responsibility for generating black money lies on the unabashed manner in which Government's licensing and regulatory powers and procedures have been used to collect massive monies for the ruling party."[8]

In fact, the main beneficiary of this type of centralized and bureau-cratically controlled economy has been India's growing middle class. The BJP has described it as an elitist economy and declared:

> The nation is more undernourished today than it was a few years ago. As a result of wrong plan priorities, the country is producing more color TV sets but not enough steel, more computers but not enough power, more fancy cars but not enough buses, more super fine fabrics but not enough cheaper varieties of dhoties and saries.[9]

The party also criticizes the urban bias in the development planning, saying that "over the years thousands of crores of rupees from the rural poor have been transferred to the urban rich, resulting in a colossal rural indebtedness."[10]

By the late 1980s the BJP came out with an economic program which sought liberalization of the economy; removal of bureaucratic control over industrial expansion; withdrawal of the state from such commercial activ-ities as running of hotels, utilities, and airlines; and turning over most of the public sector industry to private businesses unless they become profitable.

In proposing these changes, the leaders of the party were looking at the economic realities of the country. Many Indian public sector industrial units are inefficient, lose money, and are actually a drain on the national treasury, while the industries run by the private sector have been returning enormous profits. Studies have shown that "an economically inefficient public sector only drags down the state under the weight of its inefficiency and the consequent burden of internal and external debt. On the other hand, a profitable private sector can make for a strong state through the extra resources it provides."[11]

For India the Nehruvian model of economic development was a kind of sacred creed and political dogma. It was impossible for the politicians to attack the ideological assumptions underlying the Nehruvian development strategy without being ridiculed or called reactionary by India's intellectual establishment. However, emboldened by the collapse of the Soviet Union and the events taking place in Eastern Europe, L.K. Advani, the party president, strongly attacked the assumptions underlying the post-inde-pendence economic ideology, declaring "when such gales of change are sweeping Europe and the Soviet Union we are ready to debunk the shib-boleths that have misguided our post-independence destiny."[12]

In 1991, India faced a serious economic crisis resulting from an adverse trade balance, the high cost of servicing internal and external debts, a serious shortage of foreign exchange, and low credit rating in the international financial market. It was on the verge of default, and the BJP held the current and former members of the Congress (I), who had held power at the national level, responsible.

Accusing the ruling elites of India, the party leadership charged:

> These people have literally robbed the country and left its hapless citizens high and dry, staggering from one crisis to another and trapped in a vortex of high prices, murderous taxes and soaring debts. . . . The nation is on the verge of bankruptcy and has been reduced to begging for handouts from all and sundry.[13]

As stated in Chapter Three, in 1991, the Rao government introduced far-reaching economic liberalization measures. Not only did the government lift many controls on investment and industrial expansion, but it also invited multi-nationals to invest in India. The BJP welcomed the new reforms because they agreed with the party's manifesto.[14] More significantly, they looked upon the reforms as an open admission of the government's failure. Jaswant Singh, the deputy leader of the BJP in the Lok Sabha, called the new program "the most total, the most comprehensive and the most wholesale rejection of the Nehruvian model, the Nehruvian legacy, the stifling inheritance of the Nehruvian economic philosophy and thought that we have come across in the past forty years."[15]

The Congress party government's implementation of the economic program recommended by the BJP, however, created an identity crisis for the BJP. Now the question was, except for the *Hindutva*, how was the party different from the Congress (I)? Furthermore, the Rao government's 1991 economic liberalization was warmly welcomed by India's urban middle and upper classes, which had in recent years lent legitimacy to the BJP by supporting its leadership.

However, the BJP's cadre, which constitutes the party's hardcore, represents what has been termed the "messianic culture in the party."[16] This group derives its inspiration from the ascetic and austere lifestyle of the RSS *pracharaks* (instructors-propagandists).

The RSS and its *pracharaks*, most from the small towns and the lower middle classes, are alienated from the lifestyle of the westernized, English-educated, and consumption-oriented urban middle classes. The *pracharaks*, imbued with egalitarian values, seek to bridge the gap between the rich and the poor on the basis of economic and social justice. They are not attracted by the consumption-oriented Western model of economic development. They are also not in favor of large-scale industrial units, except possibly defense-related industries. They advocate establishing small and medium-size industrial units using the entrepreneurial skills of the lower middle classes. For many of them the advent of multi-nationals in India meant the loss of economic sovereignty.[17]

Thus the BJP faced a major dilemma: how to satisfy its rank and file while keeping its recently won respectability in India's English-educated establishment intact.

After considerable deliberation, in May 1992 the BJP National Council adopted a new economic policy statement entitled *Humanistic Approach to Economic Development: A Swadeshi Alternative.* While conceding that the Rao government had adopted some of the BJP's program, it pointed out that many of its important elements were not implemented. The Council charged that the Rao government did not have any comprehensive approach to take advantage of Indian genius. In its view the Congress (I) lacked adequate thinking and a clearly thought out economic philosophy, so its actions were characterized by adhoc-ism.

In contrast, in a thirty-one-page document that spelled out its new economic policy, the BJP leadership claimed that its approach to economic development originated from the country's "national heritage and from the concepts of Mahatma Gandhi's *RAMRAJYA* and Pt. Deendayal Upadhyaya's *INTEGRAL HUMANISM.*"[18] The party declared that it believed in "a new social and economic order which is non-exploitative, cooperative and harmonious and which provides full play to individual initiative and dignity."[19] The document reiterated the BJP's previous commitments such as rapid development through full employment and maximum utilization of national resources both material and manpower, with special attention to be paid to agriculture, cottage industries, and weaker sections of the society involving women, scheduled castes and scheduled tribes, backward classes and regions, and so forth. It proposed the creation of a national commission for full employment which would recommend solutions to the nation's chronic unemployment problem within five years.

Based on the values of the RSS, the BJP's new economic policy emphasized the development and enlargement of the small-scale industrial sector. Although acknowledging the importance of large-scale industries and the possibilities of their further expansion, the BJP claimed that it was the fast-growing small-scale industrial sector which would create the most export-oriented jobs. It urged the government to set up separate, full-fledged ministries at both the national and the state levels to promote small-scale industry.

The BJP leadership was not completely satisfied with the new policies of the Rao government. It recommended further liberalization by removing control over coal, sugar, tobacco, newsprint, leather, edible oil, and several other industries. In fact, said the BJP, with the exception of defense-related industries or ones considered strategic for national security or hazardous to public health, all others should be freed from government licensing.[20]

Influenced by the RSS' suspicion of foreign capital and multi-nationals, the BJP leadership pledged to protect both the private and public sectors of the national economy. Although earlier it had criticized the operation of large-scale industries in the protected market of India, it was not willing to open up the Indian market to international competition. The BJP would permit the operation of foreign capital and multi-nationals in high-tech, export-oriented and import substitution industries.[21] It excluded foreign investment from the area of consumer goods.

Two of the most striking aspects of the party's new economic policy were its rejection of unabashed consumerism, supposedly encouraged by the Congress (I) development policies, and its emphasis on *Swadeshi* (indigenousness) and *Swalambhan* (self-reliance),[22] the goals which the Nehruvian development plan had emphasized and which, according to the BJP, the Congress (I) leadership had failed to achieve. The Congress (I)-controlled government's constant borrowing from the International Monetary Fund and the World Bank was cited as a reason for their argument.

The BJP wished to distance itself from both the camps. The leadership of the party needed an alternate economic policy that would distinguish it from both the Congress (I) and the Janata Dal Left Front alignment. If the Congress (I) now paid only lip service to self-reliance and socialism and had actually embraced capitalism, the Janata Dal and the Left Front were still supporting the failed policies of the past centralized planning and the inefficient and non-productive public sectors of the Indian economy.

The party's leadership, supported by the RSS think tank, considered the International Monetary Fund and the World Bank the agents of neo-colonialism. The BJP and its associates believe that the Congress (I)'s program of economic development, in the hands of these agencies, will ultimately lead India into a "social structure and cultural life producing a greed-based, degrading and wasteful consumerist culture."[23]

Already there is what is considered by many a wasteful and vulgar display of wealth by India's super rich and English-educated upper and middle classes as well as by the ministers and the MPs of the Congress (I) and others, in the midst of extreme poverty and squalor. This type of consumption-oriented economic policies, according to the BJP, will "render sustainable development impossible in India."[24]

The BJP's Swadeshi movement, advocating the purchase or use of locally produced or manufactured products, appeals to both the intellectual and the business communities. Many Indian intellectuals, of both left and right ideological orientations, resent the domination of the international order by the West, led by the United States. Following the arguments provided by the Dependency theory[25] but without accepting its Marxist premises, they hold that the Indian ruling elite, consisting of Westernized English-educated bureaucrats, technocrats, industrialists, businessmen, and the Congress (I) party politicians, are linked with the ruling classes of the West. For their intellectual, financial, and moral support they depend on the rich nations of the West. Because of their vested interest they emulate the Western lifestyle and follow the Western model of development.[26]

Supporting the BJP's stand, the well known journalist Nikhil Chakravarty observed that the Swadeshi movement is about Indian self-confidence, about its pride in its industries; it is geared to safeguard the sovereignty of India against the predatory nature of multi-nationals. Today's multi-nationals are not much different from the East India Company of the past, according to Chakravarty.[27] On the other hand, for many Indian businessmen, Swadeshi is a cover for a protected market in which to sell their shoddy goods and to avoid international competition.

In a practical sense, however, the BJP's new economic policy is a revised version of the failed Nehruvian model of economic development which was offered as an alternative to the Soviet and the Western paths of industrialization. Like the BJP's new economic policy, the failed policies of the Congress (I) also emphasized import substitutions, self-reliance, and Swadeshi. The BJP leadership, intent on establishing its distinct identity, has failed to understand the radical changes taking place in the world economy. With a scarcity of capital in the world, there are a large number of countries seeking foreign investment, including the People's Republic of China, Russia, and the countries of Eastern Europe, which are willing to meet the conditions set by the multi-nationals. India lacks the conditions and environment which attract foreign investments. According to scholars, India's strategy of self-reliance and its distrust of multi-nationals has already left it much behind its competitors like Brazil and South Korea, which started becoming industrialized at around the same time and at the same or a lower level of economic development as India—this in spite of India's having the third largest technically trained manpower.[28]

The BJP, however, has pointed out the under-utilization of India's scientific research and especially the lack of coordination between India's scientific research establishment and industries. Even though India spends a substantial amount of money on scientific institutions and laboratories, there are not many domestic buyers of their research products. Furthermore, unlike Japan's, Indian scientists, engineers, and industrial establishment have made no efforts to improve upon their borrowed technologies.

The party leadership is right in pointing out the absence of innovation on the part of these three components of the Indian industrial establishment. But the BJP's emphasis on the development of appropriate technology is an old slogan, one which has lost relevance in the fast-paced technological revolution taking place in the world.

Agriculture and Farm Policy

In order to become a national alternative to the Congress (I) and to change its image from a party representing mainly the traders and the urban middle class to the party representing rural as well as urban sectors of the society, in 1987 the BJP's National Executive adopted a thirty-two-page document entitled *Kisanon ka adikar-patra* (A Charter of Farmers' Rights). Besides spelling out sixteen basic rights of the farmers, including the provision of minimum civic facilities such as drinking water, roads, transportation, sanitation, jobs, and a minimum wage for farm workers, it promises an allocation of seventy percent of development money provided under the Five Year Plan for agriculture and rural development.[29]

Its leadership believes that development of the rural sector is the prerequisite of a healthy, stable economy.[30] According to the BJP, fully developing agriculture and the rural economy would mean maximization of agricultural productivity, farmers free from debt, promotion of village industries, and the establishment of agro-technical networks by introducing science-based technology to small-scale industries. The adoption of such a developmental strategy, the party holds, would improve the rural life with decent housing, entertainment, and health care facilities. The goal is to bridge the gap developing between the urban and rural living standards and levels of development.[31] However, it did not spell out how the party was going to implement these programs or who would pay for them.

In order to win farm votes, the BJP pledged to write off the debts of the farmers and farm laborers, to maintain parity of price between agricultural and industrial products, and to ensure remunerative prices to the farmers.[32] Not only were such electoral promises impractical, but if implemented, they would cost the BJP urban votes, since such steps would increase food prices, especially hurting the fixed-income middle class.

The BJP also recommended simplifying the land laws, introducing land reform involving the transfer of land to the tiller, discouraging migration from rural to urban areas, building warehouses and cold storage facilities in the villages, assisting in the development of fisheries and poultry farming, and prohibiting cow slaughter on a nationwide basis. All such steps would be initiated by the state and national governments, despite the party's pledge to limit the role of the government in public life.

Reservation of Jobs for the Scheduled and Backward Castes

A quota system has been created in the government and public sectors and in the educational and technical institutions to help the socially disadvantaged sectors of Indian society. The main beneficiaries of this policy are the scheduled castes and the scheduled tribes, who have for centuries suffered indignities and discrimination in the Hindu society.

The BJP is a party dominated by upper caste Hindus. However, both on the grounds of its ideology and to enlarge its electoral base, the party leadership has made efforts to reach out to this segment of the Hindu population. To understand the party's position on affirmative action, however, a distinction must be made between the scheduled castes and socially and educationally backward castes.

The scheduled castes constitute around sixteen percent of the population of the country, and they are the most depressed sector of Hindu society. An overwhelming majority (eighty-four percent) of them live in the rural areas, where they work primarily as farm labor. Only about twenty-two percent are literate compared to the national average of forty-two percent. The literacy rate among scheduled caste women is the lowest, around ten percent compared to the thirty percent national women's average.[33] They also constitute the largest part of those who fall below the poverty line in the country.

Because of their situation, members of this segment of the Hindu population are most vulnerable to conversion to Islam, Christianity, or Buddhism. Therefore the Hindu nationalist organizations like the BJP and the RSS are quite conscious of their obligations to this group. The BJP declares that since it is "committed to a democratic and egalitarian socio-economic order,"[34] it will make massive efforts to improve the status of scheduled castes, and for this reason it proposes an activist role for the state.

The BJP supports the constitutional provisions reserving jobs in the government and public sector for the members of scheduled castes and scheduled tribes. At the same time, it stresses the need to enlarge educational facilities, especially in the rural areas, designed for the members of scheduled castes and scheduled tribes.

Affirmative action and the quota system, as practiced by the Congress (I) governments, have benefitted only tiny sections of their population. In fact, the party leaders hold that despite government actions, the law enforcement agencies have not been able to protect the scheduled castes from upper caste atrocities committed against them in the rural areas. The BJP proposed setting up mobile courts to deal speedily with the crimes committed against the scheduled castes.

In addition to the Hindu cultural traditions which sanctioned discrimination against the untouchable and the scheduled castes, poverty is recognized as another basic reason for their suffering. Although raising social consciousness about their plight is also needed, the BJP maintains that economic improvement will help them most. Therefore it favors a larger allocation of funds under Five Year Plans than the governments so far have been providing.

Its leaders want to revitalize the Special Component Plan, as adopted in the Janata Party rule in 1977, which allocated funds for the scheduled castes and scheduled tribes in proportion to their population in the country. In addition, the BJP proposes improving the working of the Scheduled Castes Development Corporations, easing the credit requirements for them, and lowering interest rates for loans.

Enormous changes have taken place in the countryside since the independence of the country, a fact which the leaders of political parties like the BJP seem to consciously ignore. With the introduction of fertilizer, new agricultural technology, and improved varieties of seeds, resulting in what is commonly termed the Green Revolution, the rich peasants and landlords have become the dominant economic and political force in India's villages. Not only do they belong to Hindu upper or middle castes, but they have also traditionally constituted the upper stratum of the rural Hindu society. Any effort by the members of the scheduled castes to challenge their authority invites the wrath of upper caste Hindus on them.

The upper and middle caste Hindus in the countryside constitute the backbone of all the centrist and right-wing political parties. They have frustrated efforts at land reforms, which the BJP so earnestly recommends to improve the conditions of scheduled caste farm laborers in the rural areas. Under such conditions, the BJP's insistence on ensuring justice for the members of scheduled castes and scheduled tribes and its support for the quota system seem simply devices to garner their votes, despite the party's assertion to the contrary.[35]

Socially and educationally backward castes, on the other hand, are not the depressed sectors of Hindu society although they constitute large segments of the Hindu population in the countryside of India. Prominent among the socially and educationally backward castes are Yadavs, Kurmis, Gujars, Telis, Koeris, Dheemars, Sonars, Lohars, and others. Yadavs, Gujars, and Kurmis are most often peasant proprietors, while Sonars, Lohars and Telis are occupational and service castes, and they are not socially disadvantaged like the scheduled castes and scheduled tribes.

When in August 1990, following the Mandal Commission's recommendations, the Janata Dal government led by V.P. Singh decided to reserve twenty-seven percent of central government jobs for the socially and educationally backward castes, it was denounced as pure political opportunism, "an act of singular political immorality,"[36] directed toward creating a solid vote bank. It was charged that such a decision would result in "apartheid, Indian style,"[37] dividing Hindus as a community in north India. The action of the Singh government was widely opposed by India's urban middle class Hindus as well as by Akhil Bharatiya Vidyarthi Parishad, the student wing of the BJP.

Initially the BJP opposed the implementation of the recommendations on technical grounds. Its leadership claimed that the Janata Dal was a minority government, and since the BJP supported the government in Parliament, it needed to consult with the leaders of their party before making such a major policy decision.[38]

Bowing to the realities of electoral politics, however, the BJP ultimately accepted the reservation policy for the socially and educationally backward castes. But it favored using additional criteria of economic conditions and poverty in a quota system so that the poor from the upper castes could also benefit from the reservation policy.

In November 1992 the Supreme Court, considering a petition challenging the constitutionality of the government's decision to implement the Mandal Commission's recommendations, upheld the decision but at the same time put a ceiling of not more than fifty percent of the jobs to be reserved under the quota system. The biggest disappointment for the Hindu leadership was, however, the fact that the Supreme Court rejected the economic criteria proposed by the BJP and others.[39]

A Uniform Civil Code and the Cultural Rights of Minorities

In May 1992 in his presidential address to the National Council of the BJP, Dr. Murli Manohar Joshi quoted Dr. B.R. Ambedkar, the person responsible for drafting the constitution of India:

It is wrong for the majority to deny the existence of the minorities. It is equally wrong for the minorities to perpetuate themselves. A solution must be found which will serve a double purpose. It must recognize the existence of the minorities to start with. It must also be such that it will enable majorities and minorities to merge some day into one.[40]

Whether because of its ideological perspective or its electoral imperatives, the BJP is perhaps the only major national party which has fervently advocated a uniform civil code for all the sectors of Indian society. It cites Article 44 of the Constitution and the Directive Principles of the State Policy which enjoin upon the state and national governments to make genuine efforts toward the ultimate adoption of a uniform civil code for the whole country.[41]

The party leadership believes that the formulation of separate personal laws for such communities as the Muslims, Hindus, Christians, and others was only a temporary arrangement. The political parties like the Congress (I) and the Janata Dal, say the BJP leaders, in search of votes of the minorities, have successfully frustrated all efforts to formulate a uniform civil code for all sectors of society and thus have helped perpetuate what the party terms "minorityism."

As an example the BJP leadership cites the passage of the Muslim Women (Protection of Rights of Divorce) Bill of 1986 into law by the Congress (I)-dominated Parliament as a result of pressure from the Muslim Personal Law Board and despite opposition from such Muslim ministers as Arif Mohammad Khan, who represented the opinion of the enlightened sector of the Muslim community. The passage of this law reversed the judgement of the Supreme Court in Shah Bano vs. Mohammad Ahmed Khan, which was a liberal interpretation of the Muslim Personal Law. And according to Justice Y. V. Chandrachud, "interpretation of law, personal or otherwise, is not only the function but the obligation of the court."[42] Muslims, however, looked upon such an interpretation as interference in the internal affairs of their community. Such steps hurt the court system, on the one hand, and helped perpetuate the minorityism on the other.

While the Congress (I) and the Janata Dal did not support the adoption of a uniform civil code to win the Muslim vote, the BJP leadership charged that the Communists, pursuing their traditional policy "to sacrifice Hindu interests at the altar of Muslim appeasement,"[43] were willing to provide reasons for a separate Muslim Personal Law, even if such a stand went against their declared ideology. The BJP, arguing that the Communists do not have the courage of their convictions, maintained that "this is what the communists were doing before independence. Those who openly supported the partition of our motherland on communal lines now pro-claim themselves as the champion of secularism and nationalism."[44]

The BJP also argued that the changes made by the Congress (I) government in the Muslim Personal Law to appease the Muslim funda-mentalists led by the Muslim League and Jamaat-i-Islami not only were against the Constitution of the country but also disrupted the uniformity in the existing criminal law and went against the interests of Muslim women. Such actions also strengthened the hand of the orthodox leaders at the expense of more enlightened and progressive Muslim leadership.

Advani, in his presidential address to the party in 1986, suggested setting up a Law Commission to study all the personal laws for different com-munities to identify the equitable elements in them, draft a uniform code, and open it to national debate.[45]

The enactment of a uniform civil code is an important element of the BJP's electoral platform, and the party has indicated that it wants to build consensus before such a law is adopted by Parliament.[46]

A recent public opinion poll conducted by the newspaper *Hindu* (Madras) and the Center for the Public Policy Studies, based on randomly sampled population, found that 81.38 percent of the people, including fifty-two percent of Muslim respondents, favor the adoption of a uniform civil code.[47] Evidently, in this respect the BJP is reflecting the popular demand.

The Constitution of India, under Article 30, allows the minorities to set up their own educational institutions to safeguard their cultural, religious, and linguistic heritage. However, the BJP's 1991 Election Manifesto de-clared that the party intends to rationalize and amend Article 30 "to ensure justice and equality to all irrespective of religion."[48] This was perceived by many as an assault on the liberal intents of the Constitution.

The BJP leaders consider these educational institutions tools used by the minorities to inculcate particularistic socialization, which undermines the universalistic values of Indian nationalism. Others consider such institu-tions of vital importance to maintain a culturally diverse and vibrant society. Such efforts on the part of the BJP to curtail the rights of re-ligious minorities raise serious doubts about its version of secularism.[49]

There may be considerable merit in the party leaders' argument for the adoption of a uniform civil code for all sectors of Indian society. But abrogation or serious modification of Article 30 will restrict the rights of cultural and religious minorities and may hurt the quality of education provided by many sectarian institutions, especially those run by Christian missions. Furthermore, at this stage of its economic development India is unable to allocate enough funds to meet the growing demand for quality education through state-run educational institutions.

The BJP also proposes replacing the minorities commission with a Human Rights Commission, which would look into all complaints of injustice and discrimination against a citizen regardless of his/her religion, caste, or sectarian orientation. Since the victims of human rights violations can come from both the majority and minority communities, a minorities commission is limited in its jurisdiction and scope since it excludes the complaints of a person who does not belong to a minority. Another problem is that it is hard to define minorities, since India has many types.

Although the human rights proposal sounds reasonable, the minorities commission was created to instill confidence in the members of religious minorities that their rights would be safeguarded in a democratic society even if the followers of Hinduism constitute an overwhelming majority.

Similarly, by incorporating Article 30 into the Constitution of India immediately after the independence, the dominant Hindu elites tried to assure the minorities that unlike in Pakistan or any Middle Eastern country, in a Hindu-majority India the cultural and religious rights of minorities would be safe from the tyranny of the religious majority.

Center-State Relations: The BJP on the Nature of Indian Federation

It is in the context of Center-state relations and the nature of the Indian federation that the BJP departs from its Jana Sangh heritage. The Jana Sangh was perhaps the only political party which favored a unitary over a federal form of government for India. It opposed the formation of a federation, fearing that it might lead to balkanization of the country.[50] The BJP has now changed its position, favoring a federal form of government for the country while seeking to enhance the powers of the states. However, whereas many political parties seek drastic restructuring of Center-state relations by transferring more powers to the states than provided in the Constitution, the BJP first sought a Center-state relation strictly according to the Constitution. Its rationale was that the authors of the Constitution tried to create a balance of "strong central authority with devolution of considerable powers to the States."[51]

However, as time passed and the party gained more administrative experience, its leaders became more willing to restrict the powers of the central government in relation to the states. The declaration of Emergency Rule by Indira Gandhi in 1975 seems to have alerted the BJP leadership to the possibility of a powerful Center leading to the establishment of an authoritarian system.

Equally significant, however, has been the government's arbitrary and partisan use of Article 356 of the Constitution to dismiss the popularly elected state governments. Even in Congress (I) state governments, as Bhagwan Dua observed, "all the Congress states were treated as nothing more than the private fiefdoms of the Gandhi household."[52]

During the regimes of both Indira and Rajiv Gandhi, in the state governments run by opposition parties, governors were used to keep an eye on the state administration. The state governors, appointed by the central government, are often discredited politicians of the ruling party at the national level. While theoretically they are supposed to function as constitutional heads of the state, experience shows that most often the governors are simply agents of the central government and work to undermine a popularly elected non-Congress (I) state government. Referring to the opposition-run state governments, Bhagwan Dua was not exaggerating when he observed that the "strategy of New Delhi seemed to be very simple: use all kinds of federal and other resources to topple them."[53]

Studies show that in the early years of the working of the Indian Constitution there was limited use of Article 356, which permits the central government to get rid of state governments. For example, between 1950 and 1967 state governments were dismissed by the central government only nine times. But from 1976-84 the frequency increased alarmingly, with thirty-five state governments dismissed. It did not matter whether the prime minister was Nehru, Indira Gandhi, or Morarji Desai; as one critic noted, "from the very beginning of the Republic there appears to have been a willingness by the Prime Minister to use Article 356 for the partisan advantage of the ruling party."[54]

In 1984 the leadership of the BJP declared that "one of the worst manifestations of Congress (I) undemocratic intolerance of the Opposition is in the field of Center-State relations," and it added that "if today, in some states, there are non-Congress (I) governments in the saddle it is by virtue of a popular verdict. But the ruling party at the Center is just not prepared to tolerate them."[55]

The dismissal of Prakash Singh Badal's Akali Dal party government in Punjab, N.T. Rama Rao's Telugu Desam government in Andhra Pradesh, and Dr. Farooq Abdullah's National Conference government in Jammu and Kashmir were cited as examples of the arbitrary use of Article 356 of the Constitution. The BJP leadership declared that such abuse of the constitutional powers by the central government against the popularly elected state governments encourages secessionist forces.[56]

Even though in its 1991 Election Manifesto the BJP did not recommend the abolition of Article 356 as demanded by many other parties, it recommended prohibiting its use for partisan purposes. However, the 1992 dismissal of the three BJP-run and popularly elected state governments in Madhya Pradesh, Rajasthan, and Himachal Pradesh by the Rao government at the Center may force the party leaders to ask for a drastic modification of Article 356, if not its abolition.

Vasant Sathe, a veteran Congress (I) leader and a former cabinet member in the Indira and Rajiv Gandhi governments, commented that the recent dismissal of the three BJP-run state governments could, indeed, be considered contrary to the provisions of the Constitution.[57] He argued that the Rao government had imposed a ban on the RSS and not on the BJP. If the BJP is a legal organization and a national party, the dismissal of the BJP-run government could be construed as a partisan action.

The partisan nature of the Rao government's action seemed to be confirmed when it took no action against the Congress (I)-run governments of Maharashtra and Gujarat after one of the worst riots in the country, although it did not necessarily result from the Ayodhya crisis.

Rioting was especially vicious and destructive in Bombay, the capital of Maharashtra state and the financial center of the county, where the law enforcement agencies failed to perform their duties. The rioting was believed to be partly the result of the actions of the Shiv Sena, a militant organization promoting the interests of Hindus of Maharashtra; the connections between the politicians and underworld; and the ongoing power struggle between different factions of the Maharashtra state unit of the Congress (I).

The BJP, in its 1984 election manifesto, pledged to "support and strengthen state Governments—and not destabilize and topple them."[58] It also recommended that the central government appoint the governors only in consultation with the state governments. Furthermore, it asked for the enhancement of the financial powers of the state, a fair allocation of central revenue among the states, and the formation of an Inter-State Council under Article 263 to settle all inter-state and Center-state disputes.[59]

In order to remove regional disparities, the BJP favors breaking up large states such as the U.P and dividing it into smaller states. It would be willing to set up an independent commission to consider forming smaller states that are economically and democratically viable.[60] In the past, after large states have been broken up, the smaller states have achieved higher growth rates than larger ones.

With their recently gained administrative experience in the states, the BJP leaders have come out more forcefully for the reappraisal of Center-state relations. Bhairon Singh Shekhawat, until November 1992 the chief minister of Rajasthan, declared for example that the political and financial centralization experiments tried during the 1970s had completely failed and had even negatively affected growth and development.[61] He demanded the return to the states of the powers taken away from them during the period of Emergency Rule. The BJP leadership especially criticized the way the Center distributes revenues among the states. While Advani complained that overcentralization had weakened national unity,[62] Shekhawat asserted that "if the states were given more power it would automatically strengthen the Union."[63]

The party leadership not only promised to implement the recommendations of the Sarkaria Commission, which had suggested an increase in the powers and responsibilities of the states, but also recommended appointing another such commission to facilitate sharing of financial resources between the Center and the states. This is necessary because, according to the BJP, many of the old practices of revenue sharing have become irrelevant and outdated.[64]

In pursuing its goal of decentralization of political and administrative powers, the party has also strongly advocated the revitalization of the local self-governing organizations including the village Panchayats, District Councils (*zila parishad*), and municipal committees. There should be no suspension of such groups as is common in the Congress (I)-ruled states. The state governments should hold frequent elections to these bodies, and they should be provided with enough powers and resources to be able to participate in the administration of the locally relevant subjects and economic development of the rural areas. Such decentralization of power, according to the party leadership, would be consistent with its ideological goals as set by Deendayal Upadhyaya, Jayaprakash Narayan, and Mahatma Gandhi.[65]

It is difficult to predict, however, if and when the party comes to power how much autonomy it would be willing to grant to the state governments. Because of its ideological heritage of the Jana Sangh, which preferred a unitary system of government, in the actual exercise of political power the party might display considerable discrepancy between its political declarations and its behavior.

Political and Constitutional Reforms

The BJP has expressed concerns about political corruption, the developing nexus between politicians and criminals, the gradual decline in respect for political institutions, and a general decline in the probity and quality of public life.

The party holds the Congress (I), and especially the Gandhi family, responsible for introducing corruption in the public life. As early as 1980 its leadership charged that "with the second coming of Mrs. Indira Gandhi corruption has assumed truly gargantuan proportions. The system of Government by the people and for the people has been changed into Government by the corrupt and for the corrupt."[66] The BJP cited the government's takeover of the bankrupt Maruti, a car manufacturing company run by her son Sanjay Gandhi and his friends, as a government bailout for a failed Gandhi family business venture.

In 1987 the leadership of the BJP once again charged that "the Rajiv government is knee deep in corruption"[67] for receiving kickbacks from Bofors, the Swedish arms manufacturing company, and for purchasing a submarine from Germany. It added that "the Rajiv government seems to have done everything possible in its power to suppress them . . . all the deals can be ultimately traced back to one source, the Nehru-Gandhi family."[68] It even accused Rajiv Gandhi of lying before Parliament.[69]

The BJP found the root cause of the corruption in the party financing and the electoral process. In 1986 Advani, then the president of the party, said:

> We hold that unless the election process is cleansed, public life cannot be clean. The roots of administrative corruption lie in political corruption, which in turn stems from electoral corruption. Four major evils pollute the electoral process. These are Money-power, Ministerial-power, Media-power and Muscle-power.[70]

Advani recommended the adoption of a nine-point reform plan. The key to reform, the party believed, was in public funding of elections, as is the practice in Germany. According to Advani, in 1973 a Joint Parliamentary Committee on Amendment to Election Law was appointed, which recommended that "a process should be initiated whereby the burden of legitimate election expenses at present borne by the candidate or the political party should be shifted to the state."[71]

Such a proposal was also supported by Madhu Dandavate, a Socialist member of the Janata Party, who asserted that if the Janata Party government had not been subverted by the Congress (I) in August 1979, his government would have instituted public financing of elections.[72] However, since the Congress (I) returned to power in 1980, no action was taken on this proposal.[73]

As seen in Chapter Three, the party also suggested using voting machines, issuing voter identification cards, lowering the voting age from twenty-one to eighteen, and holding simultaneous elections for Lok Sabha and state assemblies. In addition, the BJP recommended reconstituting the Election Commission as a multi-member body, instead of its being headed by one person, as is the practice at present.

To ensure the independence of the Election Commission, the party leadership suggested that its members be barred from holding public office after their retirement. It also recommended that the commission be empowered to penalize candidates who violate its code of conduct.

The BJP also expressed its dissatisfaction with the existing electoral system, in which the outcome is decided by simple plurality in single-member districts. Instead it favored the introduction of a mixed system—a combination of the present majority system and a list system such as is used in West Germany.[74]

Such a system would undoubtedly help the minor parties, especially if they were unable to reach an agreement on seat adjustment. However, adopting such far-reaching changes in the electoral system does not seem feasible, at least with the current volatile political situation in India.

The BJP's suggestions for electoral reforms were sound. To ensure the legitimacy of the electoral process in India, it is imperative that the Election Commission provide a mechanism for holding fair and regular elections of office holders in political parties. Also, provisions should be made for regular auditing of the party finances, and audits should be made available for public scrutiny as well as party publications.

The judiciary branch is also not above corruption. In the organization of the Indian judiciary, the authors of the Constitution were influenced by contradictory values, both coming from their British heritage. They accepted the British tradition of independence of the judiciary to ensure individual rights and freedom, but influenced by Fabian socialism, they also believed in the use of law as an instrument of social change and to establish an egalitarian social order. This has led to confrontation between the judiciary, especially the Supreme Court, and the executive backed by a parliamentary majority.

While Nehru held the judiciary in high esteem and ensured its independence, his daughter, in pursuit of unchallenged political control, sought a committed judiciary just as she sought a compliant civil service. As a result, as George Gadbois noted, the national executive of India, under powerful leaders like Indira Gandhi, employed pressure tactics including transfer to inconvenient places or inducement of promotion to bend the courts to its wishes and thus undermined the morale and independence of the judiciary.[75]

In view of these developments, the Bharatiya Janata Party vowed to restore the independence of the judiciary, in the belief that without judicial freedom, it is impossible to have the rule of law.[76] It promised to improve the judges' service conditions, increase their salaries, raise their retirement age to sixty-five, and provide them with pensions equal to their salaries while prohibiting them from assuming any public office after retirement. The loyalties of the judges have in the past been bought by inducements after retirement like appointments to political positions, such as a governor of a state or a chairman of a commission.

Presently the state chief ministers and the Prime Minister select the members of the High Court and Supreme Court judges, respectively. They are supposed to consult with the sitting justices of the High Courts and the Supreme Court, and the President of India makes the final appointments. However, the consultation is only a formality, and appointments of justices are guided by political considerations. Merit is often ignored, while political pliability is favored. As a result, state chief ministers and justices often work in tandem, undermining the impartiality and credibility of the judiciary. Even India's former Law Minister, K. Vijay Bhaskara Reddy, in 1992 complained that state chief ministers, in order to pack the state High Courts with their own men, often become embroiled with the Chief Justice of the High Court, leading to delays in appointments or leaving the positions vacant.

In 1986 the BJP leaders charged that the Rajiv government "has monkeyed so much with the appointment and transfer of High Court and Supreme Court judges recently that there was an unprecedented strike in all the courts, including the High Court."[77] The government has done little to lighten the work load of the judiciary. More than 150,000 cases are pending before the Supreme Court, and various state High Courts are burdened with 1.5 million cases, while the government has failed to fill vacancies because of political considerations.[78]

To arrest the politicization of the judiciary, the BJP recommended that the Chief Justice of India, guided by the recommendations of an independent body, should have the final say in the appointment of judges of the higher courts. To reduce the case load and provide a speedy disposition of the existing cases, the party proposes to increase the number of justices and to appoint special courts to handle certain types of cases.

Knowledgeable sources recognize that the Indian judiciary is in need of extensive reform in both structure and jurisdiction, and the suggestion of the BJP leaders to set up a high-powered commission to make recommendations for changes is a step in the right direction.

The difficulties of governance which the Indian states face today can be attributed to the decay and decline of these institutions. Many of these problems are interrelated. The connection between corrupt electoral practices and party finance has been widely documented. Similarly, the declining ability of the Center to deal with regional and local conflicts results from excessive centralization of power. India needs to take decentralization seriously. Politicization of the judiciary, administration, and law enforcement agencies results from politicians' and parties' desire to bend the institutions to their partisan goals.

However, the BJP, too, cannot escape blame. The party has defied laws, flouted court orders, and violated the spirit of the Constitution if not the Constitution itself. Furthermore, given its past record, one cannot even be sure that it would keep its promises if it came to power.

Security and Foreign Policy

Despite the BJP leaders' preoccupation with domestic issues, especially developing a nationalist ideology which could be an alternative to the nationalism of the Congress (I), the party has also done considerable work on security and foreign policy. Atal Bihari Vajpayee, who held the position of Minister for External Affairs in the Janata Party government of 1977, ran his department with sophistication in dealing with India's immediate neighbors, and he was able to protect India's national interests without his party's ideological baggage.[79]

In recent years, as stated in Chapter Two, the party has recruited the retired army generals and former members of the Indian Foreign Service, who have considerable knowledge and experience in security and diplomacy. It has set up a Foreign Policy Cell in its national office to advise the party leadership on diplomatic and foreign policy issues. In addition, its leaders have not hesitated to seek the views of academics, former diplomats, and other experts on security and foreign policy issues.

In a recent statement the BJP declared that "the security of the nation is an integrated whole: an amalgam of the internal, the economic, the social, the political, the military and the diplomatic."[80] Recognition of such interdependence would be a realistic approach to formulating security and foreign policies of the country. Industrial and economic development along with internal political stability are the keys for survival in the international system.

Identification of vital national interests, irrespective of ideology, is the first step in dealing with the problems of national security and international politics. In this area the BJP, in the words of its president Dr. Murli Manohar Joshi, is known and respected for its "no-nonsense approach to the preservation of India's unity and territorial integrity."[81]

Perception of Internal Threats to Indian Security

Political instability, insurgencies, and secessionist movements which plague strategically important border states like the Punjab, Assan, northeastern states, and Jammu and Kashmir are serious problems of internal security and threats to the territorial integrity of the country.[82] These problems have been draining the scarce resources of the Indian states. Some of these problems are interrelated, caused by systematic weaknesses and shortsighted policies pursued by the central government and by what the BJP calls the ruling party's "incompetence, ineptitude and partisan myopia."[83]

The Indian Constitution provided for excessive centralization. Whatever autonomy the Constitution granted to the states was eroded by the centralizing tendencies of the Congress party leadership. Indira Gandhi not only undermined the workings of Indian federalism but also subverted the federal structure of the Congress party in her efforts to deny the regional elites of her own party their power base. Furthermore, the Congress party leadership, as noted earlier, often subverted the authority of the state governments run by opposition parties and employed the divide-and-rule strategy. In the Punjab, for example, it was the struggle for power between the rival factions of the Congress (I) that created the opposition of Sant Jarnail Singh Bhindranwale, a fundamentalist Sikh preacher. Later Sanjay Gandhi used Bhindranwale to weaken the Akali Dal party, led by moderate Sikh leaders and representing the majority of the Sikhs in the state, to advance the cause of the Congress (I) in the Punjab.

Bhindranwale promoted Sikh separatism, leading to terrorism and demands for the formation of Khalistan, an independent Sikh state. Subsequently, in June 1984, Indira Gandhi was forced to use the army to flush out the Sikh terrorists hiding in the Golden Temple. The army action, code named Blue Star Operation, caused widespread alienation among the Sikhs.

It is hard to disagree with Joshi, who declared recently that "Had the Congress Government not toppled the duly elected governments in Punjab, not once, twice, but three times there would have been no Bhindranwale, no 'Blue Star' and no 'Black Thunder.'"[84]

The BJP seeks a political solution to the Punjab problem, opposes the demand for Khalistan, and believes that by punishing the Congress (I) functionaries who instigated and participated in anti-Sikh riots, India can win back the trust of the Sikh masses and thus solve the internal security problem in the border state of Punjab.

The security problems in Assam and to a lesser extent in the border states of the northeast, like Tripura, Manipur, and Maghalaya, have been aggravated by the influx of people from Bangladesh,[85] the BJP leaders claim.

The migration of non-Assamese into Assam created tensions among those of non-Assamese origin and the Assames, the latter believing that they were being reduced to a minority in their own state. Such a problem is not confined to Assam. In fact, frequent insurgencies in Nagaland, Tripura, and other places in the northeast are attributed to the fear that these communities might lose their ethnic-cultural identities due to the migration from outside.

In recent years such migrants have been overwhelmingly of Bangladeshi origin. Large-scale migration from poverty-ridden Bangladesh is causing major demographic and cultural/ethnic changes in the border districts of such states as West Bengal and Eastern Bihar. Estimates of the number of such illegal migrants to India range from as low as 7.6 million[86] to as high as ten to twelve million.[87]

The party considers the Hindu migrants political refugees. With the rise of Islamic fundamentalism, Hindus in Bangladesh have been increasingly subjected to harassment and indignities, so they migrate to India seeking shelter among their co-religionists.[88] Bangladeshi Muslims, also migrate to India in search of jobs, economic benefits, and farm land in tribal areas. They create communal tensions in border districts, and in the words of Hiranmay Karlekar, "many Bangladeshi infiltrators are involved in trafficking in women and drug peddling."[89] For this reason, the BJP looks upon Bangladeshi Muslims as a serious security risk for India.

Many of the border districts which were previously Hindu majority areas have now become Muslim majority. As a result, the leaders of the BJP believe that "serious efforts are going on to create a belt inhabited totally by the Bangladeshi infiltrators along the entire Indo-Bangladesh border. The pattern also reflects a silent but planned population invasion in West Bengal."[90]

Since the CPI (M) and the Congress (I) leaders provide the illegal aliens protection and enlist them as voters, the new immigrants can influence election outcomes in "more than a hundred constituencies."[91] The leaders of the parties in power in these regions are unwilling to take any action against the aliens. The BJP defense strategists consider the many foreign nationals "a potential Fifth Column" that can threaten security.[92]

The hardliners in the BJP, therefore, are demanding "operation pushback." However, since it is hard to distinguish between genuine Bangla-speaking Muslim citizens of India and Muslim Bangladeshis, the demand for their expulsion from India is unlikely to be met. The Indian state at present lacks the financial and manpower resources to undertake such a massive operation. It may also have international complications, especially involving the violation of human rights. Although the party leaders have countered this argument by citing the widespread violation of human rights of Hindus, Buddhists, and Christians by Islamic fundamentalists and the inability of the Bangladesh government to protect the minorities, the outside world pays little attention to such violations, they claim.[93]

The BJP's argument is only partly valid since many international human rights groups have expressed their concern about the minorities' plight in these countries. Without denying complicity of the Congress (I) or the Left parties in exploiting the illegal aliens for political purposes, the fact remains that migration for better economic opportunities is a worldwide phenomenon.

In the case of Jammu and Kashmir, the BJP seeks complete integration of the state into India through the abrogation of Article 370 of the Constitution, which confers special status on the state. The state law also prohibits citizens of India from purchasing property or settling in Kashmir, whereas Kashmiris are permitted to acquire property and settle in any part of India. Such arrangements were made to enable the Kashmiris to maintain their sub-national identity. The BJP leadership claims that this was only a temporary arrangement, and it creates a psychological barrier between the people of India and Kashmir. Therefore, Article 370 should be abrogated and the state of Jammu and Kashmir should become an integral part of India.

To improve security in Jammu and Kashmir, the BJP would seek the creation of three regional councils with considerable autonomy for Kashmir Valley, Ladakh, and Jammu.[94] Such a proposal has considerable merit since the people of Ladakh and Jammu differ in faith and in ethnic origin from the Kashmiris. While Muslims predominate Kashmir Valley, Hindus and Buddhists are in the majority in Jammu and Ladakh. People living in Ladakh and Jammu complain of discrimination practiced by the Jammu and Kashmir government, which has been dominated by Muslims.

There are, however, certain inherent contradictions in the BJP's position. Since the BJP's ideology of Hindu nationalism denies the existence of sub-cultural identities and seeks to create a homogeneous political culture in

India, why would it be willing to grant greater autonomy to states and sub-national or ethnic communities? While the BJP does seek greater autonomy for states, it also refuses to recognize the sub-national aspirations of such groups as Sikhs in Punjab and Kashmiris in Kashmir.

Sikh or Islamic fundamentalism and Pakistan's complicity may be reasons for the insurgencies in Punjab and Kashmir, but the main cause has been the denial of regional and sub-national autonomy by India's ruling elites. Adopting a tough stance against either Pakistan or Islamic fundamentalism in Kashmir, as advocated by the BJP,[95] is no substitute for a real policy. The Sikhs fought wars against Pakistan, and Kashmiri Muslims sided with India in three wars between India and Pakistan. The BJP seems to believe in using force and suppressing sub-national groups living on the periphery of the Indian state rather than recognizing the legitimacy of their demands. Without recognition of such realities, the BJP would not be able to solve the complex issues related to the territorial integrity of the Indian state.

Perceptions of External Threats

External military threats to Indian security, the BJP leadership perceives, come mainly from India's two neighbors, Pakistan and the People's Republic of China. While a nuclear-armed People's Republic of China may be perceived as a long-term threat to Indian security, in the short run, the BJP believes it is possible to reach an accommodation with China because of the past cultural relations of the two countries. China does not cause apprehension among the BJP policy makers.

However, since 1981 the BJP leaders, like those of the other major parties, have been expressing serious concerns about Pakistan's nuclear capabilities. Like the Congress (I) leadership, the BJP perceived that a nuclear-armed Pakistan would pose a danger to maintaining a strategic balance on the Indian subcontinent.[96]

The BJP, however, is strongly opposed to granting Pakistan military or nuclear parity with India. It was, therefore, very critical of the Rajiv Gandhi government's agreement with the Pakistani government in 1985 not to attack each other's nuclear facilities. Advani, then the party president, denounced the agreement as "a singularly ill conceived diplomatic act. It confers on Pakistan not just immunity in its military and nuclear programs, it concedes to Pakistan, for the first time, a nuclear status as ours."[97]

With the recent confirmation that Pakistan has nuclear weapon capability, the BJP has urged the Indian government to "exercise its nuclear option to restore the strategic balance in South Asia"[98] and pledges to give India's defense forces "nuclear teeth"[99] if and when the BJP comes to power. The BJP believes that Pakistan will not develop normal relations with India until it is convinced that its continuously hostile attitude toward India will result in its total destruction. Pakistan considers itself the champion of the rights of Muslims in India, so unless India adopts a tough stand toward Pakistan, it probably will not cease to interfere in India's internal affairs.

The BJP is also vehemently opposed to signing any agreement with Pakistan, under U.S. pressure, which would put a cap on India's nuclear program and open up its nuclear establishment to international inspection. Its leaders believe that under no circumstances should the Indian defense establishment give up its ballistic missile development program capable of delivering nuclear weapons to enemy territories, because such a concession would be suicidal for India.

Foreign Policy Concerns

The party leaders are critical of the Western powers for following a double standard in matters of terrorism, human rights, and nuclear non-proliferation, especially in South Asia. While some of the Middle Eastern states are punished for promoting international terrorism, the BJP charges that normal business relations are maintained with Pakistan even though Pakistan is aiding and abetting terrorism in Punjab, Kashmir, and other parts of India.

India is criticized for violating human rights in its fight against terrorism, the party asserts, while the countries of the West can practice racism against their own minorities with impunity. Israel and South Africa are never criticized for developing nuclear weapon capabilities, yet India is singled out for criticism for not signing the Nuclear Non-Proliferation Treaty (NPT). Similarly, the developed countries provide covert and overt subsidies and use protectionism for such industries as textiles, sugar, and others by fixing import quotas, while the countries of the Third World are punished for protecting their farmers and nascent industries in the name of free trade and open markets.

The BJP is projected as an anti-Muslim party. In its foreign policy, however, it recognizes that India is surrounded by Muslim countries and has to maintain friendly relations with them. The party cites the Janata Party period, when Vajpayee, the BJP stalwart, was the foreign minister.

Under Vajpayee's leadership India was able to build cordial relations with its neighbors, including Pakistan.

The leadership of the party exhibits an ambivalent attitude toward the pan-Islamic movement. In private conversations some of them admit that India does not need to fear pan-Islamism, because Islamic countries are divided among themselves on ideological, ethnic, and economic grounds.[100] In public, however, they have openly criticized the Organization of Islamic Conference for taking sides with Pakistan on the basis of common religion. The party is particularly unhappy with the OIC for its supporting Pakistan on the Kashmir issue. The BJP would strengthen India's relations with Israel, the only non-Muslim state in the Middle East, seeking to counterbalance the Muslim world.

Islamic fundamentalism is perceived by the BJP as a major threat. Islamic fundamentalist groups from the Middle East provide funds to militant groups of Indian Muslims, with substantial financial support coming from states like Saudi Arabia and Kuwait.[101] The BJP seeks a legal ban on the flow of such money to militant organizations in India.

India needs to be guided by its national interests in the formulation of foreign policy. Internal lobbies, based on ideology or religion, should not guide the decisions of policy makers. Referring to the V.P. Singh-led government's stand during the 1991 Persian Gulf crisis, M. L. Sondhi, a member of the BJP's National Executive, declared:

> What is especially unfortunate is that Indian freedom of action has been curtailed by tailoring Indian goals in the region of West Asia to what are believed to be the predominant views of Indian Muslims. Instead of developing internal consensus through open debate, India's West Asian policy has become a phenomenon of domestic appeasement of Indian Muslims, without understanding the prudent and legitimate interests of all Indians, including Indian Muslims.[102]

The impact of the Muslim lobby was not confined to the Janata Dal alone; the Rajiv Gandhi-led Congress (I) also took a pro-Iraq stance in order to win the Muslims' votes.

Foreign policy consultants of the BJP, on the other hand, are also very critical of the left parties and those Indian intellectuals who discern the evil designs of Western imperialism in all actions of the Western powers. For instance, A. K. Ray, a former Indian ambassador to Syria, asserted that "It is nonsense to suggest that there is some sort of devilish Western conspiracy to seize control of Middle East oil. . . ."[103] Realistically, Ray argued, the industrialized nations of the West are interested in maintaining stable oil prices; otherwise it would upset world economies. If the oil prices went up, it would lead to an increase in the cost of technologies and manufactured goods, and the countries of the Third World would pay the price. Therefore, the actions of the Western countries led by the United States during the Persian Gulf War were not against the interests of India, despite the loud protest made by the ideological left in India.

The BJP supported the U.S.-led action against Iraq and sought Iraqi withdrawal from Kuwait. Recognizing the strategic location of the region and the importance of Middle East oil for India, the party held that diplomatic efforts should be made to convene a West Asia Peace Conference to ensure political stability in the region by meeting the legitimate demands of Palestinians and of Israelis.[104] The BJP was the only major Indian political party which favored extending immediate diplomatic recognition to the state of Israel.

With the demise of the Soviet Union and the end of the Cold War, the BJP leadership thinks that "neither does the USA need the third world countries to contain Communism nor does the USSR have any use for its 'natural allies' in the developing world. As a result, the non-alignment movement which was created against the backdrop of a bipolar world has lost its relevance."[105] This changed situation in world politics opens up many new opportunities for India's role in global affairs. Thus the party believes that there is a need for fresh thinking in the area of foreign policy.

To be effective in international politics, however, the BJP believes that India will have to build its economic and military strength. "As long as India goes around with a begging bowl around the world, her voice in the international affairs will not be heard with respect, declared the party."[106] However, unlike the Congress (I), which in the post-Cold War era, especially under the leadership of Narasimha Rao, has shown considerable pragmatism and is pursuing vigorous economic diplomacy, the BJP's leadership has failed to recognize the nature and extent of the changes which have taken place in the global economy. It has not been able to spell out clearly how it will give an economic orientation to its diplomatic policy.

Western experts on Indian foreign policy and strategic thinking are justified in criticizing India for its lack of institutions engaged in the study and planning of long-term foreign policy and strategic goals. India has been mostly on the defensive, its thinking characterized by passivity. Even its immediate rival, Pakistan, has been successfully following an offensive strategy. Not only has Pakistan kept the territory which it occupied in Kashmir, but presently it is following a clearly designed offensive strategy to capture the whole of Kashmir in the future. Pakistan has also been successful in depriving India of the use of its superior status and resources in both international and regional politics.[107]

The party has recently proposed setting up a Policy Planning Committee to clearly identify the long-term foreign policy goals of the country as well as a National Security Council for institutionalized strategic planning of the country's defense. In contrast to the centrist parties, the BJP is willing to adopt a more aggressive posture in strategic and foreign policy thinking.

Although there are differences of opinion among the foreign policy planners of the BJP, there seems to be consensus on certain key points. For instance, most believe that while resisting the hegemonic design of the West, India does not need to seek any confrontation with the industrialized world. Even if a unipolar world is not in the interest of the countries of the Third World, it is unrealistic to think that a counter-balancing block formation can be achieved by Latin American or African countries or others. The BJP leaders support strengthening the South Asian Association for Regional Cooperation (SAARC) with the hope that a regional common market might develop, but more important is to encourage cultural and people-to-people exchange among the countries of the region.

It is also agreed that there is a need for increased cooperation between the People's Republic of China, Japan, India, and the Association of Southeast Asian Nations; India can learn a great deal from these countries.[108] The past cultural and historic ties could facilitate greater cooperation among these nations. There is room for improvement in India's relations with these countries, but the People's Republic of China may not be willing to encourage India's building cordial relations in this region. It is already working closely with the military regime of Burma, which provides shelter as well as arms to many terrorist groups active in the northeastern states of India.

Ayodhya and Ramjanambhoomi Temple: An Issue of Great Political Potential

The controversy over Ramjanambhoomi vs. Babri mosque became part of the Bharatiya Janata Party's political agenda in 1989 when in its Palmpur (Himachal Pradesh) meeting the party adopted a resolution supporting the Vishwa Hindu Parishad's claims to the site where the Babri mosque stood. "The BJP did so, says L.K. Advani, because it considered the support lent to the AIBMAC [All India Babri Masjid Action Committee] by all non-BJP parties as an extremely perverse example of minorityism."[109] It could still be debated whether it was the BJP's desire to come out in open support of an organization being maligned by all political parties and combat the pseudo-secularism of the centrist parties or it was motivated to garner Hindu votes in the forthcoming elections. There is little doubt, however, that by the mid-1980s Ayodhya had become a highly emotional issue and a powerful symbol. It was also perceived as a radical challenge to the basic foundations of India's political system.

The Ramjanambhoomi-Babri mosque episode symbolizes the way Islam was introduced in India. Ayodhya is the birthplace of Lord Ram. Lord Ram was a mythical hero of the Hindu epic of the *Ramayana*, an historical figure, and a great king, so for Hindus in India, especially in north India, he is probably the most popular and revered god and one of the many incarnations of Vishnu. His birthplace is one of the sacred places of Hindu pilgrimage.

According to tradition, the great Hindu King Vikramaditya built a temple at Lord Ram's birthplace. After a couple of centuries, when the Moughals invaded India, at the request of local Muslim residents of Ayodhya an order was issued by the Moughal ruler, Babur, to destroy the temple. Mir Baqi, Babur's general, carried out his order and in 1528 built a mosque, on the spot where the temple had stood. However, Hindus kept praying in the compound of the mosque, and Ayodhya still attracted Hindu pilgrims from all over India.

When the Moughal rule in India was in decline and the Muslim rulers of Awadh, the region in which Ayodhya was located, needed the help of Hindu nobles and notables of the region for their survival, they extended their patronage to Hindu pilgrims visiting the birthplace of Lord Ram.

In 1856 Awadh became part of the territory controlled by the East India Company and the British put a fence around the mosque, forcing the Hindus to pray on a platform raised outside the compound. During the British period there was no demand for the restoration of Ramjanambhoomi in Ayodhya.

In 1949, however, two years after the departure of the British from India, an idol of Lord Ram was installed in the mosque, resulting in major Hindu-Muslim riots that led to a government ban on entering the disputed shrine by the members of the two religious communities. The Indian judiciary became involved as both parties laid claim to the property, while the doors to the mosque remained closed.

It was in 1984, under the auspices of the Vishwa Hindu Parishad, that a movement was organized "to liberate Lord Ram from his Muslim jail."[110] A call also went out for Hindus to vote for only those parties and candidates who were willing to help the Hindus reestablish control over their places of worship. Vishwa Hindu Parishad, a revivalist and militant Hindu organization, by the early 1980s had developed enormous capabilities of mass mobilization. It used Hindu sacred symbols and ceremonies and provided a platform for Hindu holy men, sadhus, and saints to unite the Hindu community in north India. In 1986, under pressure from Hindu revivalists and to win over the Hindu voters who had become alienated from the Congress (I) because of its overturning of the Supreme Court's verdict in the Shah Bano case, the Rajiv government unlocked the doors to the shrine and allowed the Hindus to worship.

By 1989, the BJP also saw the VHP's increased ability to mobilize the Hindu voters and therefore in its Election Manifesto blamed the Congress (I) for the stalemate on Ayodhya and for not permitting the Hindus to build a temple. The tension between the two communities, it said, was the result of inaction on the part of the Congress (I) government.[111] Meanwhile, the VHP devised a brilliant strategy to mobilize the Hindu masses in support of building the temple at the site of Ram's birthplace.

The VHP called for the formation of committees in all cities, towns, and villages with a population of more than two thousand, and for elaborate religious ceremonies to consecrate bricks to be used for the construction of the temple.[112] The call was received with great enthusiasm, and millions of Hindus became engaged in religious ceremonies to consecrate the bricks through the length and breadth of the country. If the use of the ceremonies and symbols was designed to create community consciousness and a sense of solidarity among Hindus, the VHP was very successful.

The Rajiv government, with an eye to the forthcoming elections, on November 9, 1989 permitted the *shilanyas* (laying the foundation stone) of the temple in front of the gate of the mosque, and Rajiv Gandhi even started his election campaign not far from Ayodhya with a call to establish *Ramrajya.*

Shilanyas of the Ram temple deeply divided the country. The *Statesman*, an independent newspaper, termed November 9 a black day in the "history of secular India"[113] while *Indian Express*, an English newspaper with the largest circulation in the country, wrote that the ceremony demonstrated that Hindus would not put up with reverse discrimination any longer.[114] It added that if Hindus stayed united, they could bend "the state to their will."[115]

Ramjanambhoomi and Ayodhya became the central symbols unifying the Hindus and mobilizing mass support in the cause of Hindu *rashtra*, the central theme of Hindu nationalism. The sacred symbol of Lord Ram, the site of his birth under the control of the Muslim in the Babri mosque, was brought back into the Hindu consciousness as the symbol of their defeat and ultimate humiliation for the community.

The goal of restoring the sacred city of Ayodhya to its prestigious position by rebuilding the temple, destroyed by the alien invaders, was far more potent in uniting the Hindus than the cow protection movement or any other earlier movement of the Hindu nationalists.[116] The BJP was very successful in utilizing the issue both for electoral purposes and to promote its version of nationalism.

After the 1991 elections, when the BJP government led by Chief Minister Kalyan Singh was installed in U.P., the building of the Ramjanambhoomi temple was to become an issue, since the BJP had won the election with the pledge to build the temple at the site where the Babri mosque stood. Singh had frequently asserted that he would be willing to sacrifice his government for the construction of the temple.

After the demolition of the Babri mosque, Girilal Jain, a reputable intellectual and a former editor of *Times of India*, observed that since the mosque was no longer used for prayer by the Muslims and had virtually become a temple:

> The structure, as it stood, represented an impasse between what Babur represented and what Ram represents. This ambiguity has been characteristic of the Indian state since Independence. In fact, in my opinion, no structure symbolized the Indian political order in its ambivalence, ambiguity, indecisiveness and lack of purpose, as this structure. The removal of the structure has ended the impasse and marks a new beginning.[117]

Whether it would mark a new beginning or not, Jain pointed out the failure of the ideology of Indian nationalism as espoused by the secularists. Both the secularists and the Muslim leadership failed to see what this dispute represented for the Hindus. In the Shah Bano case the Muslim leadership appealed to an article of faith, the *Sharia*. As they believed it to be the word of God, it could not be subjected to rational interpretation, but they asked for historic proof to validate Hindus' claims to the site where Ram was born. Many secular intellectuals agreed with the Muslim leadership and disputed Hindus' claim as being simply based upon faith and religious traditions. While the Indian state sided with the Muslim leadership on the issue related to faith in the Shah Bano case, it refused to take a stand on the claim made by the Hindus on the basis of their faith.

The Hindu leaders had offered to relocate the mosque, which is an accepted practice among the Muslims, but the Muslim leadership did not agree. It is difficult to understand why Muslim leaders, knowing how important Ram is to Hindus, persisted in equating Ram with Babur and refused to relocate the mosque. This position taken by the Muslim leadership and the secularists helped the BJP and the Hindu nationalists sell their argument about the pseudo-secularism practiced by the Indian state.

The Rao government promptly issued an ordinance and acquired more than sixty acres of land around the disputed site. The government also promised to rebuild the Babri Mosque in Ayodhya, along with a temple. However, this promise and action once again seem to have provided a potent symbol for the Hindu militants to mobilize the community for a sacred cause. On January 25, 1993, the Sant Sammelan, an organization of Hindu holy men, issued a warning to the central government that the cultural boundaries of Ayodhya extended up to ninety-six kilometers in length and thirty-six kilometers in width and that they would fight the central government if it tried to build a mosque within that territory.[118]

The Rao government's ineptitude and the Congress (I) party's confused response to the Ayodhya controversy are evident from the fact that Hindu revivalists had already built a makeshift temple and installed idols at the disputed site. To compound the issue further, Hindus had also been allowed to worship at the new temple. It is difficult to imagine how in a Hindu majority country and in a highly emotionally charged atmosphere any party could destroy a temple and rebuild a mosque in its ruins and still hope to win election and govern effectively without causing widespread bloodshed. Only time would tell which secularist party could escape this trap, win elections, and redeem the promise made to the minority community.

Conclusions

The BJP, as the right-wing conservative party, offers itself as an alternative to the centrist parties. Its position on the role of the state in the implementation of its policies is still ambiguous. While it favors a limited role for the state in economic areas and prefers free enterprise over command economy, the BJP's strategy of self-reliance is likely to bring state regulation of the economy through the back door. Its emphasis on *swadeshi* would result in the state's providing protection for India's big and especially medium-size industries against competition from multinationals. It has embraced the present government's liberalization policies but refuses to accept the overlordship of international financial institutions. The BJP is still not clear as to how it would obtain scarce capital and modern technology.

To achieve its political goal of creating a cohesive and integrated policy, it is likely to rely more heavily on the state, especially in setting the cultural policies of the country. India faces enormous domestic problems in removing poverty, increasing literacy, providing housing for its people, controlling the relentless increase in population, and a host of de-velopment-related problems. In its policy pronouncements the BJP has paid scant attention to these vital issues. It has spent more time fighting the temple issue than offering viable solutions for the country's problems. In his June 1993 presidential address Advani tried to focus on political corruption and other economic and political issues and devoted only one paragraph of his twenty-four-page address to the temple,[119] yet given its past record, it is difficult to predict how long the BJP would keep such an emotional and vote-catching issue in abeyance. In other words, it is too early to suggest that the BJP has become serious enough to address itself to problems of nationwide concern.

In pursuit of its goal to make India a militarily powerful country, the BJP is likely to increase defense spending at the cost of India's developmental programs unless political realism prevails.

A more serious problem for the BJP is the gap between its leaders' public behavior and policy pronouncements. The BJP has tried to present itself as a well-disciplined party dedicated to stability and order in the country. It has, however, frequently sought to settle political issues in the streets rather than in Parliament. Even in Parliament its members have frequently engaged in shouting matches with their opponents, forcing the Speaker to suspend business. Unruly behavior of thousands of volunteers mobilized by the BJP and the VHP, the failure of its leaders to control them, and hysterical and irresponsible anti-Muslim speeches made by its leaders in Ayodhya raise grave doubts about the BJP's ability to govern the country effectively.

Notes

1. Bharatiya Janata Party, *Humanistic Approach to Economic Development: A Swadeshi Alternative* (New Delhi, Bharatiya Janata Party, 1992), p. 1.

2. Bharatiya Janata Party, *Economic Policy Statement* (New Delhi, Bharatiya Janata Party, 1980), p. 1.

3. R.N. Kapoor, "Voluntary Organizations in Promoting S&T in Rural Development," *Manthan* Vol. 12, No. 1 (January 1991), p. 10.

4. Govindacharya, "The Glory That Is Gone," *The Sunday Times of India*, Feb. 23, 1992, p. 14.

5. Richard Fox, "Gandhian Socialism and Hindu Nationalists: Cultural Domination in the World System," *Journal of Commonwealth and Comparative Politics*, November 1987, p. 239.

6. *The BJP Economic Policy Statement 1980*, p. 3.

7. Govindacharya, "Glory," p. 14.

8. *The BJP Economic Policy Statement 1980*, p. 11.

9. Bharatiya Janata Party, *Election Manifesto Lok Sabha Elections 1989* (New Delhi, Bharatiya Janata Party, 1989), p. 15.

10. *Ibid.*

11. Baldev Raj Nayar, *Political Economy of India's Public Sector: Policy and Performance* (Bombay, Popular Prakashan, 1990), p. 291.

12. *India Today*, March 31, 1990, p. 28.

13. Bharatiya Janata Party, *Mid-Term Poll to Lok Sabha, May 1991: Our Commitments Towards Ramrajya* (New Delhi, Bharatiya Janata Party, 1991), p. 11.

14. Bharatiya Janata Party, *Speeches on Budget 1991-92* (New Delhi, Bharatiya Janata Party, 1992), p. 15.

15. *Ibid.*, p. 16.

16. Geeta Puri, "BJP's Salvation Lies In Swadeshi Not *Hindutva*," *Indian Express*, May 10, 1992, p. 9. Also, see Bharat Bhushan, "The Dilemma of BJP: Ideological Constraints and the Prospect of Power," *Indian Express*, April 23, 1992, p. 8; and D.R. Goyal, "Economic Dimension of RSS Ideology," *Tribune*, March 27, 1992, p. 9.

17. For a sample of the RSS thinking on economic development in India and the Nehruvian model of economic planning see A.G. Modak, "Is There No Third Alternative of Development?" *Organiser*, June 21, 1992, p. 11; Daya Krishan, "Human Development Report Exposes Fallacious Western Concept of Development," *Organiser*, July 26, 1992, p. 11; Daya Krishan, "India Trapped in External Debt," *Organiser*, August 9, 1992, pp. 5 and 14; Daya Krishan, "India's Forty-Five Years of Freedom: A Tale of Economic Decline," *Organiser*, August 23, 1992, pp. 29-33; Narain Kataria, "Sangh Developing Bharatiya Model Acceptable to Modern Mind," *Organiser*, September 6, 1992, p. 11; Madan Das, "Swadeshi Panacea for All Ills," *Organiser*, October 4, 1992, p. 9; Jagdish Shettigar, "Mortgaging the Country?" *Organiser*, November 1, 1992, p. 5; and Jagdish Shettigar, "Deendayal Ji's Economic Thought and Its Relevance Today," *Organiser*, September 27, 1992, p. 9.

18. Bharatiya Janata Party, *Humanistic Approach to Economic Development*, p. 1.

19. *Ibid.*

20. *Ibid.*, p. 14.

21. *Ibid.*

22. *Ibid.*, p. 31.

23. Geeta Puri, "BJP's Salvation," p. 9.

24. Bharatiya Janata Party, *Humanistic Approach to Economic Development*, p. 29.

25. For a statement of the Dependency Theory see Andre Gundre Frank, *Capitalism and Underdevelopment in Latin America* (New York, Monthly Review Press, 1969); Peter Evans, *Dependent Development: The Alliance of Multi-national, State, and Local Capital in Brazil* (Princeton, Princeton University Press, 1979); and Fernando Henrique Cardoso and Enzo Faletto, *Dependency and Development in Latin America* (Berkeley, University of California Press, 1979). For a more recent and worldwide application of dominant and dependent relationships existing among the Third World states and rich nations of the West see Immanuel Wallerstein, *The World Capitalist System: Capitalist Agriculture and the Origins of the European Economy in the Sixteenth Century* (New York, Academic Press, 1974); *The Modern World System II: Mercantilism and Consolidation of European World Economy, 1600-1750* (New York, Academic Press, 1980); and "Rise and Future Demise of the World Capitalist System," *Comparative Studies in Society and History*, Vol. 4, No. 4 (1974). For multiple implications of the domination of the world by the

advanced nations see John Galtung, "Structural Theory of Imperialism," *Journal of Peace Research*, August, 1971, pp. 81-117.

26. For a non-Marxist critique of India's ruling elite see Rajni Kothari, "Design for an Alternative," *Seminar*, August, 1977, pp. 12-20; "The Non-Party Political Process," *Economic and Political Weekly*, Feb. 4, 1984, pp. 216-224; Sujata Patel and Krishna Kumar, "Defenders of State," *Economic and Political Weekly*, January 23, 1988, pp. 129-30; Yogendra K. Malik and Surinder M. Bhardwaj, "Ideology, Politics and Technology Policy in India," in Dhirendra Vajpeyi and R. Natrajan (eds.), *Technology and Development: Public Policy and Managerial Issues* (Jaipur, Ravat, 1990), pp. 111-142; and Yogendra K. Malik (ed.), *Politics, Technology, and Bureaucracy in South Asia* (Leiden, Netherlands, E.J. Brill, 1983).

27. Nikhil Chakravarty, "Recapture the Spirit of Swadeshi," *Organiser*, July 5, 1992, p. 13.

28. Dennis J. Encarnationa, *Dislodging Multi-Nationals: India's Strategy in Comparative Perspective* (Ithaca, NY, Cornell University Press, 1989), Chapter 5.

29. Bharatiya Janata Party, *Kisanon ka adhikar-patra* (New Delhi, Bharatiya Janata Party, 1987), pp. 31-32.

30. Bharatiya Janata Party, *Humanistic Approach to Economic Development: A Swadeshi Alternative*, p. 5.

31. *Ibid.*

32. Bharatiya Janata Party, *Bharatiya Janata Party Election Manifesto: Lok Sabha Elections, 1989* (New Delhi, Bharatiya Janata Party, 1989), p. 16.

33. Bharatiya Janata Party, *Policy Statement on the Problems of Scheduled Castes* (New Delhi, Bharatiya Janata Party, 1988), p. 2.

34. *Ibid.*, p. 3.

35. Bharatiya Janata Party, *Bharatiya Janata Party anusuchit jati morcha* (New Delhi, Bharatiya Janata Party, 1990), p. 17.

36. *India Today*, September 15, 1990, p. 35.

37. *Ibid.*, p. 36.

38. Bharatiya Janata Party, *Why B.J.P. Withdrew Support from Shri V.P. Singh Government: Speech Delivered by Shri L.K. Advani in Parliament on 7-11-1990* (New Delhi, Bharatiya Janata Party, 1990), p. 18.

39. *Hindu: International Edition*, November 28, 1992, p. 4.

40. Bharatiya Janata Party, *Presidential Speech by Dr. Murli Manohar Joshi: National Council Meeting on May 1, 2 and 3, 1992 Gandhinagar, Gujarat* (New Delhi, Bharatiya Janata Party, 1992), pp. 4-5.

41. Bharatiya Janata Party, *Presidential Address by L.K. Advani: Plenary Session, Ekatmata Nagar, New Delhi May 9, 1986* (New Delhi, Bharatiya Janata Party, 1986), p. 5.

42. Ajoy Bose, "Interview with Y.C. Chandrachud: The Supreme Court Interpreted Muslim Personal Law, It Didn't Interfere In It," in Asghar Ali Engineer (ed.), *The Shah Bano Controversy* (Hydrabad, A.P. Orient Longman, 1987), p. 80.

43. Bharatiya Janata Party, *The Great Betrayers* (New Delhi, Bharatiya Janata Party, n.d.), p. 20.

44. *Ibid.*

45. Bharatiya Janata Party, *Presidential Address by L.K. Advani*, p. 5.

46. Bharatiya Janata Party, *Election Manifesto: Lok Sabha Elections, 1989* (New Delhi, Bharatiya Janata Party, 1989), p. 9.

47. *Hindu: International Edition*, January 30, 1993, p. 9.

48. *Mid-Term Poll to Lok Sabha 1991*, p. 4.

49. *Statesman Weekly*, May 11, 1991, p. 9.

50. S.N. Jain, S.C. Kashyap and N. Srinivasan (eds.), *The Union and the States* (Delhi, National, 1972), p. 384.

51. Bharatiya Janata Party, *Our Five Commitments* (New Delhi, Bharatiya Janata Party, n.d.), p. 15.

52. B.D. Dua, "Federalism or Patrimonialism: The Making and Unmaking of Chief Ministers in India," *Asian Survey*, August 1985, p. 802.

53. *Ibid.*

54. Douglas V. Verney, "The Limits to Political Manipulation: The Role of the Governors in India's 'Administrative Federalism' 1950-84," *Journal of Commonwealth and Comparative Politics*, Vol. 24, No. 2 (July 1986), p. 176. Also, see Amal Ray, "From Consensus to Confrontation: Federal Politics in India," *Economic and Political Weekly*, October 2, 1982, pp. 1619-1624.

55. Bharatiya Janata Party, *Resolutions: National Executive Meeting 4 and 5 January, 1984 Indore (M.P.)* (New Delhi, Bharatiya Janata Party, 1984), p. 28.

56. Bharatiya Janata Party, *Our Five Commitments*, p. 16.

57. *The Statesman Weekly*, December 26, 1992, p. 5.

58. Bharatiya Janata Party, *Bharatiya Janata Party: Towards A New Polity: Election Manifesto Lok Sabha Elections, 1984* (New Delhi, Bharatiya Janata Party, 1984), p. 2.

59. Bharatiya Janata Party, *Bharatiya Janata Party: Election Manifesto: Lok Sabha Elections 1989*, p. 8.

60. Bharatiya Janata Party, *Mid-Term Poll to Lok Sabha, May 1991: Our Commitments Towards Ramrajya*, p. 10.

61. *Indian Express*, March 11, 1992, p. 3.

62. *Indian Express*, April 27, 1992, p. 10.

63. *Indian Express*, March 11, 1992, p. 3.

64. *Hindustan Times*, March 26, 1992, p. 3.

65. Bharatiya Janata Party, *Rashtriya karyakarni baithak, Palampur (H.P.) 9, 10 and 11 June 1989* (New Delhi, Bharatiya Janata Party, 1989), pp. 14-15.

66. Bharatiya Janata Party, *Statement on the IMF Loan, Review of Political Situation, Subversion of Electoral Process, War on Corruption, Election Demand for Kerala, as adopted by the National Executive on 4th, 5th and 6th December 1981 at Delhi* (New Delhi, Bharatiya Janata Party, 1981), p. 16.

67. Bharatiya Janata Party, *The Tip of the Iceberg: The Story of Three Scandals* (New Delhi, Bharatiya Janata Party, 1987), p. 1.

68. *Ibid.*

69. *Ibid.*

70. Bharatiya Janata Party, *Presidential Address by L.K. Advani: Plenary Session Ekatmata Nagar, New Delhi May 1986* (New Delhi, 1986), p. 11.

71. *Ibid.*, p. 12.

72. Interview with Math Dandavate, April 8, 1987.

73. A close associate of Indira Gandhi and one of her ministerial colleagues in an interview in New Delhi on April 7, 1987 informed this author that in the 1980 elections Mrs. Gandhi was provided campaign funds by diplomatic officials of many of the oil-producing countries of the Middle East with the understanding that she would promote and protect the interests of Muslims in India.

74. Bharatiya Janata Party, *Presidential Address by L. K. Advani 1986*, p. 13.

75. George H. Gadbois, "The Indian Superior Judiciary: Help Wanted: Any Good People Willing to be Judges?" In Yogendra K. Malik and Dhirendra K. Vajpeyi (eds.), *Boeings and Bullock-Carts: Studies in Change and Continuity in Indian Civilization, Vol. 3, Law, Politics and Society in India* (Delhi, Chanakya Publications, 1990), pp. 52-87. Also, see "The Judiciary: Crumbling Citadel," *India Today*, June 30, 1992, pp. 51-57.

76. Bharatiya Janata Party, *Election Manifesto: Lok Sabha Elections 1989* (New Delhi, Bharatiya Janata Party, 1989), p. 13.

77. Bharatiya Janata Party, *Two Years of Congress Misrule: A Charge Sheet* (New Delhi, Bharatiya Janata Party, 1986), p. 6.

78. *Ibid.*

79. Janardan Thakur, *All the Janata Men* (New Delhi, Vikas, 1977), pp. 135-143.

80. Bharatiya Janata Party, *Bharatiya Janata Party: Toward a New Polity: Election Manifesto to Lok Sabha: 1984* (New Delhi, Bharatiya Janata Party, 1984), p. 20.

81. Bharatiya Janata Party, *Presidential Speech by Dr. Murli Manohar Joshi, National Council Meeting on May 1, 2 and 3, 1992 at Gandhinagar, Gujarat*, p. 8.

82. Bharatiya Janata Party, *Statement on the IMF Loan, Review of Political Situation, Subversion of Electoral Process, War on Corruption, Election Demand in Kerala, Adopted by the National Executive Council 4th, 5th and 6th of December 1981 at Delhi*, pp. 10-11.

83. *Ibid.*, p. 6.

84. Bharatiya Janata Party, *Presidential Speech of Dr. Murli Manohar Joshi*, p. 6.

85. Bharatiya Janata Party, *National Executive Meeting December 31, 1986 and January 1, 1987: National Council Session January 2, 3 and 4, 1987 at Vijayavada (A.P.)* (New Delhi, Bharatiya Janata Party, 1987), p. 20.

86. Hiranmay Karlekar, "Influx From Bangladesh: The Bitter Harvest of Continued Indifference," *Indian Express*, April 4, 1992, p. 8.

87. Sanjoy Hazarika, "How to Solve Illegal Migration Issue," *India Abroad* (New York), November 13, 1992, p. 2.

88. Karlekar, "Influx From Bangladesh," p. 8.

89. *Ibid.*

90. Bharatiya Janata Party, *National Executive Meeting December 31, 1986 and January 1, 1987 National Council Session January 2, 3, and 4, 1987 Vijayavada (A.P.)*, p. 23.

91. *Ibid.*, p. 14.

92. Lt. Colonel Daljit Singh (Rtd.), "Bangladeshi Swarm Over India," *Organiser*, July 26, 1992, p. 6.

93. Bharatiya Janata Party, *Rashtriya karyakarni (meeting) 7, 8 and 9 October, 1988, Ahmadabad (Gujarat)* (New Delhi, Bharatiya Janata Party, 1988), pp. 8-13.

94. Bharatiya Janata Party, *National Executive Meeting, March 3, 4 and 5, 1989 Udaipur (Rajasthan)* (New Delhi, Bharatiya Janata Party, 1989), p. 13.

95. *Ibid.*, p. 14.

96. Bharatiya Janata Party, *Resolutions: BJP National Council Session, Cochin (Kerala), 25th, 26th and 27th April, 1981* (New Delhi, Bharatiya Janata Party, 1981), p. 24.

97. Bharatiya Janata Party, *Presidential Address by L.K. Advani, Plenary Session, Ekatmata Nagar, New Delhi, May 9, 1986*, p. 18.

98. Bharatiya Janata Party, *Presidential Speech by Dr. Murli Manohar Joshi: National Council Meeting on May 1, 2, and 3, 1992 at Gandhinagar (Gujarat)*, p. 8.

99. Bharatiya Janata Party, *Mid-Term Poll to Lok Sabha, May 1991: Our Commitments Towards Ramrajya* (New Delhi, Bharatiya Janata Party, 1991), p. 37. Also, see Bharatiya Janata Party, *Resolution on International Situation and India Adopted by National Executive On April 30, 1992 at Gandhinagar,* p. 1.

100. Interviews with K.R. Malkani, February 13, 1992 and Brajesh Mishra, February 17, 1992.

101. On this point see Asghar Ali Engineer, "Barelvi Muslims Support Iraq," *Hindu,* March 18, 1991, p. 5.

102. "Symposium on Gulf War-Pan-Islamism and India," *Manthan,* Vol. 12, No. 2 (February, 1991), p. 28.

103. *Ibid.,* p. 26.

104. Bharatiya Janata Party, *Rashtriya karykarni baithak 31 January 1991 tatha mahaadhivashavan 1, 2 tatha 3 February 1991, Jaipur (Rajasthan)* (New Delhi, Bharatiya Janata Party, 1991), pp. 7-9.

105. Bharatiya Janata Party, *Mid-Term Poll to Lok Sabha,* May 1991, p. 33.

106. *Ibid.*

107. George K. Tanham, *Indian Strategic Thought: An Interpretive Essay* (Santa Monica, CA, Rand, 1992), pp. 52-53.

108. Interview with Brajesh Mishra, February 17, 1992.

109. *Organiser,* January 24, 1993, pp. 1 and 15.

110. Peter Van Der Veer, "God Must be Liberated: A Hindu Liberation Movement in Ayodhya," *Modern Asian Studies,* Vol. 21, No. 2 (1987), p. 291.

111. Bharatiya Janata Party, *Election Manifesto to Lok Sabha Elections,* 1989, p. 6.

112. Hans Bakker, "Ayodhya: A Hindu Jerusalem," *Numen,* Vol. 28, Fasc. 1, pp. 98-99. On this point, also see Barbara S. Miller, "Presidential Address: Contending Narratives—The Political Life of the Indian Epics," *Journal of Asian Studies,* Vol. 50, No. 4 (1991), pp. 783-792.

113. *The Statesman,* November 11, 1989, p. 8.

114. *Indian Express,* November 11, 1989, p. 8.

115. *Ibid.*

116. Bruce Graham, *Hindu Nationalism and Indian Politics: The Origins and the Development of the Bharatiya Jana Sangh* (Cambridge, Cambridge University Press, 1990), Chapters 5 and 6. For successful utilization of sacred symbols to create a sense of communal identity at the local levels see Sandria B. Freitag, "Sacred Symbols as Mobilizing Ideology: The North Indian Search for a 'Hindu Community,'" *Comparative Studies in Society and History,* Vol. 22 (1980), pp. 597-625; and Anand A. Yang, "Sacred Symbol and Sacred Space in Rural India: Community Mobilization in the 'Anti-Cow Killing' Riot of 1893," *Comparative Studies in Society and History,* Vol. 22 (1980), pp. 576-596.

117. Girilal Jain, "Hindus Assert Themselves," *Organiser,* January 31, 1993, p. 7.

118. *Organiser,* February 7, 1993, p. 2.

119. Bharatiya Janata Party, *Lal Krishan Advani ka adhyakhsheeya bhashan June 18-20* (New Delhi, Bharatiya Janata Party Publications, 1993), pp. 1-20.

5

Organization, Decision-Making, and Supportive Groups

Political scientists who have studied political parties have delineated various factors which determine the nature of a party's organization and its decision-making process. Such factors include the circumstances under which a party is founded, the division of labor and coordination between the activities of different groups in the society supporting the party, the party's goals and ideology, and the need for specialization to deal with the environment in which the party operates. Above all, it is the struggle for power and the desire for survival which are the keys to understanding the changing nature of the party's organizational structure.[1]

While analyzing European political parties, Maurice Duverger divided them into ones having direct or indirect structures. The direct structure consists of dues-paying and card-carrying members who have signed membership applications and have been duly admitted into the party. In a party with a direct organizational structure, the members attend regular meetings of the local party organizations. The indirect structure does not have direct members but consists of various supportive organizations such as the trade unions, Friendly Societies, and other associations which have joined the party en bloc. According to Duverger, "in the 'direct' party the members themselves form the party community without the help of other social groupings."[2] Parties with indirect structures can be called federal parties, since they are created by the joining together of like-minded groups for a common cause.

Whatever the circumstances of the BJP's founding, as it operates today, it resembles Duverger's model of a federal party. Besides the primary political component, the BJP, which admits its own dues-paying members, its major non-political units are the Rashtriya Swayamsevak Sangh (RSS) and Vishwa Hindu Parishad (VHP). Whether the BJP is the political front of the RSS or the RSS is the supportive unit of the BJP is debatable, but the close interrelationship between these units suggests the federal structure of the BJP. In Indian political parlance, all of them are called the members of the *sangh parivar* (the Sangh family).

Both the BJP leaders and observers of Indian politics suggest that despite their close relationships the BJP, the RSS, and the VHP maintain considerable organizational and functional autonomy. Each seems to have its own goals, functionaries, and areas of operation. In addition, each has created various supportive organizations and agencies providing them with workers as well as financial resources to operate in their respective areas. The RSS occupies the central position; it has been compared to the sun, with all other organizations satellites that move around it.[3] The main source of the Hindu nationalism that links the three groups is the RSS, although the BJP may be able to adapt it to suit its political goals. Since the three are linked by the common ideology, a complete delineation of their functions and boundaries is difficult. The overlap of functions and personnel among the BJP, RSS, and VHP is not surprising. According to one estimate, "every second office-bearer of the party at both central and state levels is or has been either a full-time RSS *pracharak* [instructor-propagandist] or a member."[4] Thus in order to understand the functioning of the BJP, it becomes imperative to look at the functions and the role of each of these units.

We should, however, add that scholars believe that parties, even when founded to achieve certain ideological goals, over a period of time tend to develop internal bureaucracies. This leads to diversification of their aims.[5] And like any social organization, a party also develops a life of its own. As a result, organizational survival is likely to become one of its aims. In this kind of situation "the organization is perceived as a structure which responds to, and adjusts itself to, a multitude of demands from various stockholders, and which tries to maintain a balance by reconciling these demands."[6] We can suggest, therefore, that political leaders and party bureaucrats need special skills to manage the conflicting demands of the party's constituent units.

From among the Indian political parties, the BJP—like the Communist Party of India (CPI) and the Communist Party of India (Marxist) (CPIM)—is a cadre-based organization. In this respect, among the non-Communist parties the BJP occupies a distinct position. At present the party claims to have ten million members, which is not a small number for an Indian party. From among these more than one hundred thousand are active members which the party can mobilize for political campaigning.[7] The BJP possesses far superior organization than other non-Communist parties. With its distinct political ideology and highly motivated cadre, the

BJP has demonstrated its ability to undertake massive mobilization of the Hindu population of the country.

Organization of the Bharatiya Janata Party

The party's charter declares the BJP's allegiance to the Constitution of India and pledges to "uphold the sovereignty, unity and integrity of India."[8] At the same time it seeks to build a strong India "which is modern, progressive and enlightened in outlook and which proudly draws its inspiration from India's ancient culture and values. . . ."[9]

To achieve its objectives, its leaders created an organization which is open to all Indians at least eighteen years old. Any citizen of India can join the party, irrespective of his religion and sex, provided he abides by the party's rules and pays Rs.1.00 as a membership fee. The person also signs a written declaration pledging his/her faith in Integral Humanism, democracy, and positive secularism, in the concept of a nation not based upon religion, and in the use of peaceful means of social change and opposition to untouchability, and declares that he or she is not a member of any other party.

The party's basic units are organized on a residential geographic basis rather than on the basis of work place. The party's district committee keeps a register of the primary members. The membership is valid for a term of ten years or as determined by the National Executive. Every ten years the person is expected to reapply.

A distinction is made between an ordinary member and an active party member. An active member has more duties as well as rights than an ordinary member. It is only after two years in the party that a person can apply for active membership. An active member has to make a non-refundable deposit of Rs.100.00 along with his/her membership application. The president of the district party organization forwards the application, along with his recommendations, to the state party office.

The state executive will convene a special committee to review such an application and grant admission. In case of denial, the applicant has the right of appeal. The party's national organization constitutes an appeal committee, consisting of three members, at its central office to consider the appeal.

The active party member is expected to devote a minimum of twenty days in a period of two years to party work. The party's higher agencies at the local or the state level supervise the active member's work. It is only the party's active members who may seek election to the various district or state level offices.

Two Wings of the BJP Organization

The BJP has two distinct wings at both the national and state levels, the mass wings and the parliamentary wings. Figure 5.1 gives the outlines of the organization's mass wings at the national level.

The president, the highest office holder of the party, is elected indirectly by an electoral college. In the electoral college states are given representation on the basis of the number of Lok Sabha seats allocated. For instance, if a state elects ten Lok Sabha members, it will have ten electoral votes.

FIGURE 5.1 Organizational Structure of the BJP at the National Level

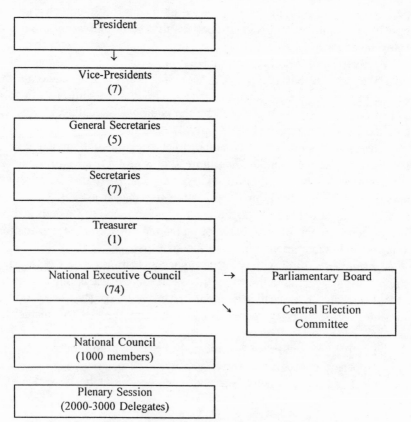

In addition, the BJP legislative party of each state will elect ten percent of the delegates from its own rank, the minimum being ten. If, however, the state legislative party has fewer than ten members, then all of them are allowed to participate in the presidential election. Similarly, ten percent of the delegates are selected from the BJP Lok Sabha members elected from the state (the minimum being three). If, however, the state has elected fewer than three BJP members to the Lok Sabha, then all the Lok Sabha members elected on the party ticket from the state will be allowed to participate in the election. The BJP parliamentary party is allowed ten percent of its representation in the electoral college from its own rank, but not more than ten in total.

The party has made special efforts to give representation in the electoral college to low caste Hindus, since the party Constitution requires that each state's delegation should give representation to the members of scheduled castes/scheduled tribes in proportion to the seats reserved for them under Indian law.[10]

The president is elected for a term of two years, and he is barred from holding the office for more than two consecutive terms. According to the party Constitution, any ten members of the electoral college can nominate an active member, with his consent, as a candidate for party president. The National Executive appoints a returning officer to conduct the election, which is done by secret ballot.

In actual practice, however, there is virtually no contest for the presidential election. It is the party elders who decide on a candidate, and their choice is usually adopted by the electoral college of the party. Atal Bihari Vajpayee, L.K. Advani and Rajmata Vijay Raje Scindia constitute a kind of inner core of party elders. Through informal consultation with each other and with other senior leaders of the party, at both the national and state levels, as well as with the leaders of the RSS, they reach a consensus on a presidential candidate. There is a deferential political culture within the party; younger leaders tend to respect the party elders.

From among the three who have held the presidency of the party, Vajpayee and Advani are known as the elder statesmen of the party with nationwide reputation. According to the party insiders, Dr. Murli Manohar Joshi, president of the party until June 1993, lacks the stature, the skill, and the political sophistication to lead the main opposition party of the country. Joshi has been characterized as "self-centered, stubborn, abrasive, and with what can best be described as a Congress mindset, which has nothing to do with ideology and everything to do with culture."[11] Joshi is a practicing orthodox Hindu while Vajpayee and Advani are described as non-practicing Hindus.

The president, besides presiding over the meetings of the National Executive, National Council, and party plenary, distributes work among the members of the Executive and other office holders. Also, he appoints the president of various *morchas* (fronts) and the cells. It is the president who calls the meeting of the National Executive and conducts negotiations with the leaders of other parties.

Office bearers of the party comprise, besides the President, seven vice-presidents, five general secretaries, seven secretaries, and one national treasurer. All these officers are appointed by the president within one month of his taking over the presidency. The president can authorize one of the vice-presidents to conduct the party business in his absence. If the president has not left such instructions, the National Executive has the right to call upon one of the senior vice-presidents to discharge the President's duties.

Most of these office bearers work in the central office of the party, which is in New Delhi. The central office conducts the day-to-day affairs of the party. Most of the vice-presidents and the general secretaries are put in charge of different sections of the party. For instance, Sundar Singh Bhandari, one of the senior vice-presidents, is in charge of the party's organization. He also serves as a link with the RSS. Many of them are asked to look after the affairs of a particular region or number of states, such as Krishanlal Sharma, another party vice-president, who is in charge of Punjab and Jammu and Kashmir affairs. A general secretary, like Govindacharya, not only maintains relations with the press and the leaders of the other parties but also plays a significant role in the formulation of the party's electoral strategies. It is the responsibility of the general secretary to convene various meetings at the request of the president, to keep records of the minutes, and to run the party's office.

All these officers are members of the National Executive Council. Sikandar Bakht, a senior vice-president of the party, is the only Muslim among the party's high-ranking officials. According the party Constitution, from among the BJP's high officials, at least two should be women and two should come from the ranks of scheduled castes and scheduled tribes. Despite these provisions, the party's top leadership positions are all held by upper caste Hindus.

The National Executive Council consists of the president and not more than seventy-four members, which include the high-ranking officials of the party. The Executive Council shall have at least seven women, and seven members should come from the ranks of scheduled castes/scheduled tribes.

The National Executive Council is the party's highest decision-making agency, provided its decisions are not overturned in the party's plenary session, which is very unlikely given the oligarchic nature of its organization and deferential nature of its political culture. It is this agency of the BJP which lays down the rules according to which all units and organs of the party work. The National Executive also provides the rules for maintenance of party accounts and their annual auditing, creates machinery, and makes rules for holding elections and filling vacancies caused by death or resignation. It assigns functions to different agencies and constitutes disciplinary action committees. It is this body which is responsible for adopting various resolutions and making decisions on policy matters.

Besides its seventy-four members, the National Executive has the right to co-opt members or invite a guest to participate in its deliberation. On several occasions many of the prominent state party leaders or chief ministers of the BJP-run state governments have been among such invitees. The 1991-93 list of the members of the National Executive released by the party's central office listed as many as 130 members.

There is considerable informality in the working of the National Executive. In consultation with the president of the party, the central office prepares the agenda for meetings. A group of party regulars, which may include some of the members of the Executive as well as the vice-presidents and the general secretaries, meets every morning in the central party office to prepare resolutions or drafts of policy statements which are subsequently presented before the National Executive for discussion. It has been reported by many of the participants that there is free and frank exchange of views. Sometimes there is sharp division of opinion that leads to heated exchanges between the members. However, decisions are made by building consensus rather than by votes. It is the senior leaders of the party like Advani, Scindia, and Joshi who play the decisive role in the formulation of the party's policies and programs.[12]

Rajinder Puri, a former member of the National Executive, once observed that "the basic principle of the organization is the dispersal of authority and accountability. But here, there is a tendency to treat everything like a family gathering, so that accountability is not pinpointed and responsibility is diffused."[13] This view of the functioning of the party at the top still holds. Although many of the participants describe the working of the National Executive as a democratic process, it appears that senior party leaders have the final say, and other members simply abide by their decisions. The National Executive must meet every three months; however, the president of the party may call it into emergency session.

The National Council is a large organization, consisting of more than a thousand delegates drawn from a large variety of party officials. Each state is given a set of representatives on a variety of criteria. For instance, a state delegation for the National Council should select representatives from its ranks equal to the number of the Lok Sabha seats allocated to the states. Such a delegation should have appropriate representation of the scheduled castes/tribes. Next, ten percent of the delegates (not exceeding ten in number) should be elected by the BJP members of the Parliament. Besides these groups, all the former presidents, all the presidents of the state party units, leaders of the BJP parliamentary party in the Lok Sabha and Rajya Sabha, BJP leaders of the state and metropolitan legislative parties, and all the members of the National Executive will participate in the National Council. Other members include national presidents of cells and *morchas* (fronts) set up by the party. The National Executive has the authority to co-opt not more than forty members outside the stated categories. All the members of the National Council pay annual dues of Rs.25.

The functions of the National Council are not clearly spelled out, although it is this body which is entitled to amend the Constitution of the party and has the power of ratification of amendments adopted by the National Executive. The National Council must meet at least once a year. The National Council seems to be primarily an annual gathering of the party office holders where the party's local and state leaders come to hear the speeches of the party's national leadership and to adopt its resolutions.

Special agencies of the BJP, with the power to perform specific functions, are the Parliamentary Board and the Central Election Committee. Since the BJP contests elections, issues party tickets to its members, and campaigns on their behalf, the party leadership needs to control the distribution of the tickets among the candidates. At the same time it seeks some degree of coordination of their activities. The functions of these two agencies complement each other.

Both agencies are set up by the National Executive. The Parliamentary Board consists of eight members; the president of the party is its chairman and the leader of the BJP parliamentary party is its member. One of the general secretaries of the party is appointed by the president as the secretary of the Parliamentary Board. It is one of the organizations which links the BJP parliamentary party with the mass wing.

The Central Election Committee contains all the members of the Parliamentary Board with eight additional members elected by the National Executive Committee. Its primary function is to finalize the list of candidates for state legislative bodies and the two houses of the Indian Parliament. Although the state election committees prepare the list of the candidates, the final decision regarding the distribution of the tickets is always made by the Central Election Committee. According to informed sources, there is considerable informal consultation between the state and the central party leadership before the list is finalized.

The evidence suggests that in the last two elections, despite centralization of the selection process, the central party leadership was unwilling to adopt a candidate unless he had a strong local support base. In the 1989 and 1991 elections the RSS workers at the district levels helped the local party leaders in the selection of candidates. Even at the state level the BJP election committees actively consulted with the state RSS leaders in picking the candidates.[14] The Central Election Committee, in cooperation with state committee, runs the party's electoral campaign. Since many of these committees contain many former RSS *pracharaks* (instructor-propagandists), in selecting candidates and running the campaigns the national BJP leaders and the RSS cooperate.

In previous years denial of party tickets did not often lead to friction since the BJP candidates had little chance of winning. However, since the electoral prospects of the party have improved, the demand for its tickets has also increased. As a result, the party faces more disciplinary problems than in the past. The party leadership is aware of this problem, yet the competition is likely to accentuate the problems within the party despite Advani's recent advice to his partymen to restrain their political ambitions in the larger interest of the party and the nation.

Morchas (fronts) and cells are special agencies of the mass wing of the party. The *morchas* are organized for women, youth, scheduled castes/tribes, and farmers with extensive networks spreading through states and districts. They function under the supervision of the National Executive, while their presidents are appointed by the party president. Each *morcha* has its own working committee, vice-president, general secretary, secretary, and an elaborate organizational structure which is replicated at the state and the district levels.[15]

Although the names or the subjects of the cells are not given in the party Constitution, party functionaries at the national level have disclosed the names of cells for such subjects as defense, foreign affairs, Punjab and Kashmir affairs, minorities, traders, intellectuals, and many others.

In 1991 at least six former lieutenant generals, two air chief marshals, and a number of other high-ranking officials, including Lt. General K.P. Candeth and Lt. General J.F.R. Jacob, joined the party. The BJP leaders quickly placed them in charge of the defense cell of the party, hoping to utilize their expertise. Since the party won elections in four states, they also created a number of study groups consisting of experts to provide advice to the leaders on various issues.[16]

The party plenary session is a very large organization consisting of around 2,000 delegates. It is held at least once in four years, although the National Executive may call emergency/special sessions. The state executives also have the right to requisition a special session by a majority vote. In such a case the president convenes the special session. According to the Constitution of the party, all the decisions made by the plenary session are binding on all the units and agencies of the party. In between the party plenary sessions the National Executive serves as the highest authority of the party.[17] Since the party plenary session is held only once every four years, the real power rests with the small, elite group represented by the president and the National Executive.

Virtually all the office holders of the party at the national and the state levels participate in the party plenary session. In addition, all the BJP members of the state legislative bodies, the members of the two houses of Parliament, and members of the state and the national councils are entitled to attend. The National Executive has the right to add to these categories of delegates, and it often does. The president of the party chairs the session. However, because of its large size this organization is not expected either to formulate policies or to undertake any serious discussion of the issues which the party or the country faces.

The Parliamentary Wing of the Party

Since the BJP has been able to elect a large number of members not only to the state legislatures but also to the two houses of Parliament, in 1988 the party adopted an elaborate constitution governing the organization and the functioning of its parliamentary wing. At the national level the official name of its parliamentary wing is the Bharatiya Janata Party in Parliament. It consists of all the members of either house of Parliament elected on the BJP ticket as well as associate members of the party.[18]

The members of the parliamentary wing have to sign a pledge to abide by the party's rule and to follow instructions issued by the party leadership. The party members also have to pay a minimum subscription of ten percent of their monthly salaries.

Organization of the parliamentary wing of the BJP. Figure 5.2 gives the organizational structure of the party at the national level, and as it indicates this wing of the BJP is headed by the leader. Under normal circumstances the leader of the Parliamentary wing should come from the Lok Sabha, the lower house of Parliament.

FIGURE 5.2 Organization of the Parliamentary Wing at the National Level

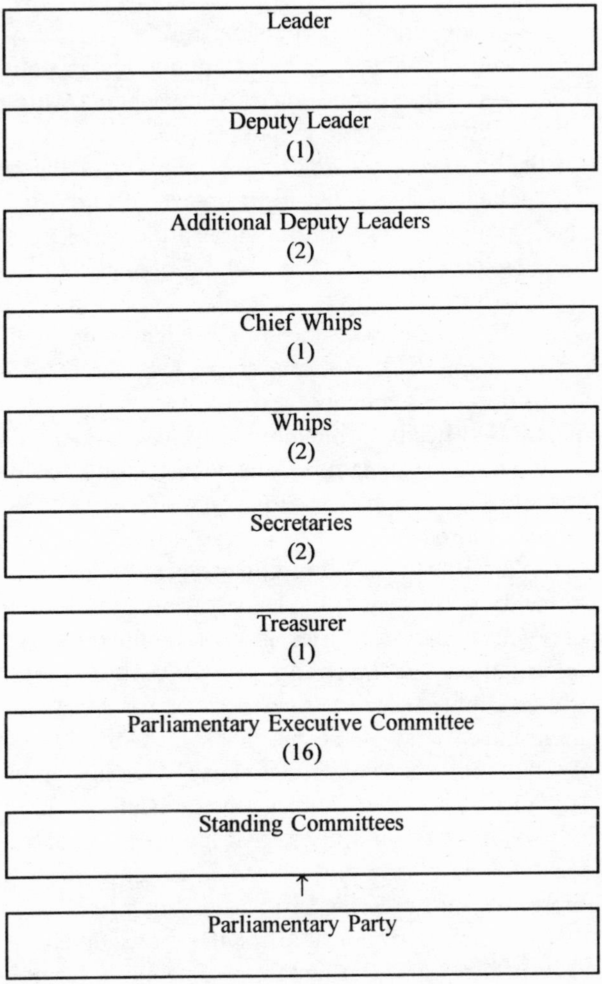

Leader

Deputy Leader (1)

Additional Deputy Leaders (2)

Chief Whips (1)

Whips (2)

Secretaries (2)

Treasurer (1)

Parliamentary Executive Committee (16)

Standing Committees

↑

Parliamentary Party

It is only under exceptional circumstances that its leader would come from the Rajya Sabha, the upper house.

In each house of the Parliament the BJP MPs elect their own leaders by a simple majority vote. They also elect other office holders such as the deputy leaders and the whips for each house. Presently, A.B. Vajpayee and Sikandar Bakht are the leaders in the Lok Sabha and Rajya Sabha respectively. Thus Vajpayee and Bakht are the leaders and deputy leaders of the parliamentary wing of the BJP. Jaswant Singh, an accomplished parliamentarian, serves as the deputy to Vajpayee in the Lok Sabha.

The chief whip and the whips assist in enforcing party instructions and see that the BJP members of Parliament follow the party policy and program. They follow standard rules of conducting the business of the parliamentary wings of the party. For instance, when a whip is issued, no BJP MP shall stay away from the meeting of the house without the prior permission of the chief whip. Similarly, a member of the parliamentary party can be expelled or suspended for a breach of party discipline.

Whereas the deputy leaders and the whips are elected every two years, the leader is elected for the full five-year term of the Lok Sabha. The leader of the parliamentary wing of the party can be removed by a vote of no confidence at the general body meeting requisitiòned by not "less than fifteen or fifty percent of the total strength, whichever is less."[19] The required quorum for such a meeting is two-thirds of the members, and the no confidence motion needs to be adopted by more than fifty percent of the members attending the meeting of the general body. While the leader is elected by a show of hands, for the passage of a vote of no confidence a secret ballot is required.

The Parliamentary Executive Committee consists of all the office holders of the parliamentary party such as the leader, the deputy leaders, additional deputy leaders, whips, and secretaries and two members elected from each house of the Parliament. If the strength of the party exceeds forty members, the party is allowed to elect one member for every ten MPs. The president of the mass wing of the party is an ex-officio member of the Parliamentary Executive as is the secretary, who is nominated by the president. It is this body which controls the legislative and parliamentary affairs of the party in the two houses. All legislative proposals, motions, and amendments made by the party law makers have to be approved by this body before they are presented in Parliament.

It is this body which is responsible for the management of the party's accounts and its affairs. The Parliamentary Executive Committee can appoint standing committees for different government ministries to make recommendations to party leadership.

At least one meeting of the parliamentary wing of the BJP consisting of all the MPs, which is also known as the general body, is to be held before the opening of each session of Parliament. The frequency of the meetings of the Parliamentary Executive Committee is determined by its leader. Meetings of both the general body and the Parliamentary Executive Committee can also be requested by the members as prescribed in its

Constitution. State-level legislative wings of the BJP follow the same Constitution and procedures as practiced at the national level.

Despite this elaborate organizational structure provided by the Constitution of the parliamentary wing of the party, in actual operation the policy formulation and distribution of powers between the two wings of the party are not yet sharply demarcated. The BJP is still primarily a mass party; at the national level it has functioned as an opposition party only. Its administrative experience is very limited, confined mainly to the state and local levels.

The BJP's nationally known leaders and members of Parliament like Advani, Vajpayee, Scindia, Bakht, Singh, Krishan Lal Sharma, J.P. Mathur, and others are also the leading members of the National Executive, the top decision-making agency of the mass wing of the party. Because of this overlapping membership between the two organizations there is constant interaction between the mass and the parliamentary wings of the party. Recently, Murli Manohar Joshi, the president of the mass wing of the party, was also elected a member of the Rajya Sabha and joined the ranks of the parliamentary wing of the party. As a result, it has been asserted by party insiders that there is complete harmony between the mass and the parliamentary wings of the party. While this may be true when the party is out of power, experience shows that when a party assumes power, a struggle for supremacy is likely to arise between the mass and the parliamentary wings of the party.

Indications are that between June 1991 and March 1992 the parliamentary wing, headed by Advani, and the mass wing, headed by Joshi, did not enjoy very cordial relations. While Advani and his parliamentary associates cooperated with the Rao government, Joshi embarked upon *Ekta yatra* (the unity march). Joshi's *yatra*, starting from the southern state of Kerala and to be terminated in Srinagar, the capital of Jammu and Kashmir state, with the unfurling of the national flag, was intended to raise Joshi to the leadership stature of Advani and to demonstrate the failure of the Rao government's Kashmir policy.

While the *yatra* might have succeeded in demonstrating the government's inability to deal with the Kashmiri militants, it was a public relations failure. The March 1992 firing of Govindacharya, a protegee of Advani, as the general secretary of the party was looked upon as an indication of an ongoing power struggle between the two wings of the party.[20] The state chief minister usually ignored the party president, Joshi, when he tried to intervene in the administrative affairs of the state.

Recently Bhairon Singh Shekhawat, who is an ideological ally of Vajpayee, refused to accept Joshi's nominees for Rajya Sabha election from Rajasthan.[21]

A more significant indication of developing conflict between the two wings, however, came from the states. In Madhya Pradesh Sunderlal Patwa, the chief minister of the state and the leader of the legislative wing of the BJP, became involved in a bitter struggle with V. K. Sakhlecha, a former BJP chief minister of the state, an organizational veteran, and Patwa's rival for the control of the party's organizational wing. Although Patwa, with the support of Kushabhau Thakre and Lakhiram Agrawal, was able to establish his control over the organizational wing, Sakhlecha was able to muster thirty-five percent of the votes to challenge the control of the ministerial wing over the organizational wing of the party.[22]

In U.P. there was an ongoing struggle for power between state chief minister Kalyan Singh and Kalraj Mishra, the chief of the state party unit, before the government resigned in December, 1992. National party president Murli Manohar Joshi and L.K. Advani were backing Mishra and Singh, respectively.[23] Dissidence also developed in other BJP-ruled states such as Himachal Pradesh and Rajasthan, where powerful and experienced chief ministers like Shanta Kumar and Shekhawat headed the state governments. However, when the party is not in power in any state, it has the tendency to close ranks behind the leaders.

State Party Organization

A state party organization is headed by a president (see Figure 5.3) who is elected by an electoral college consisting mainly of the members of the state council and some members elected for the purpose of electing the president. This electoral college gives representation to both the organizational and legislative wings of the party, although it seems to be dominated by representatives of the district and local party organizations.

The president appoints five vice-presidents, three general secretaries, five secretaries, and one treasurer. He does not have much freedom since they have to be selected from among the members of the State Executive. In practice the president is elected in consultation with the national party leadership. However, contests for the office are not unusual. The president of the state party organization has been given the same type of powers as the national party president. He is, however, subject to the control of the State Executive.

FIGURE 5.3 BJP Organization at the State Level

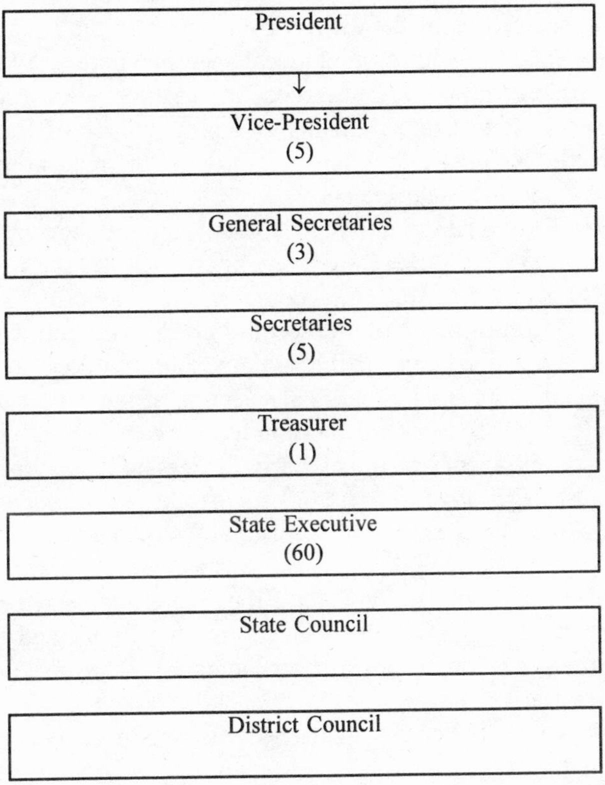

President

↓

Vice-President (5)

General Secretaries (3)

Secretaries (5)

Treasurer (1)

State Executive (60)

State Council

District Council

The State Executive consists of sixty members, including all the office holders. It should have, however, a minimum of five women members and five should come from scheduled caste/tribes. They have to be nominated by the state party president, who is in complete control of this organization. The State Executive shall meet at least once every three months.

The State Council gives representation to various constituents of the party. Local party organizations of the district receive representation based on the number of legislative assembly/metropolitan council seats allocated to the district. Ten percent of the seats are filled by the state legislative party; however, their maximum strength should not exceed ten. In case there are fewer than ten, all of them would be allowed to sit in the National Council. The BJP members elected to Parliament are given ten percent of the representation, but their minimum number should not fall below three. The State Council should also include all the members of National Council, all the former presidents of the state party organization, all the office holders of the regional committees, the leaders of the party in the state legislative assembly and state legislative council, presidents, and general secretaries of the district committees in the state and various others. The State Council must include a specified number of members of scheduled castes/tribes. It must meet at least once in a year. Each member of the State Council shall pay an annual fee of Rs.10.00 The State Council does not seem to have real power; the real power rests with the president and the State Executive.

The State Election Committee is another important agency of the state party organization. It is the State Executive which has the right to frame rules for its operation as well as its composition. The primary purpose of this agency is to recommend to the central election committee candidates for the state legislative body and the parliamentary elections and to conduct the campaigns. It also makes the final selection of the party candidates for the local elections, such as for the municipal councils and corporations. It is an important agency with key party leaders as its members.

The State Legislative Party consists of the members of the state legislative assembly and the state legislative council elected on the party ticket. It would also include those members of the legislative body who join the BJP after their election even if they were not elected on the party ticket. The state legislative party elects its own leader and other office holders in the same way as the BJP parliamentary party. The members of the state legislative party abide by the party policies, resolutions, and instructions issued to them by the party's national organization.

Although the state legislative party claims to be autonomous and the party leaders assert that the central office does not intervene in their internal affairs, in practice, the party's national leadership exercises considerable control over the state legislative party. The BJP's national leaders help resolve factional as well as leadership disputes at the state level.

The District Committee, the lowest party organization in a district, is called the local committee. It can be formed in a village or a locality with a minimum of fifty members. It has its own president and executive committee. An intermediate organization between the local and the district committees is called the Mandal committee. However, the key organization seems to be the district committee. The district is the basic unit organized for the purpose of administration in India. Political parties tend to organize themselves on a district-wide basis.

The district committee is headed by a president and consists of forty-four members. It is the elected members of the Mandal committee who elect the district president and committee members. The president, in consultation with the committee, nominates four vice-presidents, one general secretary, four secretaries, and one treasurer. The district committee shall have one woman member and at least one member belonging to scheduled castes. The BJP has been holding its organizational elections regularly.[24]

Supportive Organizations

The Rashtriya Swayamsevak Sangh (RSS) is a formidable organization providing ideological and organizational support to the BJP. In its sixty-seven-year history the RSS has been banned three times. The most recent government-imposed ban came in the wake of the demolition of the Babri mosque in December 1992. The RSS has 30,000 *shakhas* (branches) and more than 2,500 full-time *pracharaks* (instructor-propagandists). In 1975, when it was banned during Indira Gandhi's Emergency Rule, it had only 11,000 *shakhas*. According to some observers, its defiance of Indira Gandhi's authoritarian rule proved its pro-democratic credentials, and it achieved a degree of legitimacy because of the blessings which it received from late socialist leader Jayaprakash Narayan. Presently, the RSS is estimated to have the ability to mobilize around three million volunteers.[25] Whenever the ban is lifted, the organization is able to bounce back with vigor.

The RSS is active in various areas of public life, although it claims to be primarily a cultural organization. It has established numerous groups which undertake a large variety of activities. For instance, *Bharat Mazdoor Sangh* (RSS-affiliated trade union), the second largest labor organization of India, is run by Dattopant Thengdi, an RSS ideologue. It has more than three million members. The BMS was established to counter the Communist influence among the working classes. It has been very successful among the white collar workers, although it also has considerable following among the textile and transport workers. Its strongest base is the Hindi-speaking states of north India.

Since the Rao government's introduction of the economic liberalization program, the *Bharat Mazdoor Sangh* has been in the forefront of promoting the *swadeshi* movement and opposing the entry of the multinationals in India. Journalist Arun Shouri has praised the BMS as "an organization which embodies responsible trade unionism."[26]

Nevertheless, contrary to the BJP's declared policies, the BMS, reversing its earlier position, has opposed the privatization of the public sector undertakings.[27] The BMS recommends that the workers be allowed to take over the so-called "sick industries." To start with, labor should be allowed to acquire twenty percent equity and the government should amend the company law accordingly. A national commission should be constituted to determine the patterns of ownership in industries. The priority should be given to the workers in the public sector undertakings to purchase shares in the industries which the government wants to close down because of their low profitability.

Public sector industries can be owned and managed in various ways. Besides private ownership, municipal ownership, cooperatives, and joint ownership, the government and private combined can be an alternate model of industrial takeover instead of foreign takeover. The BMS leadership holds that "Productivity is based upon the will of the workers and the employers. Both factors should work in unison with the national commitment."[28]

The BMS seeks to cultivate harmonious relations between the employers and employees. It does not believe in the concept of class struggle, which, it holds, is contrary to the Hindu culture. Following Deendayal Upadhyaya's philosophy of Integral Humanism, as stated in Chapter One, its leaders hold that neither Communism nor capitalism can solve the problems faced by the Indian economy. The BMS seeks a balance between the working class's material and psychological welfare. The organization has been active in promoting higher wages for the workers and employees' compensation plans and in dealing with issues of retrenchment, plant closings, and so on.

Akhil Bharatiya Vidyarthi Parishad (ABVP: All India Students Council) is another affiliate of the RSS-BJP coalition. RSS leaders like K. P. Sudershan, Bal Apte, and Raj Kumar Bhatia led the ABVP and the *Janata Yuva Morcha* (Janata Youth Front), the youth wing of the BJP. Many of the BJP's current leaders like Govindacharya, Arun Jaitley, and Narinder Modi received their political training in the ABVP before they became active in party politics. During the 1975 Emergency Rule of Indira Gandhi thousands of its members were arrested. The ABVP is one of the fastest-growing student organizations in the country. Whereas in 1991 its membership was 300,000, in 1992 it shot up to 500,000. It presently has working units in 415 out of a total of 483 districts of the country. Similarly, out of 167 universities in the country 121 have branches of the ABVP.[29]

There are various student organizations affiliated with the political parties which are active on the campuses of Indian universities. However, whereas other student organizations are engaged primarily in campus politics and pursue student trade unionism, the ABVP seems to have a different agenda. Its primary goal is to spread the message of the RSS. For this purpose it holds a large variety of extracurricular activities such as sports clubs, symposiums, tutorial groups, health centers, and various others.[30]

It actively recruits students and faculty members for political indoctrination. As a result, it involves the students, teachers, and administrators in its activities, seeking to promote harmonious relations among the different components of the academic community. Following the Hindu traditions of the *guru-shishya* (teacher-pupil) relationship, where the student is duty bound to respect his teacher while the teacher is to look after the intellectual and physical welfare of his pupil, the ABVP's leaders perform special ceremonies to pay respect to their teachers.

The ABVP has been active in campus politics by contesting elections for the student unions. It has been successful in capturing the student unions in important universities located in Delhi, Punjab, Maharashtra, and Madhya Pradesh. Its most remarkable political activity outside of campus politics was its participation in the Gujarat and Bihar movements against the Congress-run governments.

Although it claims to be a non-political organization, in recent years it has openly criticized the Rao government's invitation to multi-nationals to invest in India, supported the RSS *swadeshi* movement, and expressed its support of the BJP on the Ramjanambhoomi issue.

In 1973 Balasaheb Deoras, the current chief of the RSS, denounced the practice of untouchability and appealed to the RSS volunteers to work towards its removal from the Hindu society. Today the RSS has set up 10,000 programs under *Seva Bharati*, an organization devoted to uplifting the members of scheduled castes. Under its auspices the RSS volunteers have started schools in which they offer vocational courses for the slum dwellers and the former untouchables while teaching them the virtues of Hinduism.

Vidya Bharati is an educational organization run by the RSS which has set up hundreds of secondary schools throughout the country. Presently, Vidya Bharati provides education for 1.2 million students and employs 40,000 teachers. It is a powerful tool of indoctrination and political socialization. While the BJP was in power, Vidya Bharati-run educational programs were adopted in Madhya Pradesh as an alternate model of education.

Seva Bharati and Vanbasi Kalyan Sangh (The Welfare Association for the Tribal) are two other prominent organizations manned by RSS volunteers. Seva Bharati has undertaken work among the slum dwellers, setting up an estimated 10,000 centers and introducing 3,500 welfare schemes. For its remarkable work among the slum dwellers the Seva

Bharati's services were recognized by the central government with a cash award and certificate of merit.[31] *Matri Chhaya,* which works under the auspices of the Seva Bharati, has set up several centers in Delhi and Madhya Pradesh to look after the welfare of children.

The tribal population has been the target of Christian missions, especially in the state of Madhya Pradesh. The RSS leaders believe that since many of the religious practices and beliefs of the tribal population are borrowed from Hinduism, they are a part of Hindu society and therefore should be protected from conversion to Christianity. The *Vanbasi Kalyan Sangh* has set up centers in more than 31,000 tribal villages.

The RSS also runs the *Bharatiya Kisan Sangh* (Indian Farmers Union) and the *Rashtriya Sevika Samita* (National Women Workers Council), and it publishes six daily newspapers and a host of periodicals in different Indian languages. It has several publishing houses located in different parts of India. The RSS undertakes a wide variety of activities for the reconstruction of the entire social life of Hindus. Politics is only one of its activities.

The RSS: The Fountainhead of Hindu Nationalism

The Rashtriya Swayamsevak Sangh was launched in September 1925 by Dr. Keshav Baliram Hedgewar, a Maharashtrian Brahmin born in 1889 in the city of Nagpur. In his youth Hedgewar was attracted by the Indian National Congress, and in the 1920s he actively participated in its activities. However, he was soon disillusioned with the policies and politics of the Congress. It was the outbreak of the Hindu-Muslim riot in 1923 that spurred him to find an alternate model of nation-building in India in contrast to what was being proposed by Gandhi and Nehru.

Deeply influenced by the writings of Lokmanya Bal Gangadhar Tilak and Vinayak Damodar Savarkar, he became convinced that the cultural and religious heritage of Hindus ought to be the basis of Indian nationhood. The essence of Savarkar's *Hindutva,* which Hedgewar adopted as the basis of Indian nationhood, is a person's acceptance of India, with its ancient cultural heritage, not only as his/her fatherland but also as the holy land. Savarkar asserted:

> To the Hindus, Hindustan being their fatherland and holy land, the love they bear to Hindustan is boundless. What is called nationalism can be defined as in fact the national communalism of the majority community. . . . Thus, in Hindustan it is the Hindus, professing Hindu religion and being in overwhelming majority, that

constitute the national community and create and formulate the nationalism of the nation.[32]

Although Savarkar and the leaders of the RSS were not able to work together, the RSS' definition of Indian nationhood reflects his concept of *Hindutva*.

The Rashtriya Swayamsevak Sangh was founded as a cultural organization, but it has a distinct political goal. The volunteers who joined the Sangh before the independence of India pledged to work towards the liberation of the Hindu nation and to safeguard Hindu *dharma* and its culture. After independence the pledge was slightly changed; now they pledge to "work for all-round progress of *Bharatavarsha* by strengthening the holy Hindu *Dharma*, Hindu *Sanskrit* [culture] and *Samaj* [society]."[33]

Despite the declaration of its political intents, the RSS for the most part stayed out of politics. Its activities were directed towards character building of its members through inculcation of discipline, the spirit of service to Hindu society and Hindu *rashtra*, and devotion to mother India (*Bharat mata*).

After Hedgewar's death in 1940 Madhav Sadashiv Golwalkar, popularly known in the RSS circle as Guruji, became the head of the organization. Golwalkar, another Maharashtrian Brahmin, was educated in Benaras Hindu University, where he had earned a Master of Science in biology. An ascetic by disposition and interested in Hindu philosophy of *Vedanta*, Golwalkar showed little interest in politics. Initially there was dissatisfaction with his style of operation, especially with his reluctance to involve the RSS in politics, and there was some defection from the organization. Nevertheless, the RSS earned enormous goodwill among Hindus with its work during the partition of India in 1947.

Golwalkar became a spokesperson of Hindu chauvinism, and his explanation of Hindu nationalism is well known:

The non-Hindu peoples in Hindustan must either adopt the Hindu culture and language, must learn to respect and hold in reverence Hindu religion, must entertain no idea but those of glorification of the Hindu race and culture, i.e. they must not only give up their attitude of intolerance and ungratefulness towards this land and its age-old traditions but must also cultivate the positive attitude of love and devotion instead—in a word they must cease to be foreigners, or may stay in the country, wholly subordinated to the Hindu nation, claiming nothing, deserving no privilege, far less any preferential treatment—not even citizens' rights.[34]

It has been frequently charged that the RSS is against the minorities, especially Muslims. Nanaji Deshmukh, a senior leader of the organization, calls the charge preposterous since it goes against the philosophy of the organization. He also denies that the RSS incites riots, adding that the RSS wants "to see India unified into a strong nation through a process of integration in which all communities join the national mainstream."[35]

Until the late 1970s the RSS did not admit non-Hindus into its ranks. It did so only in 1977, under intense public and political pressure. It is hard to deny the anti-Muslim bias in the RSS publications. The RSS heroes like Shivaji, Maharana Pratap, and Guru Gobind Singh fought against the Muslim rulers. The RSS glorifies their activities, while its villains come from the ranks of Muslim invaders and rulers.

It is often asserted by the RSS intellectuals that even after independence Muslims in India have not become part of the national mainstream. Support for the creation of Pakistan came from· the areas where the Muslims were in the minority such as U.P. and Gujarat. Most of them stayed on in India even after the establishment of the Islamic state of Pakistan, while Pakistan drove its entire non-Muslim population from its Western wing.

The RSS believes that Indian Muslims still hold on to "their pre-independence psyche and emotional attachment to Pakistan and its ideology."[36] According to RSS analysts, Indian Muslims are led by funda-mentalists and fanatic clergy, who keep preaching about the unity of *ummah* and therefore "even today the Muslim community in India tends to look at itself in isolation, far away from the national mainstream."[37] The RSS holds that *Namaz-E-Jumma* (Friday prayer) is used to denounce members of other religious communities and to teach religious bigotry. In these sermons by the Muslim clergy not even the government is spared. Furthermore, RSS members say that a large number of Muslims are educated in *Madarsaas,* funded by Saudi and Iranian money, where half-educated mullahs "brainwash children with imaginary tales of Islamic millennium. These '*Madarsaas*' are nurseries for communal fundamen-talism."[38] According to Balasaheb Deoras, even though Mahatma Gandhi appeased Muslims, the Muslims never accepted him as one of their own.[39]

Bani Deshpande, a former member of the Communist Party of India and now an RSS supporter, wrote in *Organiser* that Islam is incompatible with the ideals of a secular state. He bases this on the assertion of a Muslim intellectual that the "character of Islam is immutable and eternal and will not bend itself to any sort of remodelling for the realization of such ephemeral goals as nationalism and secularism. Both of the latter are on their way out."[40]

The BJP and the RSS believe that by accepting the basic premises of the ideology of Hindu nationalism, the Muslims of India would be assured of their honorable place in the society. Those Indian secularists, the RSS charges, who keep harping that a triumph of Hindu nationalism would result in another partition of India are indirectly encouraging the Muslim separatism. Since the Muslims do not constitute a majority in any of the states of India except Kashmir Valley, the secularists' strategy is designed to create unnecessary fear in the minds of people, according to the RSS. The Muslim population is spread all over the country. Even when the population is divided on a religious basis for each district, it is further asserted, Muslims are not concentrated in a geographically contiguous area (see Figure 5.4). Thus the creation of another Muslim-dominated state out of India is not even feasible.

It appears that the RSS leadership does not have a realistic perception of a disgruntled minority's disruptive potential. It probably would be difficult to carve another Muslim-majority state out of existing India; however, Muslims threatened by an oppressive Hindu majority might resort to terroristic activities. Since the Muslims are spread all over India, their terrorism could be far more damaging than any the country has witnessed so far. While such activities might be suicidal for the Muslims, they could also lead to the destruction of India, which Hindu nationalists claim to love so dearly.

Golwalkar kept the RSS out of active politics although he allowed many RSS workers to join politics individually. This lack of participation in politics prompted V.D. Savarkar to remark that the "epitaph for the RSS volunteers will be that he was born, he joined the RSS and died without accomplishing anything."[41]

There is evidence that the RSS was courted by right-wing Congress leaders after independence. When it was found that the RSS was not involved in the assassination of Mahatma Gandhi and in July 1949 the government lifted its ban on the organization, Sardar Vallabhbhai Patel, second only to Jawaharlal Nehru in the Congress party, persuaded the reluctant Golwalkar to let the RSS become part of the Congress. While the RSS volunteers would be involved in cultural and educational activities leading to character building among young Indians, Congress leadership would stay active in politics. Because of the opposition of Nehru, the deal fell through.[42]

Balasaheb Madhukar Dattareya Deoras succeeded Golwalkar as the RSS chief called Sar-Sangh Chalak in 1973 after Golwalkar's death. Because of his organizational abilities, Balasaheb is considered one of the ten most powerful people in contemporary India. He leads the nation's largest organization with the most devoted and loyal followers.

162

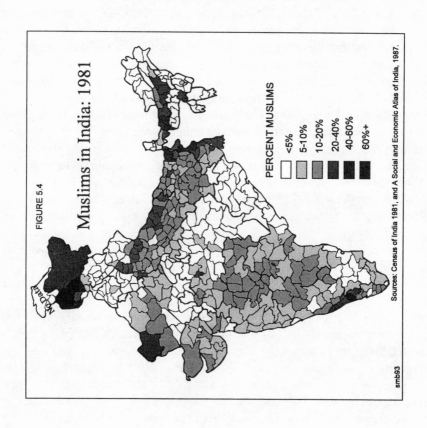

FIGURE 5.4

Muslims in India: 1981

PERCENT MUSLIMS

<5%
5-10%
10-20%
20-40%
40-60%
60%+

smb93

Sources: Census of India 1981, and A Social and Economic Atlas of India, 1987.

Balasaheb, according to one estimate, can "mobilize at least 20 million people in this country with one call."[43]

While this may be an overstatement, it is widely conceded that during his leadership the Sangh has expanded its activities and has assumed a far more politically active role. The RSS' participation in the 1974-75 movement led by Jayaprakash Narayan against political corruption and for reorientation of Indian politics on a moral basis extended the reach of the RSS into the remote villages of the country. This enabled the RSS volunteers, who originated mostly from urban India, to familiarize themselves with the problems faced by rural Indians.

Moving away from the abstract *Vedantic* traditions upheld by his predecessors, Balasaheb has employed the symbols of popular Hinduism to mobilize the Hindu population. Meanwhile, he was willing to back political parties other than the BJP if they promoted the cause of Hindus and the territorial integrity of India. Such skillful use of his organization brought the BJP back into the fold of the RSS to the extent that the BJP has virtually become the political arm of the RSS.

The RSS under Balasaheb's leadership seeks to build a powerful and modern India which could rival the West. He firmly believes that the "responsibility of building up the nation's future rests with the Hindu society and only a well organized Hindu society can discharge this responsibility."[44] Balasaheb is confident that India's future lies with the Hindu nationalists, and he warned that all those "who are under the illusion that this nation can be strengthened by belittling the Hindus, by dubbing them narrow-minded and communal, are running after a mirage."[45]

Unlike many BJP politicians who are unwilling to undertake any social reform among Hindus, Balasaheb not only denounces undesirable customs in Hindu society but believes that the RSS volunteers should actively oppose the caste system and untouchability and create harmony among the different sectors of Hindu society. The Hindu way of life, he believes, should be an example for the rest of the world. However, Hindus can set up an exemplary way of life only if there is no discrimination and segregation among them. He does not place much trust in the government's ability to bring about social revolution in India. It is rather the people's power which can bring real changes in the society and polity.

Many have grave concerns about the decline of traditional values in Indian society. This normlessness has caused a moral vacuum leading to an increase in violence and anarchy all around in the country. The RSS holds that short-sighted politicians use divisive appeals and arouse passions among different segments of the society in search of political power and votes, and that they have little concern about the future of the country and the society. The entry of criminal elements into politics has aggravated the situation. The new rich classes use their wealth to buy politicians and influence, corrupting both the society and the polity. According to the RSS, it is the non-political organizations which should take the initiative to halt this decline and restore moral values in the society.

After the BJP moved away from Vajpayee's strategy and ideology, Balasaheb inducted the best and the most dedicated of his *pracharaks* into the BJP. In the 1991 elections many of the parliamentary candidates of the BJP came from the ranks of the RSS. According to one estimate, out of 477 candidates nominated by the party, over 300 had RSS background.[46] Furthermore, the RSS workers were deeply involved in electioneering and campaigning. It was reported that only the RSS *pracharaks* were entrusted with jobs such as finances, publicity, managing polling booths, and getting people to vote.[47]

Although the BJP included some young RSS workers in its candidates for parliamentary and state legislative offices, the top party leadership at the state and the national levels is dominated by people in their mid-sixties or early seventies. Because of their training and organizational discipline, the younger generation of BJP leaders coming from the ranks of the RSS does not show any eagerness to take over the place of the party elders. While many of their contemporaries, like Bihar chief minister Laloo Prasad Yadav of Janata Dal; Subodh Kant Sahay, former union minister for home affairs; and Rajesh Pilot, the current minister for internal security in the Rao government, have come to occupy key positions in the administration, men like Govindacharya, Narendra Modi, Arun Jaitley, and many others seem willing to wait in the wings.

In 1989 India celebrated Jawaharlal Nehru's birth centenary at the same time the Virat Hindu Sammelan was convened to commemorate the birth centenary of Dr. Keshav B. Hedgewar. The events represented dramatic changes which have taken place in India since the founding of the RSS. While Nehru's vision of a secular India based on a liberal-socialist ideology is under attack, Hedgewar's Hindu nationalism, represented by the RSS, is on the rise.

Recently India's educated and westernized middle class has been strongly committed to the Nehruvian concept of Indian national identity. In the past two decades, with the spread of education and increased media exposure, India has seen an enormous expansion in the size of this class. At the same time, with the introduction of criminal elements into Indian politics by the centrist parties, members of the middle class have become disenchanted with this new breed of politicians. The RSS has successfully exploited the middle class alienation and built a strong base in this class.

The RSS has also been able to project an image of itself as an organization committed to certain basic values, its cadre being clean, incorruptible, committed to the service of the society, and devoted to the territorial integrity of the country.

The RSS is not dependent on personalities; its strength comes from its organization and the dedication of its volunteers to its ideological cause. The recent ban on the organization imposed by the Rao government (and later revoked by a tribunal) is unlikely to stop its growth and influence in Indian politics and society. The RSS has established itself as a social and political force to be reckoned with, through its sophisticated use of modern media, its various service-related activities, and its crisis management during periods of national disasters, such as its help for the Hindu refugees after the partition of the country in 1947, its cooperation with the government during the wars of 1962, 1965, and 1971, and its relief efforts during floods in Andhra Pradesh and Gujarat.

The impressive organizational abilities of the RSS are an asset for a political party like the BJP. The RSS' primary goal of mobilization of Hindus as a united community has been the cherished objective of all types of Hindu nationalists. The organization's multifarious activities endear it to Hindus, generate a strong sense of identity, and provide it a solid support base.

However, its leaders' lack of political experience makes the RSS ideologically inflexible. Many of the RSS workers have a narrow mindset. They believe, like the Muslim leaders, that issues related to faith and religion are beyond the jurisdiction of the courts. Whether this stance is a reaction against the Muslims' intransigence or not, this kind of posture makes it almost impossible for the politicians to negotiate to find compromise solutions to emotionally complex problems. Such compromise is an integral part of the political process in a democratic society, but the intertwining of political and religious issues gets in the way. Since the BJP has accepted the RSS Hindu nationalism position, it is difficult for the BJP leadership to make any claim to the practice of genuine secularism.

Furthermore, the RSS looks upon Indian Islam as an alien religion and tends to distrust almost the entire Muslim community of India. This attitude results more from deep-seated prejudices than from existing realities. The recent political behavior of some of the Muslim leaders—like Shahabuddin and Shahi Imam Bukhari of Delhi, who called for the Muslim boycott of the celebration of India's Republic Day—did not help the cause of the Muslim community. Most of the Indian Muslims, however, ignored these leaders' disruptive strategies.

In order to prove their loyalty to the Indian state, the RSS demands that Muslims join the mainstream of national life. In other words, they should seek assimilation rather than special protection or privileges for their community.

The RSS propaganda keeps denouncing Muslim leaders' unwillingness to accept the central place of Hinduism in the political and cultural life of the country. Such strong denunciations reinforce the anti-Muslim prejudices of Hindus and add to the tension existing between the two communities.

Vishwa Hindu Parishad (VHP)

The Vishwa Hindu Parishad (World Hindu Council) is another support group of the BJP and an important member of the *Sangh Parivar* (the Sangh family). Although the Rao government in December 1992 imposed a ban on its activities and froze its bank accounts, given the range of its activities and the support which the organization enjoys at the grass-roots level, it would be difficult for the present Congress (I) government to clamp down on its activities vigorously. Any suppressive action taken against the VHP is likely to be counterproductive. The government has already released its leaders.

It is this organization which has raised the slogan "Beyond caste, beyond parties, O Hindus, awake, arise and unite."[48] Along with *Virat Hindu Sammalan* and *Hindu Samajotsava,* it has organized several massive Hindu conventions and conferences to give a sense of unity to the Hindus of India. The VHP runs schools, temples, hostels, and medical centers. It carries on massive propaganda, asserting that "around ninety-five percent of those who took part in the freedom struggle were Hindus. In the war with Pakistan also, ninety percent of the casualties were Hindus. And yet Hindus are second rate citizens in their own country. Their voice does not have any weight."[49] The VHP denounces the Congress (I)-run government for spending Hindu taxpayers' money to welcome the Pope and for providing subsidies to the Muslims to make pilgrimages to Mecca, while forcing Hindus to pay pilgrimage taxes in their own country.[50]

The VHP was established in 1966 in the sacred city of Prayag (Allahabad). Its goals were to consolidate and strengthen the Hindu society, to protect and promote ethical values of Hindus, and to establish contact with the Hindus living in other parts of the world.[51] Its six objectives include elimination of the practice of untouchability; unification of all Hindus irrespective of their linguistic, regional, sectarian, and class differences; and creation of a sense of pride in the cultural heritage of Hindus. It also seeks readmission of all those Hindus who embraced Christianity or Islam in the past and are now willing to come back into the fold of Hinduism.[52]

The VHP has prepared a charter of seventeen different programs to be undertaken by the organization. These include such things as propagation of Sanskrit language, introduction of religious instruction in the universities, protection of cows, enlisting support of Hindu priests, saints and preachers to create religious consciousness among the Hindu masses, and holding frequent meetings and festivals to promote social consciousness and responsibility among followers of Hinduism.

To maintain its autonomy, the VHP bars politicians from holding any office within its organization. But this does not mean that the VHP does not have its own political agenda. Like the RSS, it seeks to bring the Muslims into the mainstream of Indian nationalism. The VHP does not oppose Islamic or Christian worship. According to its leaders, the organization is opposed only to those Muslim fanatics who adopt an anti-Hindu and pro-Pakistani attitude. In the words of the VHP leaders:

> We have no opposition to the people who accept Bharat as their motherland and who believe that [sic] the culture and traditions of Bharat as their own. Indonesians are Muslims by faith but they feel proud to participate in Ramalila or Rasalila. If the Muslims of this country also behave in a similar manner, there would be no problem whatsoever.[53]

The VHP is an ideological ally of the RSS and works in close cooperation with the Sangh. It has been able to set up its units throughout the country and has more than one-half million active workers spread all over India. It has also set up separate women's units in more than 236 districts of the country. The VHP has also established overseas units, including in the U.S., Canada, U.K., Australia, Southeast Asia, and other areas.[54] At the national level the VHP has created as many as sixteen departments dealing with such issues as religious propaganda (*dharm prasar*), service (*seva*), cow protection (*goraksha*), publicity and liaison (*prachar* and *sampark*), foreign (*videsh*), youth (*yuva*), publication (*prakashan*), Sanskrit, and central office (*kendirya karyalaya*).

It is primarily the VHP which makes claims to Hindu sacred places converted into mosques by the Muslim rulers. Ashok Singhal, the VHP general secretary, recently warned Muslim leaders against provoking a confrontation with the Hindus. And he added that "the VHP was not trying to settle the score with Muslims for their past sins but was demanding only three places of worship, i.e., Ayodhya, Mathura and Kashi, to be restored to Hindus."⁵⁵ And he assured Muslims that if they conceded these demands, they would receive full-hearted love and affection from Hindus. The most militant Hindu organization, the VHP, by using traditional symbols of popular aspects of Hindu religion, has gained enormous success in the organization of Hindus at the grass-roots level.

With the support and cooperation of the RSS it has created such organizations as *Dharm sansad* (religious parliament), *Kandriya marg darshak mandal* (central guidance council), *Dharm mandals* (religious councils), and many others. Most of these organizations consist of Hindu holy men, *sadhus* and *dharmaacharyas* (traditional scholars of Hindu religion). All these organizations are designed to create a degree of homogeneity among Hindus, who are deeply divided on sectarian, doctrinarian, caste, and class bases.

The VHP has persuaded the upper caste Hindus to undertake philanthropic activities among the members of scheduled caste Hindus and the tribals. It has brought the reformers and the orthodox together on the same platform, impressing upon them that the unity of Hindus is imperative for national survival. The VHP plays up the political dimension of religious unity while emphasizing that only through the assertion of Hindu nationalism will the majority population of the country be able to save its culture and traditions.

The primary goal of the VHP, not unlike the RSS, is political unification of Hindus. It does not seek to create a centralized religious authority with a single deity or a uniform code of behavior for Hindus, as some of its critics allege. In other words, it does not seek to eliminate the inherent pluralism in Hindu society. Its leaders know that any effort to organize Hindus with one sacred book and one prophet, like a monotheistic religion such as Islam or Christianity, is destined to fail. They realize that since Hindus are divided on a sectarian basis, eliminating doctrinal diversity is neither desirable nor practical. Religious issues, however, could be used to unite the Hindus irrespective of their caste or sect.

Like the Muslims and the Sikhs, the VHP wants to use places of worship for political purposes. It mobilized Hindu holy men to organize the highly successful *Ekatmata yagna* (integration rites) in which a holy water pitcher was carried by a member of the backward community to perform the worship of *Bharat mata* (mother India). It was observed that "the high caste Thakur women . . . rubbed shoulders with the so-called low caste sweeper women offering their worship to Ganga Mata [mother Ganges] and Bharat Mata [mother India]."⁵⁶ In another political move the VHP successfully mobilized the Hindu population for the "liberation" of the birthplace of Lord Ram. The VHP also worked ardently to create a Hindu vote bank.

Bajarang Dal, the VHP's youth wing, is its fighting arm. Consisting of lumpen elements, it reflects the contemporary political culture of India. In recent years political parties and politicians in India have become dependent upon muscle power. Gangsters, criminals, and hired hands are used frequently to achieve political goals. Vandalism displayed by the *Ram Bhakts* (devotees of Ram) and *karsevaks* (volunteers) in recent years are the BJP, RSS, and VHP versions of the vulgarization of Indian politics. The steady rise in the number of unemployed educated youth in the urban areas has added to the degenerate segment of society. The *Bajarang Dal*, more than any other group in India, is able to mobilize all these elements in the cause promoted by the VHP.

The *Bajarang Dal* has been successful in raising large amounts of money in the name of Ramjanambhoomi not only from the traders and small-scale manufacturers but also from the countryside, primarily of north India but also from south and east India.

The VHP's support of the BJP seems to be tentative. Mahant Avaidyanath, a prominent VHP leader, observed that "at the moment the only party which respects our feeling is the BJP. But nobody can say whether the party's stand remains unchanged in the future. The BJP's history shows us that its ideology has vacillated in the past."[57] The BJP is a political party, which, according to the Mahant, is guided by the percentage of the votes it receives. If the BJP finds that issues dear to the VHP have become political liabilities, it might switch its ideological stance.

Many Indian observers believe that if the BJP tries to distance itself from the VHP, the VHP leadership might launch a party of its own. The RSS leadership, however, holds that this is only a wishful assumption based upon superficial understanding of the working of members of the *Sangh Parivar*. All sister organizations are bound by the common ideology of Hindu nationalism and play autonomous roles in their re-spective areas. This may, however, be only partly valid; the BJP and the RSS both represent the Hindu middle class, which displays considerable polish and intellectual sophistication, while the bulk of the followers of the VHP come from the lower middle class and the Hindu working classes with vernacular education. They may not have much patience for the RSS and the BJP's strategic considerations.

The VHP, like the RSS workers, believes that religious matters are beyond the jurisdiction of the court. And, in such matters, the VHP would be willing to defy the courts if court decisions were imposed upon it.[58]

Many of the members of the VHP believe that the Constitution of India not only does not conform to the values of Hinduism but is blatantly anti-Hindu. It would not be surprising if the VHP demanded the revision or even rewriting of the Indian Constitution.

From among the two prominent members of the RSS family, namely the VHP and the BJP, the VHP is believed to have better access to the top leadership of the RSS than the leaders of the BJP have. "Even the fulcrum of the financial power of the family has shifted towards the VHP, which has collected enormous amounts of money worldwide, mainly from the expatriate Indians in the West. To this money, the BJP has no access; it has to collect money the way other parties do,"[59] said Ashis Nandy.

The VHP is headed by Shivnath Katju, the son of the late Congress leader Kailashnath Katju. Because of Katju's illness, Vishnu Hari Dalmia, its acting president, and Ashok Singhal, its general secretary, have become its most outspoken representatives. Vinay Katiyar is the leader of the *Bajarang Dal*. Many of the VHP's leaders like Katiyar and Mahant Avaidyanath are also BJP members of Parliament.

Deendayal Shodh Sansthan (Deendayal Research Institute)

One of the sister organizations of the RSS family is the Deendayal Research Institute (DRI), which works quietly as an autonomous think tank. The organization is headed by the RSS stalwart, Nanaji Deshmukh, who in 1977 declined a cabinet position in the Janata Party government. After spending more than thirty years in active politics, in 1978 he retired from party politics and devoted himself to social and constructive work on the Gandhian line. Deshmukh found politics to be too power oriented to play a constructive role in the process of nation-building. He thought that by launching educational institutions and working at the grass-roots level one could play a more constructive role in the reform and revitalization of the society. He spent most of his time working first in Gonda, a backward district of U.P. which was also his parliamentary constituency. Later he took up developmental work in the tribal area of Bihar, and now he has shifted his focus to Chitrakut in Madhya Pradesh, where he is setting up an agricultural university.[60]

Founded in 1972 in memory of Pandit Deendayal, the former Jana Sangh leader and founder of the philosophy of Integral Humanism, the DRI directs its activities in search of "a philosophy of life and socioeconomic structure suited to the present age."[61] The organization is dedicated to translating Deendayal's dream of a strong, prosperous, and dynamic India into reality.

The intellectuals associated with the DRI believe that under the imperative of politics India has drifted away from the ideals of the freedom movement. Both the establishment intellectuals and their Marxist critics are influenced by the Western model of development. Both are captives of the ideology and the thought process introduced by the colonial masters. With the collapse of Communism and the crisis faced by capitalism, these intellectuals believe that people worldwide are seeking alternative modes of thinking and living styles, and they should lead in the search and "collectively re-learn from our own heritage."[62]

At this stage of India's development, according to the DRI intellectuals, there are three autonomous and dynamic forces working within Indian society: the intellectual and academic community, the political process, and voluntary grass-roots movements. Each has its shortcomings. While the academic and intellectual community proposes theories and holds discussions, it is completely divorced from political realities. Politics and parties are often vehicles of cheap rhetoric and populism directed towards winning elections in the pursuit of power. The grass-roots voluntary organizations, though attracting the most dedicated workers and performing useful services, lack coordination.

According to the DRI researchers, regular and constant interaction is needed to strengthen and coordinate these three forces. "Any genuine effort at nation-building must involve all the three simultaneously. What is urgently needed now is to generate an intellectual movement which would act as a bridge between these three streams,"[63] they suggest.

The DRI is engaged in presenting position papers and policy options as well as publishing scholarly journals like *Manthan*. The organization is engaged not only in theoretical formulations and in offering alternate models of economic and political development but also in social experimentation. It has set up various pilot programs in agricultural development, rural industries development and training, the *Go-Vikas* (Cow Development) project, poultry training-cum-production center, rural and tribal mobile eye care units, and several village development projects. Its Appropriate Technology Research Center is working on extracting edible oil from non-traditional sources.

The DRI, in many ways guided by the Gandhian philosophy and methods of economic development, does not believe that government aid is needed to implement rural development programs. Generally its members have a negative view of politics and believe that politicians tend to forget the people as soon as they acquire political power.

Combining the Gandhian philosophy with the thinking of Deendayal
Upadhyaya, the DRI emphasizes creating a balance between the ecological
needs of the society and developmental goals. Since a majority of Indians
live in rural areas and are dependent on agriculture and cottage industries
for their living, the institute focuses on these subjects.

There does not seem to be any direct linkage between the DRI and the
BJP. However, the leading intellectuals at the institute are ardent BJP supporters. Frequently they provide intellectual rationale for the political activities of the BJP leaders. Nanaji Deshmukh, for instance, while calling
the demolition of the Babri mosque unfortunate "to the extent that it was
not part of the proposed *karseva* agenda," at the same time felt that there
was no need to be apologetic about it.[64] The expression of profound regret
by Advani and other leaders of the *Sangh Parivar* should be looked upon
as the natural reaction of genuinely secular people. Following the BJP line
of argument on the Babri mosque, Deshmukh asserted that it was the
pseudo-secularist elements and the media which had projected it as an issue
of Hindu-Muslim conflict.

The DRI is frequently consulted by the RSS leadership; in fact, there is
constant interaction between the senior leaders of the two organizations.

Supportive Organizations, the BJP Factions, and Political Decision-Making

The decision-making process within the BJP is influenced by interaction
among various elements, some of which are embedded within the party itself and others of which originate from the supportive organizations. Even
though the party leaders tend to deny the existence of factions within the
BJP, faction formation is natural to all organizations. In previous chapters
we have outlined the ideology- and strategy-based factions and divided
them into three categories: liberals, moderates, and hardliners.

Since the BJP is controlled by leaders who are well into their late sixties
and early seventies, age may be another factor in the formation of factions.
The 1992 transfer of Govindacharya, the BJP's popular general secretary,
to Tamil Nadu brought out age-based differences within the party. While
the transfer was welcomed by party old guards, it was deeply resented by
the party's young Turks. It was perhaps to satisfy them that Govindacharya
was brought back to New Delhi. Linkages with supportive organizations
such as the RSS, ABVP, VHP, BMS, and *Bajarang Dal* and leaders' work
experience with the mass or parliamentary wing could also lead to factions
within the party. Since there are various reasons for the formation of

factions and many members may have cross-cutting affiliations, membership is fluid in these factions. Factional alignments also change with changes of strategy.

Leaders like Atal Bihari Vajpayee, Jaswant Singh, and Sikandar Bakht who belong to the liberal faction of the party are not likely to have close relations with organizations like the VHP. Since many of the leaders of state legislative wings like Kalyan Singh, Shanta Kumar, and Bhairon Singh Shekawat have to deal with state administrations, they were anxious to demonstrate their administrative abilities and establish the credentials of the BJP as a ruling party. They were aware of the fact that "Ram is no substitute for governance."[65] Naturally they were not enthused about the hard line on the construction of the temple adopted by the leaders of the VHP.

The state leaders recognized that if the BJP is to replace the Congress at the national level, they have to act as a responsible opposition party. In their view there can be no defiance of law or the courts or resorting to agitation and demonstrations—in short, no street-level politics.

Advani was recently asked, "Do you think the BJP will come to power in the next election?" After a moment of hesitation he answered, "That is not the issue. The real question is: are we ready for power?"[66] Many Indians have been looking for an alternative to the Congress (I), and many felt the need for a conservative alternative to the centrist parties. The experienced politicians and party leaders would have liked the BJP to meet this need. Murli Manohar Joshi's close association with the VHP is not welcomed by the party's liberal and moderate factions. While the hard-liners led by Joshi were unable to exercise restraint, they thought that the issues could be settled in the streets.

Despite all the militant rhetoric, the BJP has all the disadvantages of a federal party. Subgroups like the VHP and the *Bajarang Dal* are mass organizations; their followers are not regular BJP cadre and are not even subject to the control of the RSS. For the VHP the rise of the BJP to the position of power is secondary. It has a different agenda. Ashok Singhal, the VHP general secretary, and Vinay Katiyar, the *Bajarang Dal* chief, lack the political sophistication displayed by Vajpayee or Advani. For Vajpayee and Advani, the party's liberal and moderate leaders respectively, what is more important is to spell out a grand national vision for the country. They believe that the BJP cannot work with the populist and the sloganeering tactics of the VHP.[67] They have come to realize that "with Hindu *rashtra* definitely entering the agenda as the logical alternative to the demolished pillars of the Nehruvian edifice,"[68] the BJP has an historic opportunity to present its own blueprint for the emerging India. They would like to distance themselves from the hardliners of the VHP.

Although the Ramjanambhoomi issue, the moderates thought, might have emotional appeal, it could not be a substitute for real policy alternatives for the party. However, the positive reaction of Hindus after the demolition of the Babri mosque surprised not only the BJP moderates but even the leadership of the RSS. A public opinion poll conducted by *India Today* and *Marketing* and *Research Group (MARG)* after the demolition of the mosque showed that the BJP made significant gains among the voters of the crucial states of U.P., Bihar, Madhya Pradesh, Rajasthan, Haryana, and even Orissa and West Bengal. Although 52.6 percent of the people nationally disapproved of the demolition of the mosque, in the Hindi-speaking states of north India a majority of the voters (54.2 percent) supported it. Furthermore, a majority of Indians (53.3 percent) disapproved of the Rao government's decision to rebuild the mosque. The survey concluded that "perhaps the biggest difference in this poll from earlier ones is the spread of the BJP message into the villages. Earlier a predominantly urban party, now its share of the rural votes is as high as its share of urban votes."[69] This reaction was an expression of anger and alienation of a large number of Hindus over the way politics was being conducted in India. It did not seem to be an overnight reaction but a disgust and anguish which had been building up over a period of time.[70]

This episode provided credibility to VHP leaders like Ashok Singhal and hurt the moderates within the party. The mood of the Hindus was changing faster than the leadership within the BJP and the RSS were able to gauge. As a result of these developments, the *Bajarang Dal* has been able to marginalize the ABVP, the more moderate and sophisticated student wing of the RSS. It appears that it is now the RSS which is able to stitch together the different factions of the BJP and the supportive organizations into a cohesive political force. The intellectual leadership of the RSS, which by its social origin and training is conservative and well disciplined, may not like the lumpen elements of the *Bajarang Dal* or the Hindu holy men mobilized by the VHP, but it has been able to play a decisive role in coordinating the activities of these different organizations. The National Executive of the RSS, headed by Balasaheb Deoras and H.V. Sheshadhari, the chief and the general secretary respectively, brings the leaders of the BJP like Murli Manohar Joshi, Sundar Singh Bhandari, and Ashok Singhal, the general secretary of the VHP, together to help work out their differences. Although not much is known about the process whereby the decisions are reached, sources close to these groups stress the influential role played by the elder of the family, Deoras.

For sorting out factional disputes within the BJP at the national level, the RSS office located on Jhandewala Estate in New Delhi and headed by professor Rajinder Singh is frequently contacted to mediate. It is the RSS, thus, which provides the guidance, the intellectual stimuli, the motivation, the cadre, and the seasoned leaders for the BJP. Under the existing situation the party leadership may maintain a degree of autonomy in the management of its internal affairs and in the formulation of policies and strategies suited to capture political power, but it is unlikely to stray far from the ideological lines laid down by the RSS leadership. Much of the party's success is likely to be dependent on its leadership's ability to reconcile the conflicting goals of its constituent units and to maintain its internal cohesion by adopting flexible strategies to capture political power.

Notes

1. Angelo Panebianco, *Political Parties: Organization and Power* (Cambridge, Cambridge University Press, 1988), Chapter 1.

2. Maurice Duverger, *Political Parties* (New York, John Wiley and Sons, 1954), p. 5.

3. *India Today*, May 15, 1991, p. 16. Also see Swapan Das Gupta, "Hedgewar's Legacy: Limitation of Elitist Hinduism," *Statesman Weekly*, April 8, 1989, p. 12.

4. Panebianco, *Political Parties*, Chapter 1.

5. B. Abrahamsson, *Bureaucracy or Participation: The Logic of Organization* (London, Sage Publications, 1977), p. 118.

6. *Ibid.*

7. Bharatiya Janata Party, *Report of the General Secretary: Bharatiya Janata Party National Council Session, 18-20 June, 1993, Banglore* (New Delhi, Bharatiya Janata Party, 1993), p. 7.

8. Bharatiya Janata Party, *Constitution and Rules* (New Delhi, Bharatiya Janata Party, 1991), p. 1.

9. *Ibid.*

10. *Ibid.*, pp. 8-10.

11. Smita Gupta, "BJP: Power Games," *Illustrated Weekly of India*, May 2-8, 1992, p. 5.

12. Interviews with K. R. Malkani, February 13, 1992; K. L. Sharma, February 25, 1992; Sundar Singh Bhandari, March 12, 1992; and J. P. Mathur, March 4, 1992.

13. *India Today*, February 23, 1983, p. 27.

14. *India Today*, May 15, 1991, p. 16.

15. Bharatiya Janata Party, *Constitution and Rules*, pp. 51-54.

16. Interview with Sundar Singh Bhandari, March 12, 1992.

17. Bharatiya Janata Party, *Constitution and Rules*, p. 13.

18. Bharatiya Janata Party, *Bharatiya Janata Party in Parliament: Constitution*, (New Delhi, Bharatiya Janata Party, 1988), p. 2.

19. *Ibid.*, p. 2.

20. S. K. Pande, "The Power Play: The Tussles in the BJP," *Frontline*, May 8, 1992, pp. 32-35. Also see "The Mirror Cracks," *Illustrated Weekly of India*, March 2-8, 1991, p. 5.

21. *India Today*, July 31, 1992, p. 27.

22. Taroon Coomar Bhadari, "Sunderlal Patwa: A Losing Game?" *Illustrated Weekly of India*, March 2-3, 1992, pp. 5-6.

23. *Sunday*, May 10-16, 1992, pp. 23-38.

24. *India Today*, January 15, 1982, p. 79.

25. *India Today*, July 31, 1992, p. 27.

26. *Organiser*, October 18, 1992, p. 9.

27. *Organiser*, July 12, 1992, p. 14.

28. *Organiser*, January 24, 1993, p. 7.

29. *Organiser*, June 21, 1992, p. 12.

30. Walter K. Andersen and Shridhar D. Damle, *Brotherhood in Saffron: The Rashtriya Swayamsevak Sangh and Hindu Revivalism* (Boulder, Westview Press, 1976), p. 120.

31. *India Today*, January 15, 1993, p. 35.

32. Quoted in Prabha Dixit, "Ideology of Hindu Nationalism," in Thomas Pantham and Kenneth L. Deutsch (eds.), *Political Thought in Modern India* (New Delhi, Sage Publications, 1986), p. 133.

33. K. R. Malkani, *The RSS Story* (New Delhi, Impex, 1980), p. 200.

34. Quoted in Craig Baxter, *The Jana Sangh: A Biography of an Indian Political Party* (Philadelphia, University of Pennsylvania, 1969), p. 31.

35. Nana Deshmukh, *RSS: Victim of Slander* (Vision Books, 1979), p. 15. For a different view see A. G. Noorani, "Banning Party Means No Compromise," *Statesman Weekly*, December 19, 1992, p. 5.

36. S. K. Bandhu, "Indian Muslims and National Integration," *Organiser*, October 13, 1992, p. 13.

37. *Ibid.*

38. *Ibid.*

39. *Organiser*, October 18, 1992, p. 8.

40. Bani Deshpande, "Sarvdharm sambhva: Illusion or Reality?" *Organiser,* December 20, 1993, p. 13.

41. Quoted in Swapan Das Gupta, "Hedgewar's Legacy," p. 12.

42. Andersen and Damle, *Brotherhood,* pp. 55-56 and Malkani, *RSS Story*, pp. 56-58.

43. *Probe India,* January, 1989, p. 36.

44. *Organiser,* October 18, 1992, p. 6.

45. *Ibid.*

46. *Illustrated Weekly of India*, April 23-27, 1991, p. 2.

47. *India Today*, May 31, 1991, p. 16.

48. *India Today*, May 31, 1988, p. 31.

49. Anand Pandya, *Hypocrisy of Secularism* (Karnavati, Vishwa Hindu Parishad Prakashan, 1990), pp. 10-11.

50. *Ibid.*, p. 6.

51. M. P. Degvekar, "The Origin and the Growth of Vishwa Hindu Parishad," *Hindu Vishwa*, Vol. 25, No. 12 (August, 1990), p. 11.

52. Vishwa Hindu Parishad, *Vishwa Hindu parishad ke uddeshya, karya tatha uplabhdhiyan* (New Delhi, Vishwa Hindu Parishad, n.d.), p. 2.

53. Degvekar, "Origin," p. 13.

54. *Vishwa Hindu parishad ke uddeshya,* p. 2.

55. *Organiser,* October 15, 1992, p. 9.

56. Acharya Girjakishor, "A Glimpse of the Ekatmata Yagna," *Hindu Vishwa,* Vol. 23, No. 12, p. 52. Also see "Hindu Militant Revivalism," *India Today,* May 31, 1988, pp. 30-39.

57. *Statesman Weekly,* April 27, 1991, p. 12.

58. *Organiser,* August 30, 1992, p. 9.

59. Ashis Nandy, "Three Propositions," *Seminar,* February, 1993, p. 3.

60. *Indian Express Sunday Magazine,* April 5, 1992, p. 3.

61. Deendayal Research Institute (New Delhi, Deendayal Research Institute, n.d.), p. 1.

62. Deendayal Research Institute, "Towards an Alternative Discourse: A Draft for Discussion" (New Delhi, Deendayal Research Institute, n.d.) (typed), p. 2.

63. *Ibid.,* p. 3.

64. *Organiser,* January 31, 1993, p. 15.

65. *India Today,* November 30, 1991, p. 21.

66. Swapan Das Gupta, "Prepare for Power," *Sunday,* December 27, 1992, January 2, 1993, p. 9.

67. *Ibid.,* p. 8.

68. *Ibid.,* p. 9.

69. *India Today,* January 15, 1993, p. 15.

70. "The BJP Supporters: The Invasions of Scuppies," *India Today,* May 15, 1991, pp. 18-19.

6

Electoral Performances: National and State Levels

The splitting and merging of political groups and parties, only to split again, has been the characteristic process of party formation in India. The Bharatiya Janata Party (BJP) of today or the Bharatiya Jana Sangh (BJP) of the past, though credited as having relatively more discipline, also could not escape this pattern. Although it did not face any major split in the past, there were occasions when the rank and file revolted against the official dictates of the party high command. The BJP's seat adjustment with Charan Singh's Lok Dal in the Haryana state elections in 1982 and with the Janata Dal in the 1989 Lok Sabha elections, for instance, were perceived by many local units as detrimental to the party's interest. But the BJP's strategy of forming alliances with the opposition, as seen in Chapter Three, was designed to minimize its losses. For in the "first past the post" system of elections, the ruling Congress party, according to the BJP, has benefitted most because of divisions in non-Congress votes.

In this chapter we intend to explore how far the Bharatiya Janata Party's optimism of early 1980 was borne out when it actually entered the electoral arena as a separate party in May 1980. What level of performance did it achieve in the elections that followed through most of 1980? What changes has the party undergone during the course of different elections and with what consequences? And, finally, given the premises the party is presently operating under and the gains it has registered during the last two elections, what prospects can it envisage for its future? These along with queries about its social bases are the issues we intend to examine in the pages that follow.

Vidhan Sabha Elections Held Between 1980 and
1984 Lok Sabha Elections

Of all the political parties, the BJP was the one caught most unprepared when elections to nine Vidhan Sabhas (the state legislatures) were announced in April to be held in May 1980. Despite the fact that national executives were constituted by taking people from both Jana Sangh and non-Jana Sangh backgrounds, state executives were yet to be finalized. With merely two weeks' time to complete the complicated task of candidate selection (inviting applications, scrutinizing them by constituencies, selecting the most suitable ones, and allotting the party symbol), the party depended heavily on the leaders and organizational units of the erstwhile Jana Sangh to facilitate this job in time. Notwithstanding the short notice and unpreparedness, the party was able to select its candidates without causing any serious conflict detrimental to the smooth running of the election campaign.

In all, 2,237 legislative seats spread over nine states (Uttar Pradesh-425, Bihar-324, Madhya Pradesh-320, Rajasthan-200, Gujarat-182, Maharashtra-288, Punjab-117, Orissa-147, and Tamil Nadu-234) were contested in May 1980, and the BJP with all its ambitions to emerge as a national alternative to the Congress could field candidates in only 1,430 constituencies. Failing to put up candidates in as many as 807 Vidhan Sabha constituencies of different states may be construed as a weakness of the party, but the fact that it contested more seats than the Jana Sangh did in these states prior to its merger with the Janata Party indicates the BJP's gain in attracting people at least to contest under its symbol. It may be noted that prior to its merger, the Jana Sangh contested 1,263 seats as opposed to the BJP's 1,430 in the 1980 elections from these states. Interestingly, the major share of the increased number of BJP candidates came from the states of Gujarat, Madhya Pradesh, and Maharashtra, in that order.

Despite the fact that the BJP was able to field more candidates than the Jana Sangh in elections held between 1972-75 in these states, its electoral performance did not show any improvement. On the contrary, the party witnessed decline both in seats and in votes. Compared to the 165 seats won by the Jana Sangh in elections held during 1972-75 in these states, the BJP won only 148 seats in 1980. The Party lost heavily in Uttar Pradesh, where it could win only eleven seats as against sixty-one the Jana Sangh had won in the 1974 elections. Similarly, its strength came down from eighteen to nine seats in Gujarat and from twenty-five to twenty-one seats in Bihar elections. The same fate was met by the party in terms of votes.

Losses suffered in these states were more or less compensated for by the gains it made in Rajasthan (from eight seats to thirty-two), Madhya Pradesh (from forty-eight seats to sixty), and Maharashtra (from five seats to fourteen).

It may be noted that excepting Maharashtra, the party gained only in those two states (Madhya Pradesh and Rajasthan) where the Jana Sangh component of the Janata Party headed the state governments prior to and during the elections. Similarly, of the three states where the BJP suffered loss, two states' (Uttar Pradesh and Bihar) governments were headed by the Lok Dal component of the Janata Party while in the third, Gujarat, the Congress (O) headed the state government. Thus during the short spell of the Janata Party rule, whether in the center or in the states, it was practically a coalition government, and parties having a greater share in power strengthened their political bases in their respective states.

Notwithstanding the heavy losses in Uttar Pradesh, Bihar, and Gujarat, the party's overall performance in the 1980 Vidhan Sabha elections was quite satisfactory. Compared to the Jana Sangh's performance in elections held prior to 1977, it not only increased its members in the state legislatures of Madhya Pradesh, Rajasthan, and Maharashtra but also gained in votes and saved security deposits in a greater number of constituencies. Even in the states where the party's strength in legislatures went down, its popular support did not decline much. While there was only marginal decline in Uttar Pradesh and Bihar, the party polled more votes in Gujarat, maybe because it put up more candidates this time. But the fact that of the 127 seats it contested in Gujarat in the 1980 elections only sixty-six of its candidates lost their security deposits reflects the expansion of the BJP support base in the states (see Table 6.1).

Exactly two years later, four more states (Haryana, Himachal Pradesh, West Bengal, and Kerala) went to the polls in May 1982. Enjoying the benefit of its Jana Sangh legacy, the BJP was credited with eleven and twenty-four members in the state legislatures of Haryana and Himachal Pradesh, respectively. Intending to exploit the glory of the Jana Sangh's past, its present organizational strength, and its appeal for "Gandhian socialism," the party was hoping to expand its support bases, at least in these two north Indian states. In order to avoid splits in the non-Congress votes, the BJP worked out seat adjustments with the Lok Dal and agreed to contest only twenty-four of ninety Vidhan Sabha seats in Haryana while giving only about a dozen of sixty-eight seats to its partner in Himachal Pradesh.

182

TABLE 6.1 Performance of BJP in Vidhan Sabha Elections 1980-1991
(Number of Contestants, Elected and Forfeited Deposits, and % votes polled)

Vidhan Sabha Elections

Name of State	1980	1982	1983	1984	1985	1987	1988	1989	1990	1991
A&N Islands	-	-	-	-	-	-	-	-	-	-
Andhra Pradesh	X	X	80-3-62 2.8	X	10-8-0 1.6	X	X	12-5-0 1.7	X	X
Arunachal Pradesh	0-0-0	X	X	6-1-0 7.7					X	X
Assam	X	X	0-0-0	X	37-0-34 1.1	X	X	X	X	#-10-#
Bihar	246-21-173 8.4	X	X	X	234-16-172 7.5	X	X	X	221-39-# 11.0	X
Chandigarh	-	-	-	-	-	-	-	-	-	-
Dadra & Nagar Haveli	-	-	-	-	-	-	-	-	-	-
Daman & Diu	-	-	-	-	-	-	-	-	-	-
Delhi	X	X	50-19-0 37.0	X	X	X	X	X	X	X
Goa	-	-	-	-	-	-	-	-	-	-
Gujarat	127-9-66 14.0	X	X	X	124-11-63 15.0	X	X	X	143-67-# 26.4	X

Haryana	X	24-6-4 7.7	X	X	X	X	X	X	X	X	#-2-# 10.3
Himachal Pradesh	X	67-29-11 35.2	X	X	57-7-8 30.6	X	X	X	X	51-46-0 42.7	X
Jammu & Kashmir	X	X	27-0-20 3.2	X	X	29-2-20 5.1	X	X	X	X	X
Karnataka	X	X	110-18-71 7.9	X	115-2-100 3.7	X	X	X	114-5-# 4.1	X	X
Kerala	X	69-0-67 2.8	X	X	X	116-0-113 5.6	X	X	X	X	130-0-126 4.7
Lakshadweep	-	-									
Madhya Pradesh	310-60-59 30.3	X	X	X	312-58-53 32.4	X	X	X	X	270-219-# 39.2	X
Maharashtra	145-14-74 9.4	X	X	X	67-16-14 7.3	X	X	X	X	105-42-# 14.6	X
Manipur	X	X	X	13-0-11 0.7	X	X	X	X	X	X	X
Meghalaya	X	X	0-0-0	X	X	X	X	0-0-0	X	X	X
Mizoram	X	X	X	X	X	0-0-0	X	X	0-0-0	X	X
Nagaland	X	X	X	X	X	2-0-2 0.2	X	X	0-0-0	X	X
Orissa	28-0-25 1.4	X	X	X	67-1-60 2.6	X	X	X	X	64-2-# 3.9	X

(continues)

TABLE 6.1 (continued)

						Vidhan Sabha Elections				
Name of State	1980	1982	1983	1984	1985	1987	1988	1989	1990	1991
Pondicherry	0-0-0	x	x	x	3-0-3 .1	x	x	x	x	9-0-9 .8
Punjab	x	x	x	x	26-6-12 5.0	x	x	x	x	x
Rajasthan	123-32-22 18.6	x	x	x	118-39-10 21.2	x	x	x	120-86-# 25.2	x
Sikkim	x	x	x	x	0-0-0	x	x	x	x	x
Tamil Nadu	10-0-10 0.1	x	x	15-0-14 0.2	x	x	x	35-0-34 0.4	x	99-0-83 1.7
Trioura	x	x	4-0-4 0.1	x	x	x	10-0-10 0.2	x	x	x
Uttar Pradesh	400-11-283 10.8	x	x	x	347-16-249 9.9	x	x	278-54-154 11.7	x	416-223-35 34.0
West Bengal	x	54-0-53 0.6	x	x	x	57-0-56 0.5	x	x	x	292-0-241 11.4
Total	x	x	x	x	x	x	x	x	x	x

#Exact figures are not available.

Source: V.B. Singh and Shankar Bose, *Elections in India: Data Handbook on Lok Sabha Elections, 1952-89 and State Elections in India: Data Handbook on Vidhan Sabha Elections, 1952-85 (Five Volumes)* (New Delhi: Sage Publications); Election Commission of India, *Report of the Ninth General Elections to the House of People in India 1989 (statistical)*, 1990; *Report on the Tenth General Elections to the House of People in India 1991 (statistical)*, 1993; *India Today*, July 15, 1991, pp. 40-48; Provisional result sheets of the Election Commission; and PIB Reports.

While both parties, by and large, adhered to their alliance commitments in Haryana, the understanding in Himachal Pradesh broke down completely largely due to the defiant mood of Lok Dal candidates who refused to withdraw from constituencies assigned to the BJP. As a result, the BJP contested almost all the seats (sixty-seven of sixty-eight) in Himachal Pradesh.

Since the Janata Party government led by Shanta Kumar in Himachal Pradesh was virtually a Jana Sangh government, its performance during its short rule (1977-80) came as a big help to the BJP in this election. Implementation of different developmental programs including the provision of water to large parts of the population, a plan which had remained on paper during the Congress rule, paid rich dividends to the party.[1] Primarily for this reason the Congress, which won all four Lok Sabha seats and polled more than fifty-two percent of the votes in the state in the 1980 Lok Sabha elections, was locked in a very bitter contest when people were to elect representatives to form the state government.

Except for the confusion in seat adjustments with the Lok Dal in the early stages of the campaign, the party did quite well in this election. Out of its sixty-seven candidates, twenty-nine won and only eleven of them forfeited their security deposits. It polled 35.2 percent of the popular vote (see Table 6.2). In contrast, only six of twenty-four candidates could win in Haryana where the party's understanding with the Lok Dal went quite well. The poor showing in Haryana may be attributed largely to non-political issues setting the tone of elections in the state. As described by Kumar, "Politically, it is one of the most meaningless elections fought in the region. . . . Even political affiliation of the candidate is secondary. His caste and his equation with community leaders is more important."[2] And the BJP with its urban leadership could not match the skills of the Haryana Congress leaders known for their expertise in linkage building in rural society.

In the West Bengal and Kerala elections, the BJP had neither a foothold in these states nor great ambitions. "The modest objective of the party" in these two states, according to Advani in one of his press conferences in Kerala, "was to create the nucleus for a third force."[3] Accordingly, the party put up candidates in sixty-nine out of 140 constituencies in Kerala and in fifty-four out of 294 in West Bengal. Interestingly, the senior leadership of the party took part in campaigns to guide and advise the party workers and to educate the masses.

TABLE 6.2 Performance of BJP in Lok Sabha Elections 1980-1991
(Number of Contestants, Elected and Forfeited Deposits, and % votes polled)

Name of State	Lok Sabha Elections		
	1984	1989	1991
A&N Islands	0-0-0	0-0-0	1-0-1 4.9
Andhra Pradesh	2-1-0 2.2	2-0-0 2.0	41-1-34 9.6
Arunachal Pradesh	0-0-0	0-0-0	2-0-2 6.1
Assam	2-0-2 0.4	Elections not held	8-2-4 8.6
Bihar	32-0-22 6.9	25-9-6 13.0	51-5-27 16.0
Chandigarh	1-0-1 5.6	1-0-1 12.3	1-0-0 28.8
Dadra & Nagar Haveli	0-0-0	0-0-0	1-0-0 35.4
Daman & Diu	2-0-2 3.0	0-0-0	1-1-0 31.9
Delhi	5-0-0 18.8	5-4-0 26.2	7-5-0 40.2
Goa	With Daman & Diu	1-0-1 0.7	2-0-1 15.6
Gujarat	11-1-0 18.6	12-12-0 30.5	26-20-0 50.4
Haryana	6-0-4 7.5	2-0-0 9.3	10-0-9 10.2
Himachal Pradesh	3-0-0 23.3	4-3-0 45.3	4-2-0 42.8
Jammu & Kashmir	1-0-1 1.7	2-0-2 7.2	Elections not held
Karnataka	6-0-2 4.7	5-0-4 2.6	28-4-5 28.8
Kerala	5-0-5 1.8	20-0-20 4.5	19-0-19 4.6
Lakshadweep	0-0-0	0-0-0	0-0-0
Madhya Pradesh	40-0-3 30.0	33-27-1 39.7	40-12-0 41.9
Maharashtra	20-0-5 10.1	33-10-6 23.7	31-5-6 20.2

(continues)

TABLE 6.2 (continued)

Name of State	Lok Sabha Elections		
	1984	1989	1991
Manipur	1-0-1 7.0	1-0-1 2.3	2-0-2 8.1
Meghalaya	0-0-0	0-0-0	2-0-2 6.9
Mizoram	0-0-0	0-0-0	0-0-0
Nagaland	0-0-0	0-0-0	1-0-1 3.0
Orissa	4-0-4 1.2	6-0-6 1.3	21-0-18 9.5
Pondicherry	0-0-0	0-0-0	1-0-1 2.0
Punjab	3-0-2 3.4	3-0-0 4.2	41-1-19 6.5
Rajasthan	24-0-6 23.7	17-13-4 29.6	25-12-0 40.9
Sikkim	0-0-0	0-0-0	0-0-0
Tamil Nadu	1-0-1 0.1	3-0-3 0.3	15-0-14 1.7
Trioura	1-0-1 0.8	1-0-1 0.6	2-0-2 3.0
Uttar Pradesh	50-0-41 6.4	31-8-13 7.6	84-51-4 32.8
West Bengal	9-0-9 .4	19-0-19 1.7	42-0-34 11.7
Total	229-2-112 7.4	226-86-88 11.5	477-120-190 20.0

#Exact figures are not available.

Source: V.B. Singh and Shankar Bose, *Elections in India: Data Handbook on Lok Sabha Elections, 1952-89 and State Elections in India: Data Handbook on Vidhan Sabha Elections, 1952-85 (Five Volumes)* (New Delhi: Sage Publications); Election Commission of India, *Report of the Ninth General Elections to the House of People in India 1989 (statistical)*, 1990; *Report on the Tenth General Elections to the House of People in India 1991 (statistical)*, 1993; *India Today*, July 15, 1991, pp. 40-48; Provisional result sheets of the Election Commission; and PIB Reports.

But as the results show, only two of the BJP's candidates in Kerala and just one in West Bengal could save their security deposits and polled as low as 2.8 percent and .6 percent of the total valid votes in these states, respectively (see Table 6.2).

In 1983, six more states and one Union Territory (Andhra Pradesh, Assam, Jammu and Kashmir, Karnataka, Meghalaya, Tripura, and Delhi) went to the polls. The BJP did not put up any candidates in Assam and Mehgalaya and contested only four of sixty seats in Tripura, where too all of its candidates lost their security deposits. In both south Indian states, Andhra Pradesh and Karnataka, the party put up large numbers of candidates and also performed better than previous performances of the Jana Sangh. Three of the eighty candidates in Andhra Pradesh and eighteen of the 110 in Karnataka were elected. Another fifteen in Andhra and twenty-one in Karnataka were able to save their deposits, indicating a first step in gaining a BJP foothold in the south.

Encouraged by their performance in the south, particularly in Karnataka, the party entered the Delhi electoral contest with rejuvenated confidence. Although it formed an alliance with the Lok Dal (Charan Singh) by allotting six of the fifty-six metropolitan seats to that party, confident as it was, it declined all offers from other parties. But as the campaign progressed, the Congress began to attract voters. The shift of the Sikh voters (about fourteen percent of the total electorate in Delhi) in favor of the Congress party coupled with complacency among BJP workers, especially after the successes in the south, as Kedar Nath Sahani and Madan Lal Khurana agreed, tilted the balance in favor of the Congress party.[4] The BJP won only nineteen seats and polled thirty-seven percent of the votes to thirty-four seats and 47.5 percent for the Congress. A major setback, alleged many BJP leaders, came from "the RSS cadres who did not throw their phalanx behind the BJP candidates who did not belong to their hard core."[5]

The lackadaisical attitude of the RSS cadres seen in Delhi continued in the elections held in Jammu and Kashmir. There too, as one of the senior BJP leaders confessed, "the greatest threat the BJP was facing was from its hardcore workers [meaning the RSS] who were not campaigning for the party candidates and in some cases were tacitly supporting the Congress (I) candidates."[6] The BJP suffered badly, losing security deposits in twenty of the twenty-seven constituencies it contested, and polled only 3.2 percent of the total votes. It could not win a single seat from an area where the Jana Sangh had a fairly good base, especially in the Jammu region of the state. The election results from this region thus indicate a remarkable shift in the choice of the Hindu electorate who voted for the Congress instead of the BJP, a shift which was also seen in several bye-elections held later in the year.[7]

1984 Lok Sabha Elections

Hindu backlash following Indira Gandi's assassination put the Congress in a commanding position in the 1984 Lok Sabha elections. Anti-Sikh riots sparked in many parts of the country, while unifying Hindus in favor of the Congress also earned Rajiv Gandhi a good deal of sympathy, especially from women, for losing his mother for the cause of the nation.

In addition Rajiv's appeal to voters, "How can the opposition which cannot unite itself keep the county united?"[8] and pledges, "*Hum is hatya ka badla lenge*"[9] (We will avenge the assassination), helped to organize and agitate the masses in favor of his party. Indira Gandhi's death, which resulted in, as Hasan Suroor puts it, "life after death for Congress (I),"[10] made the 1984 elections quite easy for the Congress. The opposition, divided as they were, made its task still easier. Commenting on the 1984 elections, Vajpayee agreed that the divided opposition, which had lost its credibility because of prolonged and intermittent talks about merger, alliance, adjustment of seats, and so on, had helped the Congress win.[11]

Whatever anger and dissatisfaction people had with the Congress rule not only disappeared with Indira Gandhi's assassination but were even converted into a sympathy wave for Rajiv in the 1984 elections. The short spell of his rule preceding the 1984 elections was, in fact, quite satisfactory. His promise of a clean administration and technological advancement on the one hand and his platform that the Congress party alone could keep the country united and strong on the other paid rich dividends to the party.

The BJP was the only other party that received over seven percent of the total votes in 1984. The Janata party polled 6.7 percent, followed by the Communist Party of India (Marxist) and the Lok Dal, which polled 5.7 percent and 5.6 percent, respectively.

In sum, of all the opposition parties the BJP fielded the most candidates (229) in this election. A maximum number of candidates were put up in the states where the party, as part of the Janata Party, had either led the government or shared power with other components of the Janata Party during the Janata phase. Accordingly, it contested all forty seats in Madhya Pradesh, twenty-four of the twenty-five seats in Rajasthan, three of the four seats in Himachal Pradesh, five of the seven seats in Delhi, thirty-two of the fifty-four seats in Bihar, fifty of the eighty-five seats in

Uttar Pradesh, eleven of the twenty-six seats in Gujarat, and twenty of the forty-eight seats in Maharashtra.

The party had local seat sharing adjustment with other opposition parties on a selective basis. For example, it shared seats with Charan Singh's Lok Dal in Uttar Pradesh, Bihar, Haryana, Himachal Pradesh, and Delhi. It also worked out electoral adjustments with Telugu Desam in Andhra Pradesh; with the Janata Party in Gujarat; and with the Janata Party, Congress (S), and Peasant and Workers Party in Maharashtra. There were efforts to avoid further division of the non-Congress votes in other areas, too. But since the opposition parties failed to form a united front to oppose the Congress, they could not capitalize on the general resentment against the party in power.

Viewed from this perspective, the BJP's performance in Madhya Pradesh, Rajasthan, Himachal Pradesh, Delhi, and Gujarat was satisfactory. It polled more than eighteen percent of the votes in all these states and very few of its candidates lost their security deposits, indicating a formidable support base of the party in a large number of constituencies. For example, of the total eighty-three candidates put up from these states only nine of them lost their security deposits (see Table 6.2). Similarly, in Maharashtra, twenty candidates fielded by the party polled 10.1 percent of the votes and as many as fifteen of them saved their deposits, meaning that each one of them polled more than 16.6 percent of the votes in their respective constituencies.

Compared to these states the party failed miserably in Uttar Pradesh and Bihar, where only nineteen of the eighty-two candidates put up (ten of thirty-two in Bihar and nine of fifty in Uttar Pradesh) could save their security deposits. In both these states, the BJP polled less than seven percent of the votes (6.9 percent in Bihar and 6.4 percent in Uttar Pradesh). The fate was similar in Haryana where it contested six seats, lost deposits in four and polled only 7.5 percent of the total votes. In all three states, the Lok Dal of Charan Singh emerged as the main opposition party by polling 13.7 percent in Bihar, 21.6 percent in Uttar Pradesh, and 19.1 percent in Haryana. But like the BJP in Madhya Pradesh, Rajasthan, Himachal Pradesh, Delhi, Gujarat, and Maharashtra it could not convert these votes into many seats. It won only two seats in Uttar Pradesh and one in Bihar, while it drew blanks in Haryana.

Despite the sympathy votes for the Congress party, the opposition parties have themselves to blame for their dismal performance. Besides the division in the opposition votes, the BJP's poor performance, especially in its strong belts, was caused largely by half-hearted support from the RSS workers. Nanaji Deshmukh's appeal to the RSS to support Rajiv Gandhi created a lot of confusion among the RSS workers.[12] Added to this, the BJP's effort to woo Sikh voters in Delhi drove away many Punjabi Hindus who formed the backbone of the party and, as the results showed, it polled very badly in the areas considered strong pockets of the Jana Sangh in earlier elections.[13]

Notwithstanding these setbacks, the BJP, by polling 7.4 percent of the total valid votes in this election, to some extent proved its claim to emerge as an alternative to the Congress party. And its successes in mustering popular support against the Congress by polling 30.0 percent in Madhya Pradesh, 23.7 percent in Rajasthan, 23.3 percent in Himachal Pradesh, 18.8 percent in Delhi, and 18.6 percent in Gujarat undoubtedly boosted its members' morale.

Vidhan Sabha Elections Held Between 1984 and 1989 Lok Sabha Elections

The overall performance of the BJP in the 1984 Lok Sabha elections and the grudging support it received from the RSS forced the party to rethink its strategies. Accordingly, the BJP, at its national executive meeting in early January 1985, as stated in Chapter Three, showed an inclination to move closer to its Jana Sangh identity than its immediate past of the Janata identity. The BJP's decision to revive the Jana Sangh's demand to repeal Article 370 of the Indian Constitution was an indicator of this decision.[14] The leaders' decision not to be a part of any national front showed another shift in its strategy to emphasize the party's separate identity, in an attempt to regain the confidence of the traditional supporters of the Jana Sangh.

With these minor changes in its outlook and strategies the BJP entered the Vidhan Sabha contests in March 1985, and to its satisfaction, as Table 6.1 would suggest, it recouped its losses somewhat in these elections. Of eleven states (Andhra Pradesh, Bihar, Gujarat, Himachal Pradesh, Karnataka, Madhya Pradesh, Maharashtra, Orissa, Rajasthan, Sikkim, and Uttar Pradesh) and one Union Territory, Pondicherry, that held elections in March 1985, the BJP put up candidates in all except Sikkim. The BJP put up 155 fewer candidates than it had in previous Vidhan Sabha elections in these states, mainly because it entered into seat adjustment with Telugu Desam in Andhra Pradesh and with the Progressive Democratic Front in Maharashtra. Excepting these two states, there were only minor changes in the number of candidates fielded from previous elections.

The overall performance of the party remained more or less the same as in the previous elections in these states. Of the 1,481 candidates the BJP put up, 174 won and only 732 lost their security deposits as opposed to the previous election, when 197 of the party's 1,636 candidates won and 846 lost their deposits. Thus, while about twelve percent of its total candidates won both times, the party improved its performance slightly in saving its deposits in larger numbers of constituencies. Only 49.3 percent of its candidates lost deposits in the 1985 elections compared to 51.7 percent in the previous election.

Despite the comparable electoral performance of the BJP in the 1985 state elections and its recovery from the setbacks of the 1984 Lok Sabha elections, the party suffered heavy losses in Himachal Pradesh and in Karnataka. It won seven seats in Himachal Pradesh and only two in Karnataka compared to twenty-nine and eighteen seats respectively in the previous election. Not only did it lose seats, but its share of votes also declined. In both the states the decline in votes was less than five percent (from 35.2 to 30.6 percent in Himachal Pradesh and from 7.9 to 3.7 percent in Karnataka), but the party lost twenty-two seats in Himachal and sixteen in Karnataka.

The party lost heavily in Himachal Pradesh not because of its own follies but because of the change in the state Congress leadership from Ram Lal to Virbhadra Singh. During his two-year tenure (1983-85) as chief minister, Singh not only performed better than his predecessor but was also able to lead the party's election campaign unitedly. In Karnataka, however, the BJP's losses may be attributed to its own tactical mistake in aligning too closely with Ram Krishna Hegde and his government, hoping that this alignment would project the party's secular image and help it bargain for seat adjustments with the Janata Party in the coming election. But to the party's dismay, when the elections came Hegde preferred to align with the Communist parties, thus isolating the BJP. As a result, while anti-Congress voters sided with Hegde and his allies, the BJP could not capitalize on the follies of the Hegde government which, in fact, survived and functioned with BJP support.

The BJP also suffered a loss in Bihar but to a lesser extent. Compared to twenty-one seats in the previous election, it won only sixteen this time. It also fielded twelve candidates fewer and polled 7.5 percent of the total votes as against 8.4 percent in the last election. Besides Himachal Pradesh, Karnataka, and Bihar, the performance of the BJP improved. For example, from merely three seats in the last Vidhan Sabha its representation went up to eight in Andhra Pradesh, as a result of electoral adjustments with the Telugu Desam. Compared to 1983, when it contested eighty seats but won only three and lost deposits in sixty-two constituencies, it contested only ten seats this time, out of which it won eight and lost no deposits.

The party witnessed electoral improvement in other states, too. It won more seats and saved its security deposits in a larger number of constituencies, indicating an expansion of its support bases in different parts of the country.

Results of the Punjab and Assam Vidhan Sabha elections, which were held separately in September and December 1985, respectively, also suggest BJP progress. In Punjab it won six seats as against only one in the previous election. Although there was no formal adjustment with any party, the BJP and the Akali Dal decided informally to avoid a split in the non-Congress votes. Accordingly, the BJP, which put up forty-one candidates in the previous election, fielded only twenty-six this time. In Assam, even though it failed to win any seat, the fact that it put up thirty-seven candidates, three of whom were able to save their security deposits, supports the party's claim to have emerged as a national party.

The gradual increase in the BJP support and its representation in state legislatures continued in the 1987 elections as well. Six states (Haryana, Jammu and Kashmir, Kerala, Mizoram, Nagaland, and West Bengal) went to the polls in 1987, and the BJP made a grand recovery in Haryana. It was the only state where it worked out seat adjustments with the Lok Dal. Out of twenty seats it contested, the BJP won sixteen and accounted for 17.8 percent of the total valid votes in the state (see Table 6.1).

Its recovery in Jammu and Kashmir was not as dramatic as in Haryana, but here too, it was able to win two seats and get 5.1 percent of the votes as against 3.2 percent in the last election. It did not put up any candidates in Mizoram and contested only two seats in Nagaland but fielded 116 candidates in Kerala and fifty-seven in West Bengal, compared to sixty-nine and fifty-four, respectively, in the last election. As Table 6.1 shows, it increased its share of votes from merely 2.8 percent to 5.6 percent in Kerala but had no impact in West Bengal.

In 1988 only two states, Meghalaya and Tripura, went to the polls, and the BJP could not make any inroads in them. While it did not field any candidate in Meghalaya, all of its ten candidates lost their security deposits in Tripura.

The states of Tamil Nadu, Mizoram, and Nagaland, which voted in January 1989, did not add any feathers to the BJP's cap. While the party did not put up candidates in Mizoram and Nagaland, its effort to carve out a support base in some pockets of Tamil Nadu also went in vain when thirty-four of its thirty-five candidates lost their security deposits. Even the support assured from a local Hindu organization (Hindu Munnani), which was believed to have created a Hindu vote bank in the districts of Kanniya

Kumari, Tirunnelveli, and Chidambaranar,[15] proved inconsequential as the party could claim only .4 percent of the total valid votes in the state.

While the Congress won in Mizoram and Nagaland, its humiliating defeat in Tamil Nadu (it polled 20.2 percent of the votes and won only twenty-six of the 234 seats in the state) helped the opposition parties to recover their morale and fighting power against the Congress. Using rising prices, the crushing burden of the national debt, and the Bofors bribery scandal as rallying points to discredit the Rajiv Gandhi government, almost all opposition parties also worked out specific strategies to expand their individual support bases.

The BJP's tacit support of Vishwa Hindu Parishad's *Ramshila pujan* program served to unite Hindus and to mobilize their support for the party. The overwhelming enthusiasm about the program, particularly in Hindi-speaking areas, encouraged the BJP to exploit the Hindu sentiments politically. Accordingly, a pledge to construct the Shri Ram temple at Ayodhya became one of its main election promises. By the time the elections to the ninth Lok Sabha were announced, the BJP had become a force to reckon with, at least in north India. It was the primary reason why the National Front (formed by five parties: the Janata Dal, Congress [S], Telugu Desam, Dravida Munnetra Kazhagam, and Asom Gana Parishad), despite bitter opposition from the left parties, was not able to exclude the BJP from an alliance to fight against the Congress in the forthcoming Lok Sabha elections. All opposition parties were thus forced to bury their individual differences for the time being.

1989 Lok Sabha Elections

Thus the National Front, particularly the Janata Dal, had to enter into electoral adjustment with this party despite its reservations about the BJP's stance on Ramjanambhoomi and its pro-Hindu posture. The growing popularity of the BJP in the north Indian states and in Gujarat had forced the Janata Dal to accommodate the BJP in its alliance to avoid division in the non-Congress votes. The CPM too, despite its persistent effort to isolate the BJP politically, "acquiesced in a *de facto* Janata Dal-BJP alliance. Most important, its strategy of forging an alternative to the Congress which excludes the BJP has failed. Its commendable anti-communal initiative has run out of steam, at least for the moment,"[16] as one writer put it.

As the election process began, the gap between the Janata Dal and the BJP decreased. Although they could not arrive at a perfect alliance, they succeeded in forging seat adjustments in many constituencies of Andhra

Pradesh, Bihar, Gujarat, Haryana, Himachal Pradesh, Jammu and Kashmir, Madhya Pradesh, Rajasthan, Uttar Pradesh, and Delhi. Out of these ten states, while there was complete understanding in six, in the remaining states they put up candidates against each other in some constituencies. In all other states except Maharashtra, where the BJP shared seats with Shiv Sena, it fought the 1989 Lok Sabha elections individually.

In all, the BJP contested 226 Lok Sabha seats in this election. While eighty-six of them won and eighty-eight lost their security deposits, the party received 11.5 percent of the total valid votes. This share went much beyond the expectation of the party. Statewide analysis of its performance, as shown in the Table 6.2, shows that it contested only two seats (these were the only seats allotted to the BJP by the Telugu Desam) in Andhra Pradesh and lost both. But it is interesting to note that in both the constituencies it polled over forty percent of the votes. Exactly the same was the case in Haryana.

While there was mixed response to the party in Uttar Pradesh, Bihar, and Maharashtra, it received overwhelming support in Gujarat, Himachal Pradesh, Madhya Pradesh, Rajasthan, and Delhi, where most of the candidates put up by the party romped home, securing over fifty percent of the total valid votes in their constituencies. It contested twelve seats in Gujarat, and all of them won with over fifty percent of the votes. The story was the same in Rajasthan, where all of its winners (thirteen out of seventeen contested seats) were elected by the majority of voters in their constituencies. In Madhya Pradesh, twenty-seven of its thirty-three candidates were elected and eighteen of them secured over fifty percent of the votes. In Himachal Pradesh and Delhi too, all of its winners except one were sent to the Lok Sabha by the majority of electors.

In Maharashtra, too, the BJP made impressive gains. Thanks to its alliance with the Shiv Sena it expanded its support base in rural Maharashtra. It contested thirty-three of the forty-eight seats in the state and ten of them were elected. Only six of the thirty-three candidates put up by the party lost their security deposits. In all, the party polled 23.7 percent of the total valid votes in the state, a remarkable performance indeed.

The story was not as impressive in Uttar Pradesh and Bihar, however. In both these states, despite seat adjustments with the Janata Dal, in many constituencies they pitted their candidates against each other. The mood of the people being what it was, the Janata Dal was the most favored party in both these states. Even the weaker Janata Dal candidates or ones put up by it under friendly contests performed quite well. As a result, many of the BJP candidates were defeated because of division in the non-Congress votes. In Uttar Pradesh, it contested thirty-one seats (of these, about twenty in alliance with the Janata Dal), won only eight and lost deposits in thirteen constituencies. Its share of votes increased to 7.6 percent, only 1.2 percent more than it polled in the 1984 Lok Sabha elections. The party did slightly better in Bihar, where it won nine of the twenty-five seats it contested. Moreover, only six of its candidates lost deposits, and its share of votes increased to 13 percent as against only 6.9 percent in the 1984 elections (see Table 6.2).

In the rest of the states like Karnataka, Kerala, Orissa, Tamil Nadu, and West Bengal the BJP contested alone. As none of them had any significant BJP support base, most of these candidates performed miserably. Out of the total of fifty-six candidates put up by the BJP from these states, only one could save his security deposit in this election. Interestingly, in none of these states could it poll over five percent of the votes, indicating the weakness of the party in southern as well as in northeastern states.

However, its spectacular gains in most of the Hindi-speaking states and in Gujarat and Maharashtra put the BJP on a very sound footing. Although, in an aggregate sense, it increased its share of votes from 7.4 percent in 1984 to 11.5 percent in 1989, its phenomenal success in five states (Gujarat, Himachal Pradesh, Madhya Pradesh, Maharashtra, and Rajasthan) and in the union territory of Delhi heightened the BJP's hope to emerge as a national alternative to the Congress.

Vidhan Sabha Elections Held Between 1989 and 1991 Lok Sabha Elections

Vidhan Sabha elections in three states (Andhra Pradesh, Karnataka, and Uttar Pradesh) were held simultaneously with the Lok Sabha elections in November 1989. Following the Lok Sabha pattern of seat adjustments among the non-Congress parties, the BJP was allotted twelve seats by the Telugu Desam in Andhra Pradesh, to which it agreed. While the BJP was left all alone in Karnataka, somehow it arrived at a limited understanding with the Janata Dal in Uttar Pradesh: that both parties would avoid fielding candidates against prominent leaders and sitting members of the other party. Accordingly, the BJP contested 114 Vidhan Sabha seats in Karnataka and 278 in Uttar Pradesh, in contrast to the 400 and 347 seats it sought there in the 1980 and 1985 Vidhan Sabha elections, respectively.

It improved its performance in all three Vidhan Sabha elections. In Andhra Pradesh, five of the twelve candidates put up by the party won. In Karnataka, too, it won five seats as against only two in the previous election. It also improved its share of votes from 3.7 percent in 1983 to 4.1 percent. Similarly, in Uttar Pradesh, as against only eight seats and 7.6 percent votes in the Lok Sabha elections, it won fifty-seven Vidhan Sabha seats and 11.7 percent of votes in the state elections held simultaneously (see Table 6.1).

Soon after the formation of the National Front government at the Center, Vidhan Sabha elections to eight more states (Bihar, Gujarat, Himachal Pradesh, Madhya Pradesh, Maharashtra, Manipur, Orissa, and Rajasthan) and the union territory of Pondicherry were held in February 1990. Encouraged by its performance in the Lok Sabha elections, the BJP appeared confident to concentrate its power in just a couple of those states. At the same time, its impressive performance in the previous election had increased its bargaining power vis-a-vis the Janata Dal in seat adjustments to overthrow the Congress in these states. Moreover, the minority status of the National Front in the Lok Sabha and the BJP's support of it from outside put the BJP on still firmer ground.

But the party was fully aware that despite its heavy seat losses, the Congress party's share of votes in the 1989 Lok Sabha elections was over forty percent, marginally less than its 1980 tally which did not fall below thirty-five percent even in Hindi-speaking states, so a division of the non-Congress vote would spell disaster for the ruling alliance at the Center. Accordingly, the Janata Dal and the BJP agreed to adjust with each other, at least in states where local differences were containable. Since the BJP was already committed to continuing its alliance with the Shiv Sena in Maharashtra and the Janata Dal strongman, Biju Patnaik, was not agreeable to accommodating the BJP (as he did during the Lok Sabha elections in Orissa), there was no adjustment between the Janata Dal and the BJP in these two states. Having no base whatsoever, there was no tussle between the two in Manipur and Pondicherry.

Out of the remaining six states besides Bihar, there was an understanding between the Janata Dal and the BJP to put up common candidates against the Congress party. Although large numbers of candidates from both the parties filed their nominations against each other and many of them, despite directives from their parties, did not withdraw from the contest, the adjustment continued and the election campaign, by and large, was carried jointly.

Statewide analysis of the results of the Vidhan Sabha elections of February 1990, as shown in Table 6.1, suggests that the BJP made handsome gains in all the states. It not only increased its strength in different state legislatures but also gained an absolute majority in two states. In Himachal Pradesh, where it contested fifty-one of the sixty-eight seats, forty-six of them won. Similarly, out of 320 seats in Madhya Pradesh it contested in 270 constituencies and in 219 of them it won. The long cherished dream came true when the BJP formed its government in both these states.

In Gujarat and Rajasthan, where the BJP and Janata Dal had problems in seat adjustment, both parties strove hard to gain supremacy and contested more seats than were assigned to them; as a result, both lost quite a few seats which they could very easily have won. Imperfect adjustments notwithstanding, the BJP and the Janata Dal together won the majority of seats in these states as well. Sixty-seven of the BJP's 143 candidates in Gujarat and eighty-six of its 120 candidates in Rajasthan won. While it achieved the distinction of the single largest party in Rajasthan, the Janata Dal acquired this status in Gujarat. As a result, the parties formed coalition governments in these two states.

The BJP had a perfect alliance with the Shiv Sena in Maharashtra. The BJP, which had been accorded senior partner status during the Lok Sabha polls, this time in the Vidhan Sabha elections was allotted only 105 seats as against 183 seats for the Shiv Sena. Since the Progressive Democratic Front, consisting of the Janata Dal, Shetkari Sangathan, Peasants' and Workers' Party, Communist Party of India, and Communist Party of India (Marxist), was also a potential claimant for the non-Congress votes, the effectiveness of the BJP-Shiv Sena combination, to a great extent, was neutralized. And together they could win only ninety-three seats (BJP forty-two and Shiv Sena fifty-one). Accordingly, the percentage share of the BJP vote also declined; it received only 14.6 percent as against 23.7 percent of the votes in the 1989 Lok Sabha elections.

Despite the BJP's failure in states like Manipur and the Union Territory of Pondicherry, insignificant gain in Orissa, and not so impressive performance, as expected, in Maharashtra and Bihar, the results of the Vidhan Sabha elections of February 1990, by and large, went in its favor. Its successes in the 1989 Lok Sabha elections and the Vidhan Sabha elections that followed do not make the BJP the only major gainer in these contests, but the party also is "indeed being increasingly viewed as the major alternative to the Congress."[17]

1991 Lok Sabha Elections

Differences in outlook of the two supporting parties of the National Front government, the BJP and the CPI-M, became apparent in the drama[18] played by the Janata Dal leaders when they were electing a leader to fill the post of the prime ministership. The event contained in it the seeds of premature dissolution of the ninth Lok Sabha, and subsequent events amply proved these apprehensions. The struggle for power and self-aggrandize-ment of the Janata Dal leaders, as discussed in Chapter Three, leading to a hasty decision on the Mandal Commission's recommendation to reserve twenty-seven percent of the government jobs for "other backward classes," hastened the disintegration of the Janata Dal. It also sent alarming signals to the other parties to withstand the onslaught of the game plan of the pro-Mandal leaders.

The BJP, anticipating the negative results of its association with the V.P. Singh government and threatened by the consolidation of the backward castes through the Mandal politics of the Janata Dal, perhaps had no option but to return to its old source of identity, *Hindutva*, and went all out to agitate, organize, and mobilize Hindus to ensure their support. Encouraged by the rich dividends it received from the *Ram shila pujan* ceremony during the previous Lok Sabha elections in 1989, the BJP launched Advani's *Ram rath yatra* from Somnath to Ayodhya, during which the party symbol was prominently displayed to increase religious fervor among the Hindus and to mobilize their support for the party. With the over-whelming response to the *rath yatra*, on the one hand, and efforts of the other parties to brand the BJP a communal party on the other, the BJP hardened its stand on the temple issue still further. Unlike in the 1989 Lok Sabha elections, this time the party firmly promised to construct the Shri Ram Temple at Ayodhya.

By the time the elections to the tenth Lok Sabha were announced, the BJP was well set to exploit its Hindu identity. Accordingly, it entitled its manifesto *Towards Ram Rajya*. The party president, Murli Manohar Joshi, also promised that the temple would be constructed at the Janambhoomi in Ayodhya as soon as the party came to power. As the campaign progressed, the BJP coined slogans such as "*Jo Hindu hit ki baat karega, wahi desh par raj karega*" (Only those will rule the country who would look after the interests of Hindus) and "*BJP ko lana hai, ram rajya banana hai*" (To bring the Ramrajya in the country, bring the BJP to power) to encourage the *Hindutva* feeling of the majority community. While these campaign promises echoed the feelings of Hindu fundamentalists, its slogan, "*Sabko dekha baar-baar, hamko parkhen ek baar*" (You have tested all others many times; why not test us only for once?), appealed to all the sections of the society.

As the campaign progressed, the BJP outsmarted all other parties on almost all the fronts. Three video tapes—one on Advani titled *The Man India Awaits*, a second on the BJP titled *The Right Alternative*, and the third, an edited version of the controversial video prepared by the Jain Studios on the events at Ayodhya in October-November 1990—were extensively circulated.

Tactically, while the party's religious cards were blatantly being played by leaders like Ashok Singhal, Uma Bharati, Sadhvi Ritambhra, and many more at regional and local levels, the star campaigners of the party, Vajpayee and Advani, were propagating the party's ideology and program to present the BJP as the right alternative. For example, Advani, while welcoming 1500 Muslims who joined the BJP in April 1991, explained in a public meeting at Bilaspur, Madhya Pradesh that "the problems of all Indians, irrespective of caste and religion, were identical and his party's ideology was to solve them as humanitarian problems without adding political or communal overtones to them."[19] The top-ranking BJP leaders also made their stand clear on the construction of the Sri Ram Temple. Vajpayee, for example, explained that "Ayodhya is not a poll issue, but a matter of faith."[20]

The BJP contested over 400 Lok Sabha seats, which it never had before, not even during its Jana Sangh days. Of the 477 seats it contested in the 1991 Lok Sabha elections, it won 120 of them. Its popular support had also increased; compared to the mere 11.5 percent in 1989, it won twenty percent of the votes in 1991. The proportion of candidates losing their security deposits, however, remained the same, about thirty-nine percent. But because the number of contestants in the 1991 elections had almost doubled, its performance showed an improvement. In addition to the 120 seats won, in as many as 167 constituencies the BJP polled more than 16.33 percent of the votes, indicating a potential increase in popular support in many Lok Sabha constituencies.

A statewide analysis of the 1991 Lok Sabha elections, as presented in Table 6.2, would suggest that excluding Himachal Pradesh and Maharashtra, where it lost both seats and votes, the party gained at least in votes in all other states. That is to say, even though it lost a few seats in some of the states, its overall share of votes increased. For example, its members from Bihar decreased to five in 1991 from nine in 1989, but its share of votes increased from thirteen to sixteen percent. Similarly, it lost one seat in Rajasthan, but its poll percentage went up from a mere 29.6 in 1989 to 40.9 percent in 1991. Even in Madhya Pradesh, where it lost heavily in seats, it gained in votes.

The party achieved the distinction of getting over fifty percent of the votes in Gujarat, where it also won twenty of the twenty-six Lok Sabha seats and no lost deposits. The case was similar in Uttar Pradesh, where despite stiff competition, the BJP polled 32.8 percent of the votes and won fifty-one of the eighty-five Lok Sabha seats while only four of its eighty-four candidates lost their security deposits. In Delhi, too, it polled over forty percent and won five of the seven seats. Similarly, it captured the lone seat of Daman and Diu Union territory and polled over one-third of the total valid votes. In Dadar and Nagar Haveli, although it did not win, it polled 35.4 percent of the votes.

The party expanded its base in the south as well, winning four seats in Karnataka and one in Andhra Pradesh and polling over twenty-eight percent and nine percent of the votes, respectively. Three major states of the eastern zone—Assam, West Bengal, and Orissa—where the party had a weak support base in the past also contributed to the BJP's success. While it won two of the fourteen seats in Assam, it also made inroads in West Bengal, the bastion of the left front, by polling 11.7 percent of the votes. In Orissa, too, it polled about ten percent of the votes (see Table 6.2).

In brief, in the tenth Lok Sabha elections the BJP not only increased its seats from eighty-six to 120 but also garnered support from one-fifth of the total electors in the country who voted in the 1991 elections. Notwithstanding the setbacks of seats lost in Bihar, Madhya Pradesh, and Maharashtra, its popular support base, measured by the percentage of votes polled, either increased or remained the same. It may be noted that most of the seats lost by a very narrow margin in Madhya Pradesh and Maharashtra were those in elections in the second phase, i.e., after the assassination of Rajiv Gandhi. And, finally, the substantial gains the BJP made in the southern as well eastern zones of India amply proved that the party had potential to emerge as a national alternative to the Congress. (See Figure 6.1 for the BJP's support base.)

Vidhan Sabha Elections Held in 1991

Elections to state legislatures of Assam, Haryana, Kerala, Tamil Nadu, Uttar Pradesh, West Bengal, and Pondicherry were held simultaneously with the Lok Sabha elections in 1991. The BJP fielded quite a large number of candidates in the Vidhan Sabha elections as well. Out of the six states and one Union Territory that went to polls, the BJP improved upon its previous performance in all except two. Despite the fact that it put up more candidates, its share of votes declined in Haryana and Kerala. As against sixteen seats in the previous house it could win only two this time in Haryana.

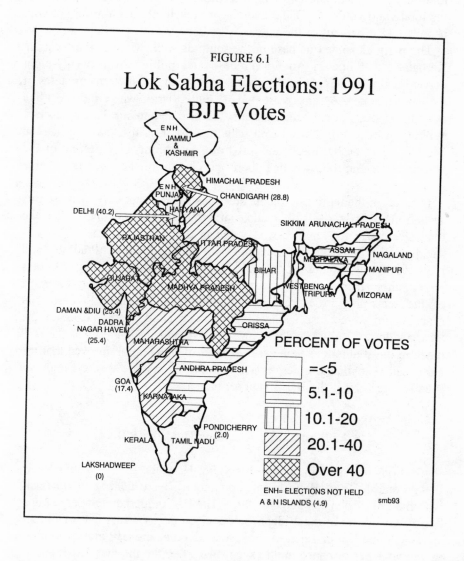

FIGURE 6.1

Lok Sabha Elections: 1991 BJP Votes

ENH
JAMMU & KASHMIR

HIMACHAL PRADESH

ENH PUNJAB

CHANDIGARH (28.8)

DELHI (40.2)

HARYANA

RAJASTHAN

UTTAR PRADESH

SIKKIM ARUNACHAL PRADESH

ASSAM

MEGHALAYA

NAGALAND

MANIPUR

BIHAR

GUJARAT

MADHYA PRADESH

WEST BENGAL

TRIPURA

MIZORAM

DAMAN &DIU (25.4)
DADRA & NAGAR HAVELI (25.4)

ORISSA

MAHARASHTRA

ANDHRA PRADESH

GOA (17.4)

KARNATAKA

PONDICHERRY (2.0)

KERALA   TAMIL NADU

LAKSHADWEEP (0)

PERCENT OF VOTES

	=<5
	5.1-10
	10.1-20
	20.1-40
	Over 40

ENH= ELECTIONS NOT HELD
A & N ISLANDS (4.9)

smb93

In Kerala there was no question of losing a seat because it held none, but its popular support went down to 4.7 percent from 5.6 percent previously. In Tamil Nadu and Pondicherry it was not much different; had it not put up more candidates this time, its share of votes, which showed slight improvement over its earlier performance, would have been nullified.

In contrast, the BJP performed remarkably well in Uttar Pradesh, Assam, and West Bengal. For the first time, the BJP fielded more than fifty candidates in Assam and ten were elected. Interestingly, nine of these came from Barak Valley districts, an area considered to be a stronghold of the Congress party in Assam. The two Lok Sabha seats it won were also from this region. Similarly, the party made spectacular gains in West Bengal, where it polled about twelve percent of the total valid votes. Of the 292 candidates it fielded, fifty-one were able to save their security deposits. The fact that the BJP was able to get over 16.33 percent of the votes in fifty-one constituencies was a clear signal that the party had entered the bastion of the left front.

Of all the states, Uttar Pradesh turned out to be the most favorable for the party. As mentioned earlier, it won fifty-one of the eighty-four Lok Sabha seats where elections were held.[21] Similarly, the party contested 416 of the 420 Vidhan Sabha seats and won 223. Interestingly, only thirty-five of its candidates lost their deposits. In a multi-corner contest which the state witnessed in the 1991 Vidhan Sabha elections, the BJP's success in polling thirty-four percent of the total valid votes in the state was a remarkable performance. A detailed analysis of results at the constituency level suggests that the BJP cut very heavily into the upper caste support base of the Congress party. Notwithstanding the proclamations of the Janata Dal and the Samajvadi Janata Party, the BJP was able to mobilize fairly substantial support from the castes characterized as backward. As the results have shown, it had alienated the Muslims in a very real sense but had attracted support from almost all sectors of the majority community.[22] What is thus reflected is that the BJP not only gained power in Uttar Pradesh but also carved out its support base across caste lines, which the party with its organizational base may very well sustain.

To investigate its support base further, we have examined the BJP performance in urban and Muslim constituencies. To do so, we have identified Lok Sabha constituencies with forty percent or more urban population and constituencies with thirty percent or more Muslim population, and the votes polled by the BJP in the 1991 Lok Sabha elections were aggregated against them in Table 6.3.

TABLE 6.3 Performance of BJP in Urban and Muslim Constituencies in the 1991 Lok Sabha Elections

S.No.	Name of State	% 1991 Urban Population	% 1981 Muslim Population	% Votes Polled by Bharatiya Janata Party		
				in the State	in Urban Constituencies (with 40% or more urban population)	in Muslim Constituencies (with 30% or more Muslim population)
1.	All India	25.7	11.4	20.0	27.5	22.1
2.	A&N Islands	26.8	8.6	4.9	-	-
3.	Andhra Pradesh	26.8	8.5	9.6	22.7	23.4
4.	Arunachal Pradesh	12.2	.8	6.1	-	-
5.	Assam	11.1	No Census held in 1981	8.6		
6.	Bihar	13.2	14.1	16.0	33.3	25.1
7.	Chandigarh	89.7	2.0	28.8	28.8	-
8.	Dadra & Nagar Haveli	8.5	1.9	35.4	-	-
9.	Daman & Diu	46.9	4.5	31.9	31.9	-
10.	Delhi	89.9	7.7	40.2	40.2	-
11.	Goa	41.0	15.6	17.4	-	-
12.	Gujarat	34.4	8.5	50.4	50.9	-
13.	Haryana	24.8	4.1	10.2	14.9	12.0
14.	Himachal Pradesh	8.7	1.6	42.8	-	-

				Elections were not held		
15.	Jammu & Kashmir	23.8	64.2	28.8	34.5	-
16.	Karnataka	30.9	11.1	4.6	5.5	6.6
17.	Kerala	26.4	21.3	-	-	-
18.	Lakshadweep	56.3	94.8	-	-	-
19.	Madhya Pradesh	23.2	4.8	41.9	47.9	-
20.	Maharashtra	38.7	9.3	20.2	37.3	
21.	Manipur	27.7	7.0	8.1	5.6	-
22.	Meghalaya	18.7	3.1	6.9	-	-
23.	Mizoram	46.2	0.5	-	-	-
24.	Nagaland	17.3	1.5	3.0	-	-
25.	Orissa	13.4	1.6	9.5	-	-
26.	Pondicherry	64.1	6.1	2.0	2.0	-
27.	Punjab	29.7	1.0	16.5	-	
28.	Rajasthan	22.9	7.3	40.9	49.0	-
29.	Sikkim	9.1	1.0	-	-	
30.	Tamil Nadu	34.2	10.3	1.7	3.3	-
31.	Tripura	15.3	0.3	3.0	-	-
32.	Uttar Pradesh	19.9	15.9	32.8	51.3	39.0
33.	West Bengal	27.4	21.5	11.7	11.1	17.1

Urban Population and BJP Voting Patterns

It is generally held that the BJP, like the Bharatiya Jana Sangh, is primarily an urban-based party. To some extent, it was true in the early days of the Jana Sangh but not afterwards, when it emerged as a major political party because it expanded its support base beyond the bounds of urban areas (see Table 6.3). The same has been the case with the BJP. It does have an urban bias in its organizational set-up, a characteristic feature of all political parties, and since it is backed by the RSS, which is organizationally very strong in urban areas, the party has performed better than other parties in areas with larger shares of urban population. The results of the 1991 Lok Sabha elections, as plotted in Table 6.3, corroborate this.

The share of BJP votes in constituencies with forty percent or more urban population comes to 27.5 percent, as against the national total of only twenty percent. In all states except West Bengal the BJP's performance in urban constituencies has been either better than or equal to its overall performance in the state. For example, as against the state average of only 9.9 percent of the votes in Andhra Pradesh it polled 22.7 percent in constituencies with forty percent or more urban population. Similarly, it polled almost the double of its state average in Bihar. In Maharashtra and Uttar Pradesh, too, its poll percentages in urban constituencies were much higher than its state average; to be exact, it polled 37.3 percent and 51.3 percent in urban constituencies as against the state average of 20.2 percent and 32.8 percent in Maharashtra and Uttar Pradesh, respectively. Likewise, its performance in urban constituencies of Haryana, Karnataka, Madhya Pradesh, Rajasthan, and even Tamil Nadu were significantly better than its state average (see Table 6.3).

Muslim Population and BJP Voting Patterns

Despite its proclamation of positive secularism, the BJP has remained the most disliked party for the Muslims. Its avowed stance on *Hindutva*, its promise to construct the Sri Ram temple at the disputed site in Ayodhya, and its religious appeal to unite the Hindus to oppose minority-ism of other national parties in the 1991 elections have driven the Muslims still further away. As a result, the Muslims have come out openly against the BJP, particularly in the areas where they constitute a sizable number.

In an emotionally charged atmosphere, when one group asserts, the other reciprocates.

We tested this hypothesis by examining the BJP performance where Muslims constitute over forty percent of the population. In general, where over forty percent of the voters vote against the BJP and the party must compete with others for the remaining votes, its chances for even average support are minimized. But that is not the case with the Muslims; on the contrary, the BJP has performed better in these constituencies. As against its average support of 19.9 percent, the party has polled over twenty-two percent of the votes in Muslim constituencies (see Table 6.3). Although such constituencies are few, in Andhra Pradesh, Bihar, Uttar Pradesh, and West Bengal the BJP polled much higher in Muslim constituencies than its state average. Even in states like Haryana and Kerala it polled better in Muslim constituencies, indicating the tendency of the majority to unite and support the BJP against the assertion of a minority.

To sum up, we can make the following observations. First, the BJP, which came into existence soon after the 1980 Lok Sabha elections and wanted to establish its secular credentials independent of its Jana Sangh legacy by opting for Gandhian socialism to resolve India's socio-economic and political problems, found little success in the elections that followed. Second, its poor performance in elections in the early 1980s, the growing popularity of the late Indira Gandhi among the Hindus for her bold steps against the Sikh militancy, and the dwindling RSS support for the BJP forced it to revive its *Hindutva* identity and to put more emphasis on Deendayal Upadhya's Integral Humanism than on Gandhian socialism. Third, encouraged by the popular response to its *Hindutva* posture, the party went all out to exploit the Hindu sentiments of the majority community for electoral gains. Fourth, the failure of the National Front government and inability of the Congress to refurbish its popular image provided an excellent ground for the BJP's slogan, "*Sabko dekha baar-baar, hamko parkhen ek baar*" (You have given many chances to other parties, give only one chance to us), which helped the party attract support in the 1991 elections. Fifth, its better performance in urban and in Muslim constituencies suggests that the party has potential to attract urban people who are generally better informed than their rural counterparts and that it can unite the majority to its favor to oppose the minorityism of other national political parties.

The BJP's Performance in the 1993 State Elections

Results of the six Vidhan Sabha elections came as a big surprise to the BJP. Except in the Delhi elections, the party suffered a setback in all other states. Its slogan *"Ramrajya ki or: Aj panch Pradesh, kal sara Desh"* (Towards Ramrajya: today five states, tomorrow the whole country) came to naught when it lost in Himachal Pradesh, Madhya Pradesh, and Uttar Pradesh and could improve only marginally in Rajasthan.

This was the first legislative election since Delhi's change of status from union territory to statehood. The BJP contested all seventy seats and won forty-nine of them, polling 43.5 percent of the votes. Compared to its performance in the 1991 Lok Sabha elections, it polled 3.3 percent more this time. The Janata Dal, receiving only 1.2 percent of the votes in 1991, got 12.8 percent in the 1993 elections. The Janata Dal, the Samajvadi Party, and the Bahujan Samaj Party cut into the support base of the Congress party, particularly the *dalits* and the Muslim vote, which proved advantageous for the BJP in the "first-past the post" system of election.

The BJP contested all sixty-eight seats in Himachal Pradesh. It won only eight of them. In contrast, it contested only fifty-two seats in 1990 and won forty-six. In the 1990 Vidhan Sabha and 1991 Lok Sabha elections its poll percentages had been 42.9 and 42.8. It secured 36.2 percent of the votes this time. With a 6.7 percent loss in its popular support, the party lost thirty-eight seats. A comparison of the 1990 and the 1991 results shows that the BJP's vote share remained the same. But then, it had contested only fifty-two seats in 1990, whereas in 1991 its Lok Sabha candidates ran for office in all sixty-eight Vidhan Sabha segments. Similarly, the BJP Lok Sabha candidates won only in thirty-four Vidhan Sabha segments, showing a loss of eighteen seats in 1991. This declining trend continued and the party lost heavily in 1993.

In the 1990 elections, the BJP contested only 266 seats in Madhya Pradesh. It won 218 and received 38.4 percent of the votes. However, in 1993, it contested all 320 seats and it could only win 116 of them. In fact, the party suffered a setback in the 1991 Lok Sabha elections. The BJP Lak Sabha candidates won in 131 assembly segments while the Congress party carried 180. It polled 41.5 percent of the votes while the Congress got 45.2 percent. In 1993, the Congress won 177 seats and about forty-one percent of the votes while the BJP won 116 seats and polled about thirty-nine percent of the votes (see Table 6.4). Between 1991 and 1993, the BJP lost fifteen seats and about two percent of the votes.

TABLE 6.4 **Performance of BJP in Vidhan Sabha Elections, November 1993**

Name of State	Number of Seats	Seats Contested	Seats Won	% Votes
Delhi	70	70	49	43.5
Himachal Pradesh	68	68	8	36.2
Madhya Pradesh	320	320	116	39.0
Mizoram	40	8	-	N.A.
Rajasthan	200	197	95	39.5
Uttar Pradesh	425	425	177	33.4

Source: Compiled from *India Today*, December 15, 1993, pp. 26-39 and *Organiser*, December 19, 1993, p. 3.

The BJP contested 197 of 200 seats in the state of Rajasthan in the 1993 elections. In the remaining three constituencies, it supported independents. While all BJP-supported independents won, only ninety-five of its own candidates were able to win. The BJP polled 39.5 percent of the votes, which is just one percent more than polled by the Congress party. The Congress won seventy-six seats while of the remaining twenty-five (excluding the three won by the BJP-supported independents), six were won by the Janata Dal, one by CPI (M) and eighteen by the independents. An analysis of the voting pattern shows that the BJP secured 41.5 percent of the votes in the 132 constituencies it contested in 1990 and added another 3.4 percent in these segments in 1991. In addition, it polled thirty-four percent of the votes in the 1991 Lok Sabha election in those segments which it did not contest in 1990. In the 1993 election, the party basically maintained its 1991 performance and secured seats and votes from almost all the regions of the state. The party's gain was largely at the cost of the Janata Dal. The non-Congress Jat voters seemed to have shifted from the Janata Dal to the BJP. Similarly, the BJP performed better in urban constituencies and also in the districts that have a higher literacy rate.

Based on its state government's performance and the likely division of the non-BJP votes in the 1993 elections, the BJP strongly believed that it would return to power in overwhelming majority in the Uttar Pradesh elections. Its leader, Kalyan Singh, the former chief minister of the state, actually stated that anything less than 220 seats would be considered a defeat of the party in the state. The failure of the non-BJP parties to form an alliance to unify their votes in fact enhanced the BJP's prospect in this election. While the Samajvadi Party of Mulayam Singh Yadav and the Bahujan Samaj Party of Kanshi Ram formed an alliance, the unified Janata Dal (the Janata Dal-B, Janata Dal-A, and Chandra Sekhar faction of Samajvadi Janata Party merged to form the Janata Dal just before the 1993 elections) and the Congress party failed to arrive at any understanding to oppose the BJP's political position.

As the election campaign progressed, all other parties attacked the BJP's pro-Hindu position and fervently appealed to the electors to defeat the BJP's divisive politics. But the BJP, having achieved the task of demolishing the Babri mosque at Ayodhya, did not play its *Hindutva* card very blatantly. Emphasizing its governmental performance, the BJP's promise to accomplish Ramrajya through better policies and programs, rooted in the Indian cultural tradition, formed the main body of its election campaign. Confident of its victory, the BJP's mild *Hindutva* posture in the campaign was designed to distance itself from the VHP and Bajrang Dal on the one hand and to expand its support base on the other. As the results suggest, there was hardly any gain for the party. While it received 31.6 percent of the votes in 1991, it polled only 33.4 percent in 1993. It failed to attract new voters to its fold. On the other hand, failure of the Congress and the Janata Dal to effectively divide the non-BJP votes helped the SP-BSP alliance to defeat the BJP candidates in a large number of constituencies. The only region where the Janata Dal effectively divided the non-BJP votes was Western Uttar Pradesh and, as expected, the BJP gained in this region.

The Muslims (15.9 percent) and the scheduled castes (21.1 percent) played a decisive role in this election. They along, with the Ahirs, one of the most prominent among the backward castes, extended almost total support to the SP-BSP combination. The BJP, however, received overwhelming support from the upper castes. Despite the fact that the state *Vyapar Mandal* (traders' association) appealed to the traders to support the SP-BSP party, which had promised to abolish the sales tax, the BJP's urban base did not decline since it was able to retain most of its urban seats. However, in rural areas it lost because the party failed to attract new voters from among the backward castes who, in all probability, decided to distance themselves from the BJP's upper caste domination. The results are reflected in the eastern and the Oudh regions of the state, which gave 107 of the 199 seats to SP-BSP as opposed to only sixty-eight for the BJP.

In brief, the results of the November 1993 elections, which are being interpreted as "secular victory" or as a "defeat of communalism," shook the confidence of the BJP leadership. Even though the party's popular support base seems to be intact (it has increased its vote share in U.P., Delhi, and Madhya Pradesh and lost marginally in Rajasthan), its capacity to win seats declined. In most cases, it is the consolidation of backward castes and the *dalits* who, by joining hands with the Muslims, tilted the balance against the BJP.

An aggregate analysis of votes polled by parties in all the five states (U.P., M.P., Himachal Pradesh, Rajasthan, and Delhi) shows that the BJP secured 36.2 percent as against 26.2 percent, 9.1 percent, and 16.6 percent by the Congress, Janata Dal, and SP-BSP respectively.

The BJP leadership has offered various explanations for the setbacks it suffered in the November 1993 state elections.[23] While some of these explanations may be partly valid, one cannot overlook the less than satisfactory performance of the BJP governments in the four states as one of the main causes of its failure to recapture power in U.P., Madhya Pradesh, and Himachal Pradesh. Although the promise to construct the Ram temple in Ayodhya might have been a motive for many Hindu faithful to vote for the party in the previous elections, the voters also expected the BJP to revitalize the administration, to remove corruption in public life, and to undertake development projects to promote their welfare. People expected the BJP governments to deliver more than had the Janata Dal or the Congress (I) governments during their terms of office. However, the BJP governments failed to meet popular expectations; people found that they were no better than the Congress (I) governments.

While the Kalyan Singh government in U.P. took half-hearted steps to improve law and order in the state, it failed to prevent the demolition of the Babri mosque. It is known that the BJP government had given firm assurance to the Supreme Court and to the National Integration Council that no damage would be done to the Babri mosque. The government was duty-bound to protect the property rights of a religious minority, whatever the nature of the dispute might have been. The Singh government failed to carry out these responsibilities.

The basic duty of a government is to enforce law and to maintain order. The BJP leadership in U.P. was aware of the demoralization of the civil bureaucracy and the continuous politicization of the law enforcement agencies under the previous regimes. However, directly or indirectly, by condoning the actions of Hindu militants, it failed to enforce the law and maintain public order and thus contributed further to the decay of political institutions. It was so preoccupied with the temple issue that it did not pay much attention to the economic development of the state.

The BJP government in Madhya Pradesh made concerted efforts to bring about radical transformation in the educational and cultural policies of the state. Not only did it grant autonomy to various RSS-backed schools, but it recruited hundreds of RSS members into the education, culture, and public relations departments of the state. In its zeal to implement the RSS cultural policies it neglected the economic development of the backward castes and the tribal populations of the state. Furthermore, the BJP government, like the previous Congress (I) governments of the state, also was constantly plagued by infighting, which did not help in improving the image of the party in the eyes of the voters.

Shanta Kumar, as the chief minister of Himachal Pradesh, enjoyed a clean image; however, his government alienated two important and powerful segments of the state population, namely the civil servants and the apple growers. While the BJP government successfully crushed the state employees' strike, it also withdrew state subsidies to the apple growers, leading to the massive rejection of the BJP at the polls by these powerful groups. It was only Bhairon Singh Shekhawat in Rajasthan who, while withstanding the pressure of the RSS and following a pragmatic approach, gave a credible performance. As a result, the BJP under his leadership was returned as the largest party in the Rajasthan legislature, and he was able to form a government with the support of the independents.

By losing power in three states of north India, especially in U.P. and Madya Pradesh, and by the poor performance of its governments, the BJP lost an opportunity to prove itself as an effective alternative to the Congress (I) or the other centrist parties.

Notes

1. See Varsha Banyal, "Congress (I)—BJP Head-on Clash Likely: Himachal," *The Economic Times*, May 10, 1982, p. 5.

2. Prem Kumar, "Haryana Prospects: Congress (I) Fights Back to the Wall," *The Statesman*, May 11, 1982, p. 4.

3. *Indian Express*, May 9, 1982, p. 3.

4. *The Statesman*, February 14, 1983, p. 1.

5. Sukumar Dutta, "The Latest Election Results Hold the Same Old Lessons," *Amrit Bazar Patrika,* February 15, 1983, p. 5.

6. Harpal Singh Bedi, "PM Takes Away BJP Votes," *The Telegraph*, June 13, 1983, p. 5.

7. See reports on the Sonepat Lok Sabha bye-election where the BJP supporters were found to be supporting the Congress (I) instead of the BJP leadership, which joined hands with Charan Singh's Lok Dal. *Times of India*, December 25, 1983, p. 3.

8. *Indian Express*, December 2, 1984, p. 1.

9. *The Telegraph*, November 19, 1984, p. 3.

10. *The Statesman*, November 17, 1984, p. 2.

11. *The Statesman*, January 20, 1984, p. 2.

12. *Times of India*, December 9, 1984, p. 4.

13. *Indian Express*, November 17, 1984, p. 4.

14. See also Walker K. Andersen and Shridhar D. Damle, *The Brotherhood in Saffron: The Rastriya Swayamsevak Sangh and Hindu Revivalism* (New Delhi: Vistaar Publications, 1987), pp. 234-35.

15. *Indian Express*, January 5, 1989, p. 1.

16. Praful Bidwai, "CPM's Electoral Calculus: Opposition Unity at any Cost," *Times of India*, October 27, 1989, p. 6.

17. Surjit S. Bhalla, "Lok Sabha and Assembly Polls: The Real Winner is the BJP," *Indian Express*, March 7, 1990, p. 6.

18. In order to deny a chance to Chandra Shekhar to contest for the post, the V.P. Singh faction proposed Devi Lal, who was unanimously elected. According to the game plan, Lal declined, expressing his inability, and proposed V.P. Singh's name for the prime ministership.

19. *Indian Express*, April 15, 1991, p. 1.

20. *Indian Express*, April 20, 1991, p. 1.

21. U.P. has eighty-five Lok Sabha and 425 Vidhan Sabha seats. Elections were completed in all except the Meerut Lok Sabha seat and the five Vidhan Sabha seats falling in it.

22. For details see V.B. Singh, *Political Fragmentation and the Electoral Process: 1991 Elections in Uttar Pradesh* (Delhi: Ajanta Books International, 1992), Chapter V.

23. See various articles in *Organiser*, December 12, 1993 and December 19, 1993.

7

Conclusion: Summary, Assessments, and Prospects

The Changing Nature of the Ideology of Nationalism and Political Parties

Ideologies are revised and changed. The ideology of nationalism is no exception. The recent emphasis on Hindu national identity has been described as an ideology of Hindu communalism. The basic idea of Hindu nationalism as propagated by the BJP, that the Hindu community and its cultural heritage have an ancient origin, has been challenged as a myth created in the recent past. It has been charged that the "Hindu communal ideology which [claims] legitimacy from the past, namely, that there has always been a well-defined and historically evolved religion which we now call Hinduism and equally clearly defined Hindu community,"[1] has no historic validity. Hindus, unlike Muslims, Christians, and Jews, do not have a single book which contains divine knowledge. There is no single prophet, and there is no single unified religious authority embodied in a church. Hindus are divided into several sects, each with its own book, prophets, saints, and traditions. There is no homogeneous Hindu society, since the caste system has created deep social cleavages. It is impossible to unite Hindus on a religious or cultural basis, let alone to create a sense of national identity among them.

It is possible to turn this argument around and note that not long ago it was argued that there was no such thing as an Indian nation. It was frequently asserted that Indian nationalism was a creation of a few Western-educated Indians. It had no real foundation since Indian society was divided into racial, ethnic, linguistic, and religious groups. India was and still is looked upon by many as a loose conglomerate of nations and races. Indian nationalism is also of recent origin.

Historians agree, however, that starting in the nineteenth century, with the improved means of communication and the diffusion of the Western concept of nationalism following the introduction of the Western system of education, Indian elites started the process of invention and reinterpretation of Indian history and traditions.

The process of "inventing" traditions means generally "a set of practices, normally governed by overtly or tacitly accepted rules and of a ritual or symbolic nature, which seek to inculcate certain values and norms of behavior by repetition, which automatically implies continuity with the past."[2] Some invented traditions can be supported by history while others cannot; there may be only a mythical basis. Invention or creation and rediscovery of myth is a part of the nation-building process. As the pace of social change increases, so does the frequency of reinterpretation or invention of traditions, since the process helps reduce the chaos that often accompanies rapid social change.

According to Eric Hobsbawm, since the industrial revolution the invented traditions belong to "three overlapping types: (a) those establishing or symbolizing social cohesion or the membership of groups, real or artificial communities, (b) those establishing or legitimizing institutions, status, or relations of authority, and (c) those whose main purpose was socialization, the inculcation of beliefs, value systems, and conventions of behavior."[3] It is invented traditions which underlie the ideology of modern nationalism. Ideologies of nationalism in India are no exception to this rule.

As stated earlier, Hindu nationalism was closely related to the Hindu cultural revival movement, which invented the Golden Age, tracing its existence back to the Vedic period. Cultural revival and nationalism resulted from the elites' dissatisfaction with the conditions existing within the society. They sought to create a sense of cohesion within a society which was fragmented and lacked a sense of purpose. Internalization of Western values had created a crisis of identity, and they turned to Sanskritic traditions to forge a sense of national identity. They also sought to enhance the status of the community. Historical evidence shows that "emergence of nationalism was related to preoccupation with status."[4] Thus self-assertion, acculturation, and nationalism became intertwined.

Hindu writers and intellectuals idealized ancient Hindu culture and invented various traditions to mobilize Hindus. Bengali nationalists, like writer Bankimchandra Chattopadhyaya, created Hindu heroes and Muslim villains and wrote songs using Hindu symbolism to forge a sense of Hindu national identity. Bal Gangadhar Tilak's use of the Ganapati festival in Maharashtra was another example of the use of traditional religious symbols to mobilize the Hindus in the cause of Hindu nationalism. Whether Hindus were a real or an invented community, the creation of these literary heroes, political interpretation of religious traditions, and use of Hindu religious symbols were meant to create a pan-Indian Hindu identity. Muslims were not only excluded but also completely alienated from this early version of national identity.

In contrast to the traditions inherited from the past which were more precise and socially binding for the various sections of Hindu society, the newly invented traditions of Hindu nationalism were generally vague and ill defined. However, they were frequently used to socialize the new generations of young Hindus, to inculcate new beliefs, values, and norms of behavior—to create a universalistic spirit of Hinduism. Nationalism is often described as an expression of sentiment; it is basically a psychological predisposition conditioned by a common culture. Culture, on the other hand, is a system of ideas, signs, and associations as well as ways of behaving and communicating.[5]

Early leaders of Hindu nationalism were evidently engaged in the task of building an "imagined community." In the words of Benedict Anderson, nationalism is

> imagined as a community because, regardless of the actual inequality and exploitation that may prevail in each, the nation is always conceived as a deep, horizontal comradeship. Ultimately it is this fraternity that makes it possible, over the past two centuries, for so many millions of people, not so much to kill, as willingly to die for such limited imaginings.[6]

According to Anderson, roots of such a commitment to nationalism are found in the culture of the society. Kinship and religion become essential ingredients of such an imagined community.[7]

National identities are founded basically on symbols and on a certain set of ideas which are embedded in the culture of the society. Rituals, which are an integral part of popular Hinduism and its non-elite culture, are used for popular participation, leading to the formation of collective identities. Hindu nationalists, both in the nineteenth century and in contemporary India, have successfully used these rituals to consolidate collective identity. Societies with long historical traditions and rich cultural heritage do not borrow wholesale from external sources. However, reaction against the external cultural values itself is a creative process and as a result, the "new system of values that emerges is necessarily influenced by the one to which it is a reaction."[8] India's westernized Hindu elites, however, do not seem to have much tolerance for the use of these religious symbols and rituals.

From the start India's nationalist elites, who were predominantly Hindus, according to Ashis Nandy became divided into two groups: "the modernists and the restorationists. Both were defensive about their Indianness, but each chose to cope with their anxieties in a distinctive way. The former sought national salvation in total Westernization, the latter in revivalism."[9] In their style the modernists embodied a mixture of Brahminism and English utilitarianism. They also represented the tolerant, absorptive, and eclectic nature of Hinduism. The revivalists' style "gave salience to the Kshatriya identification and world image, and deemphasized the syncretic Upanishadic imageries which had till then dominated the political idioms."[10] Bankimchandra Chattopadhyaya, Swami Dayananda Sarswati, Swami Vivekanada, Aurobindo Ghosh, Bal Gangadhar Tilak, Lala Lajpat Rai, and others represented a militant version of Hinduism which sought to reassert the Hindu cultural and national identity.

In both the pre- and post-independence periods these two versions of nationalism, one representing tolerant and eclectic and other militant and revivalist Hinduism, coexisted. While Gandhi and Nehru recognized the composite nature of Indian culture and basically projected the form of Hindu culture which is liberal, eclectic, and absorptive, they differed in their perceptions of the nature of the Indian state and the role of religion in Indian society.

Gandhi was a devout Hindu who believed in religious tolerance, holding that all religions contain eternal truth. Deeply influenced by the devotional traditions of Vaishnavism and popular Hinduism, Gandhi believed that Indian politics had the moral capacity to sort out relations between different communities living in the society. He propagated the inculcation of ethical values based upon religions into politics and the creation of a decentralized polity with autonomy for different cultural communities existing within India. As noted in the first chapter, however, it was the Nehruvian concept of a centralized socialist state based upon the European version of nationalism which became the dominant political ideology. This emphasized separating religion from politics and creating a political system legitimatized on a rational-secular basis.

There are various ways to explain the recent rise and reassertion of militant Hindu nationalism as represented by the Bharatiya Janata Party at the center stage of Indian politics.

It has been argued that basically there is little difference between the versions of nationalism espoused by the Congress and the Bharatiya Janata Party, except that one represents tolerant and eclectic and the other militant and aggressive Hinduism. According to Nandy and Jain, both the Indian and the Hindu nationalists, represented by the Congress and the BJP, respectively, are committed to the idea of a centralized nation-state based upon the European version of nationalism.[11] Both groups promote the concept of a nation-state under which the numerical majority would impose its will on the minorities and would refuse to concede even the legitimate demands of the minorities, whether linguistic or cultural. According to this group, both the so-called centrist political parties, like the Congress and the Janata Dal, and the militants, led by the Bharatiya Janata Party, believe in maintaining the territorial integrity of the country and are willing to use state power to suppress insurgencies waged by religious or ethnic minorities. A democratic polity, with an open and free society, is only an instrument to achieve national glory.[12]

Both versions of nationalism represent majoritarian secularism. And for the majoritarian secularists "there exist no hard and fast principles of secularism, or, for that matter, anti-secularism. Their secularism is shaped by political expediency, by elections, by leadership struggles and by social conflicts at hand. At some moments they might espouse secular values as the cure for conflict, while at others, they might hold that religion itself is secular and that tradition is in tune with the actual spirit of Indianness."[13] As a result, the Congress party did not need to adopt an openly pro-Hindu stance, since it was self-evident to the members of the majority community.

Thus, from among the centrist parties, the Congress (I)'s monopolistic claim to secularism, if not completely baseless, is at least doubtful. Even though the Congress claimed to be an organization representing all Indians, it was overwhelmingly dominated by Hindus. Hindus supported the organization since they believed that the Congress could protect their interests better than such organizations as the Hindu Mahasabha or the Jana Sangh. Such Congress leaders and freedom fighters as Vallabhbhai Patel, Rajendra Prasad, Purushottamdas Tandon, K.M. Munshi, Govind Ballabh Pant, and several others could easily be called Hindu nationalists. Especially after the creation of Pakistan, both in their orientations and attitudes, they turned pro-Hindu.

Following their arguments one can assert that the Congress (I)'s record in dealing with the minorities and meeting the cultural-nationalist aspirations of Hindus might look slightly less aggressive than that of the right wing of the BJP. It is the Congress (I)'s functionaries who have been implicated in the massacre of more than 3,000 innocent Sikhs after the 1984 assassination of Indira Gandhi by her Sikh bodyguards to "teach them a lesson." Most of them have yet to be brought to trial despite the repeated demands made by the aggrieved Sikhs and civil libertarian groups.

Furthermore, indications are that more anti-Muslim riots have been engineered in the Congress (I)-ruled states than in the states ruled by the opposition parties. For instance, during the twenty months of Congress (I) chief minister V.P. Singh's rule in U.P. (1980-1982) there were as many as ten Hindu-Muslim riots resulting in the loss of around 200 Muslim lives, whereas during the fourteen months Kalyan Singh led the BJP's rule there was only one riot, in which twenty-eight Muslims lost their lives. The monthly average of Muslims killed under four chief ministers of U.P., namely V.P. Singh (Congress I), N.D. Tiwari (Congress I), Mulayam Singh Yadav (Janata Dal/Samajwadi Party) and Kalyan Singh (BJP) was the lowest during the BJP rule.[14] Despite its claim to be committed to secularism and its recent denunciation of the parties organized on the basis of religion, it is the Congress (I) which has frequently entered into electoral and ministerial alliances with religious parties like the Muslim League and the Sikh Akali Dal.

Furthermore, it was the Congress governments in U.P. and Bihar which adopted and promoted Hindi as the language of administration and instruction and denied Urdu, a language identified mostly with the Muslims, the status of second language in these two states. It was only before the 1989 elections that the Congress (I)-led U.P. government officially recognized Urdu as the second language of the state, in order to win Muslim votes.

In addition, the serialization of Tulasidas' version of the *Ramayana* on Indian television during Rajiv Gandhi's rule provided unprecedented support for an emotional upsurge of Hindu pride. Whether the Rajiv government intended it or not, it was a skillful use of modern media to create Hindu cultural consciousness on a pan-India basis and gave Hindus a new sense of cohesion. Subsequent serialization of the *Mahabharat*, another Hindu epic, and *Chanakya*, the story of the ancient Hindu emperor Chandra Gupta's minister, though not as popular as the *Ramayana*, also aided Hindu solidarity.

The Congress (I) gave Muslims only token representation in the national or the state governments and made no significant efforts to improve their economic or educational condition. According to B. Sen Gupta, while in the past the Congress sponsored the largest number of Muslim candidates for Parliament, it was mostly in areas where they did not have any chance of winning. Muslim interests in Parliament or in government were not protected by the Congress (I) Muslim members of Parliament; rather it was the Hindu M.P.s of the Left parties who came to their aid.[15] Asghar Ali Engineer was not off the mark when he wrote that "the politics of power reduced the Muslims to mere vote-bank. No political party, neither the

Congress nor the Janata Dal, took any concrete measures to uplift them educationally and economically."[16]

According to this view, after Nehru's death India practically turned into a Hindu *rashtra,* and there is no basic difference in the nationalist ideology espoused by the Congress (I) and the BJP. The two political parties represent the power struggle between the two groups of Hindu elites, one westernized and anglicized upper class Hindus looking more towards the West for cultural inspiration and the other vernacular-speaking Hindus with lower middle class origins, rooted in the culture of the country.[17] Both use different symbols and slogans, but basically they represent the two different traditions of nationalism which originated in the nineteenth century.

In the militant Hindu version of nationalism, all religions such as Buddhism, Jainism, and Sikhism originating in India are considered part of Hindu cultural traditions. All these religions share the concept of reincarnation, a cyclical rather than linear progression of time, the concept of *karma,* and obligations based on *dharma.* Indian nationalism as represented by the more moderate Hindus in the Congress party, on the other hand, holds that Hinduism is part of Indian civilization and all other religions in India, including Islam and Christianity, despite originating outside of India, have been deeply influenced by Hinduism.

However, even though both these arguments have a degree of validity, it would be unrealistic to equate the Congress with the BJP in its attitudes towards the minorities, especially the Muslims. Whatever the flaws of the Nehruvian model, the Congress did not propound religious intolerance, which Hindu nationalism does. Extremists among the Hindu nationalists show little tolerance for the dissidents even within their own ranks. It was the Congress leadership which adopted a basically secular Constitution, recognizing the right of minorities to practice and preserve their cultural heritage. Even the contemporary Congress leadership does not repudiate the pluralistic nature of Indian society, nor has it ever denied the composite nature of Indian culture. It refuses to use Hinduism as the sole criterion of Indian nationalism. In public rhetoric it still proclaims its faith in the Hindu belief upheld by Gandhi that all religions contain truth.

Such an assertion, however, may not conform to the fundamental teachings of Islam and Christianity, the two religions born outside of India, which believe that only their way is the true way to discover the divine. Especially with the recent rise of Islamic fundamentalism inside and outside India, the Islamic creed, in the ultimate analysis, would reject both the Nehruvian concept of secularism and the Gandhian belief of equality of all religions. The Islamic view of their scripture, that "the very words of the Koran are 'uncreated,' literal dictation of the eternal thoughts of God and not subject to modification by translation or interpretation,"[18] does not conform with either Nehru's secularism or Gandhi's religious pluralism. It is this paradox which helps the Hindu nationalists challenge the secularists' version of Indian nationalism.

The rise of the BJP as an alternative to the Congress and the reassertion of militant Hindu nationalism is a complex phenomenon. It can not be explained only by a class-based interpretation[19] or as the last-ditch efforts by the upper caste Hindus to protect their interests from aggressive demands made by the politically mobilized lower caste.[20]

The proponents of the Nehruvian nationalism tended to ignore, if not reject, the religious and cultural content of Hinduism as the mainspring of Indian civilization, placing undue emphasis on the contributions of Islam, Christianity, and the West to Indian civilization. Some have argued that despite the contributions of these non-Hindu sources to Indian civilization, the essence of Indian culture is determined by Hinduism. K. M. Pannikar, a noted historian, observed that "In essence . . . the history of Indian effort towards the building up and maintenance of a specially Indian civilization has to be the history of the Hindu mind and its achievements."[21] Since the Nehruvian concept of Indian nationalism in recent years became a kind of empty vessel, the BJP and Hindu nationalists returned to the revivalist traditions developed in the nineteenth century. Employing the manipulative process of reinterpretation of the traditions of Ramrajya and strategic use of the myth of the Ramjanambhoomi, they have been successful in exposing the softness of the ideology of nationalism developed by westernized Indians.

They claim that acceptance and adoption of Hindu culture does not require giving up Islam or any other faith. D. B. Thengdi, an ideologue of Hindu nationalism, stresses that "There is no incompatibility between Hindu national culture and the individual faith of Muslims. Our culture welcomes all religions, all prophets. Again, the Indian Muslims are not aliens ethnically. They are the flesh of our flesh and the blood of our blood."[22] They believe that past history provides enough evidence that even the aliens became acculturated and assimilated into Hindu India. This version of nationalism, based upon the reinterpretation of Hindu traditions and culture, intends to continue socializing the minorities in the dominant culture, leading to their ultimate assimilation in the national mainstream. The contemporary cultural and political crisis in India caused by the reassertion of Islamic fundamentalism, the BJP and the Hindu nationalists claim, demonstrates the stark failure of the westernized ideology of nationalism.

Some of the causes for the rise of BJP and the revival of Hindu nationalism may be found in the failure of many of the policies of the Congress, in the degeneration of the Congress system itself, and in the consequent decay of the Indian state.

Decline of Idealism within the Congress

The loss of vision by the Congress party and the domination of its organization by powerful personalities turned many of the members of this great party into weak followers dependent on their leaders for winning elections and capturing political power. The organization abandoned many of its ideals and goals. Ideologies might be utopian, but they set up certain ideals and high goals, which have emotional appeal. Leaders of great parties and movements either set examples by their conduct or offer great and innovative ideas to lead. It was the force of Gandhi's personality and the example of his high moral conduct as well as the force of Nehru's ideas and vision which provided the ideology and leadership to the Congress party in the nation-building process.

According to Swami Vivekananda, "the basis of all systems, social or political, rests upon the goodness of man. No nation is great or good because Parliament enacts this or that, but because its men are great and good."[23] An individual's conduct in politics, it was stressed, should be based upon sound ethical principles. Although not *all* government leaders in the post-independence period adhered to these principles in public life, it was expected that politics was not simply the pursuit of political power to achieve personal ends but was to be directed towards the common good. When this failed to happen, the loss of idealism became pervasive at the grassroots level. District and state Congress party workers became deeply engrossed in the pursuit of their kinship or client-oriented interests.

The subsequent domination of the party by Indira Gandhi and her centralized control over the party stifled both independent party leadership and new and innovative ideas. Amoral pursuit of political power became the norm. Sanjay and Rajiv Gandhi, who exercised political power as the leaders of the Congress party, whether on a constitutional or extra-constitutional basis, had no roots in the culture of the society nor any grounding in Hinduism or in Islam. They were men without vision and commitments. They lacked even broad policy perspectives rooted in the culture of the country. The practice of manipulative politics within both the party and the government became common.[24]

Corruption and Criminalization of Politics

Rajmohan Gandhi, a grandson of Mahatma Gandhi, observed in 1984 that politics in India was no longer a calling or a commitment. Instead it could be seen "as a trade or industry in which men are purchased, repackaged and sold and which hires public relations men and media managers for the purpose, or an investment with large risks and vast profits."[25] He called upon the opposition leaders, especially Chandra Shekhar, to provide leadership for the reconstruction of Indian society. Because "it is India's habit to take its ethics from the ruler's throne, the political platform has also served as the pulpit or the reformer's perch."[26]

It was V.P. Singh who, in 1989, talked about value-based politics. Shekhar joined his Janata Dal, though reluctantly, since he did not have any other option. The subsequent amoral political behavior of Singh, Devilal, Shekhar, and Rajiv Gandhi caused widespread disillusionment in India's articulate middle class and intellectual establishment. Politics had earlier been termed by Rajmohan Gandhi a disease which was characterized "by the use of power to perpetuate power, married with the use of power to make money, intertwined with the use of money to gain power."[27] This was perhaps the most apt description of the degeneration of the secularist politics practiced by Rajiv Gandhi, Shekhar, Devilal, and other leaders of the Congress and the Janata Dal. They showed complete disregard for probity in political behavior.[28]

The development of a nexus between criminals, politicians, and political parties led the *Economist* to comment on the 1991 electoral contest that "Indian voters now believe that virtually all politicians are crooks. They may take the view that the Gandhi mafia can provide the stability that small-time crooks cannot."[29] U.P. and Bihar, the two north Indian states, rank at the top in percentage of members of the legislative bodies with criminal records. According to one estimate, whereas in 1984 the U.P. legislative body had only seven percent of its members with criminal records, in 1990 their number went up to thirty percent.[30] In fact, no political party in U.P. can claim that it shelters no criminal.[31] Such a situation is not confined to Bihar and U.P. alone; no state legislative body in India can claim to be completely free from criminal elements within its ranks.

At the time of elections politicians hire *goondas*—hoodlums—to mobilize the voters and to capture voting booths. The criminalization of politics has demoralized the law enforcement agencies, undermined the authority of the courts, and rendered the civil administration ineffective. According to the *Economist*, "This criminalization of politics gathered momentum in the 1980s, to the disgust of voters. Congress is the greatest culprit, though others are not far behind."[32]

Institutional Decay and Disintegration
of the Ruling Coalition

Organizational decay also led to the disintegration of the broad coalition on which the Congress party was based. The Congress organization was dominated by a coalition of urban middle classes and the land-owning groups of rural India. These two dominant groups were able to bring diverse sectors of Indian society under their leadership. With the establishment of the Nehru-Gandhi family's control over the vast organization, the absence of organizational elections within the party, increased corruption, and criminalization of politics led to the alienation of the urban middle class from the Congress.

Also leading to anomie and disenchantment were the decay and decline of political institutions through the politicization of the bureaucracy and judiciary, disrespect and disregard for the presidency and the Parliament of the country shown by both Rajiv Gandhi and Chandra Shekhar, and the inability of the state governments to perform effectively. Alarmed by the increasing political violence and anarchy in the country, the urban middle class started looking for alternatives to the Congress. In contrast to the Congress and the centrist parties, the BJP and its leadership, with a clean image, became an attractive alternative.

Apprehensions about Territorial Integrity

Hindus also became increasingly apprehensive about the territorial integrity of the country. Alarmed by the rise of a variety of secessionist movements, especially in Punjab and Kashmir, led by Sikh and Muslim fundamentalists, respectively, and supported by Pakistan, many Hindus became skeptical about the wisdom of the post-independence ideology of secular nationalism followed by the Congress and the Indian state.

Benign neglect by both the Congress (I) government and the media of the thousands of Kashmiri pundits who were forced by the Muslim fundamentalists to flee Kashmir Valley, leaving behind their ancestral homes and properties, further alienated the Hindus in north India from the ideology pursued by the Congress. The recent flight of Hindus and Sikhs from Afghanistan, where the Islamic fundamentalists have taken over, confirms their fears that the party and its ideology are inadequate to protect the interests of Hindus. Surrounded by the Islamic world as India is today and with the increasing Muslim fundamentalism within and outside of India, the politically conscious Hindu middle class seems to have developed a siege mentality.

Mobilization of Peripheral Sectors of Indian Society

The electoral process, the ongoing democratization, and the drive to modernize the society have enhanced the political awareness of many disadvantaged and hitherto unmobilized sectors of Indian society. Many tribal people and the *dalits* (the economically and socially depressed sectors of Hindu society), helped by increased media exposure and education, are becoming organized and making demands on the political system. They no longer display the traditional deferential attitudes towards the upper caste/middle class Hindus. And the political system's inability to meet their demands has led to an increase in the anarchy within the society, consequently increasing the anxieties and insecurities of the middle class upper caste Hindus. As a result, they look for a party which at least gives the appearance of being led by austere and puritanical leadership and followed by a disciplined cadre.

It is in the context of these developments that one can understand the rise of a party like the BJP and the reassertion of militant Hindu nationalism. This has also led to sharp divisions among the leaders of political parties, in India's articulate intellectual community and in the general population. Central to the contest for power has become the place of the Muslim minority in Indian politics and the cultural contents of the Indian state where Hindus constitute an overwhelming majority of the population.

Muslim Minority in a Hindu Majority State

Muslims in India are not a pampered minority. Economically, educationally, and socially, most of the Muslims constitute an under-privileged sector of Indian society. Although they form only twelve percent of the population, they are not a small minority, since they account for around 110 million of India's large population.

Over the centuries Hindus and Muslims have coexisted. Their relations have varied from harmony to hostility. Muslims have contributed and are still contributing to the enrichment of Indian literature, art, music, and other aspects of Indian culture. It is hard to imagine an India devoid of Muslim cultural contributions. It is true that Islam, as practiced in India, has been exclusivist as well as syncretic. Rural India, however, has witnessed greater cultural and social interchange between the members of the two communities than urban India.

It was in rural India that a large majority of Muslims lived among a neighborhood populated by respectable Hindu castes and even practiced a kind of quasi-caste system closely resembling their Hindu neighbors. However, as Louis Dumont points out, this kind of coexistence failed to produce a "general ideological synthesis"[33] even during the period when Muslims constituted the ruling class. Partial synthesis between the two systems of religion resulted in the creation of new sects among Hindus without their acceptance of monotheism. "On the Muslim side, the orthodoxy, the articulate monotheism of Islam was constantly reaffirmed from two sources: the revealed book upon which the tradition is based, and the contact with the Muslim world outside . . ."[34]

In the pre-partition India the urbane and educated Muslims were afraid of the Hindu *raj* while in rural India the Muslims enjoyed a sense of security which was based upon a compromise between the two communities. This compromise, though in existence for centuries, did not result in consensus on the fundamental values on which the societies are built. However, according to Dumont, partition "put an end to their mutual compromise,"[35] increasing the insecurity among Muslims even in rural India.

The ideology of Indian nationalism, as promoted by the secularist and liberal elites of India, was an effort to create a new value system. Such an ideology, they believed, Hindus and Muslims would be able to share. The core of this ideology, as noted earlier, was an idealized version of a European liberal state which was supposed to be neutral in religious affairs. However, in the context of Indian society the state was also expected to play an activist role facilitating the modernization of a traditional society through social reforms. In other words, the state was expected to enact a body of laws providing equal rights for its citizens irrespective of their creed, caste, and gender.

Hindu nationalists question whether the Muslims, with the change of the power equation between the members of the two communities, can live in a Hindu-majority state. Can the minority community understand the complexity as well as the richness of the culture of the majority community?

Can they ever accept the idea of a liberal state where social and political issues would be discussed on a rational basis? Can they place the national interests of India above Islamic interests?

Hindu nationalists stress that the ideology of Indian nationalism, based upon the British concept of liberal democracy and Fabian socialism, might or might not have been suitable for Hindus, but it could not have been acceptable to Muslims. According to this view, "the concept of nationalism . . . is fundamentally alien to Islam, emphasizing as it does loyalty to the rival principle of international *ummah*."[36] While criticizing the western concept of the legitimacy of the political authority as developed by the liberal-rationalist school, G. Hossein Razi asserts that it is not applicable to societies based upon Islam since "Islam created a religion and a state at the same time. Its constitutional theory stands in sharp contrast to that of Christianity, which is represented by the doctrine of two swords."[37]

Unlike Christianity, Islam does not make a separation between spiritual and temporal affairs. Accordingly, it is asserted that the behavior of Indian Muslim leaders shows that they tend to play the Islamic card while dealing with the Indian state. The Indian state can pursue secular policies so long as they do not affect Islam and the nature and the structure of the Muslim community in India based on its distinct traditions and cultural heritage.

In other words, Muslims feel they should not be subjected to the state's authority to promote modernization, secularization, and the scientific spirit. In this way the contemporary Muslim leadership in India tends to reject one of the basic elements of the ideology of Indian nationalism.

Even Nehru, despite his awareness of Islam's contribution to Indian culture, his great sympathy for the Muslims, and his desire to bring them into the mainstream of Indian national life, was concerned about their resistance to accepting ancient Indian cultural traditions as part of their cultural heritage. For instance, in his address to the students of Aligarh Muslim University on January 24, 1948, he expressed his pride in India's ancient heritage and its remarkable ability to absorb invigorating ideas coming from other cultures, and then he asked his Muslim audience:

> How do you feel about the past? Do you feel that you also share it and [are] inheritors of it and, therefore, proud of something that belongs to you as much as to me? Or do you feel alien to it and pass it by without understanding it or feeling that we are the trustees and inheritors of this vast treasure? . . . You are Muslims and I am a Hindu. We may adhere to different religious faiths or even to none; but that does not take away from that cultural inheritance that is yours as much as it is mine.[38]

In the same spirit Abid Hussain, a Muslim intellectual, had pleaded with his co-religionists to end their isolation in the national life by making efforts to have an understanding with the Hindus, who constitute the majority community. They should identify themselves with the Indian past "including the cultural life of Hindus—their own,"[39] thereby "bringing themselves in harmony with the soul of India."[40] Evidently Indian Muslims have not yet developed such an understanding of the culture and traditions of Hindus. Their inability to come to terms with the pre-Islamic heritage of India, according to Hindu nationalists, jeopardizes Indian nationhood.

There is a sense of alarm among many Hindu intellectuals that "Muslims, on the whole, have remained frozen in their attitude, as illustrated by their passionate adherence to the Muslim Personal Law; they owe it to themselves to explain why this remains the case after more than four decades of life under secular political order . . ."[41] Muslims in India, in other words, need to do serious introspection before blaming the Hindu nationalists for propagating bigotry.

The ban on Salman Rushdie's *The Satanic Verses* is given as another case in point. It has been pointed out that if the book had not been banned "by the [Indian] Government when the demand came from the Muslim leaders it would have led to a serious situation and even rioting and bloodletting."[42] More disturbing, however, was the fact that in 1992 Professor Mashirul Hasan of Jamaia Millia, the well known Muslim nationalist institution, commented in an interview that even though he personally disapproved of Rushdie's book, as a matter of principle no book should be banned in a liberal and free society. Muslim students of the institution not only protested his remarks and demanded his resignation but also resorted to violence.[43] No prominent leader of the Muslim religious establishment in India condemned the students' action.

Freedom of intellectual debate and discussion are the essence of academic life, especially in a liberal state. This incident "sent a chill down the spine of many liberals belonging to the majority community, who now fear that they too can come under pressure from the fundamentalist elements."[44] Whether Hindus are more tolerant of dissent or not, and whether such violence was incited by Muslim politicians or not, the incident is cited as an example of Muslims' intolerance of dissent.

Although Nehru dealt harshly with Hindu bigots and vehemently criticized such organizations as the Hindu Maha Sabha and the Jana Sangh, he recognized the contradictions between the tolerant traditions of Hinduism and the inflexibility of Muslim orthodoxy. He observed that "the philosophy and the world outlook of the old Hindus was amazingly tolerant . . . The Muslims had to face a new problem, namely how to live with others as equals . . . They came into conflict with Christendom and through hundreds of years, the problem was never solved. In India slowly a synthesis developed. But before it could be completed other influences came into play."[45]

According to the proponents of Hindu nationalism, like Girilal Jain, the conflict between Islam and Christianity was never resolved despite the fact that both have monotheistic belief systems. Similarly, the conflict between Islam and Hinduism, before and after the arrival of the British in India, also remained unresolved.

Nehru might have been sensitive to the Muslims' resistance to modernization and acceptance of a rational and secular way of life. Nehru was so deeply influenced by the Soviet experience and liberalism of Europe, however, that ignoring his own reservations, he held on to the belief that Muslims would ultimately respond positively to the modernization process where the social and political issues could be handled on a rational basis. However, according to Girilal Jain and others, it is evident from the recent behavior of the Muslims that even after four decades of independence "Muslims have not come out of their ghetto psychology."[46] In other words, they have not yet accepted the ideology on which the Indian state is based.

Indian Muslims, especially their leaders, rallied in support of Saddam Hussein during the Persian Gulf war. It was observed that "all across the country, the cry of 'Jai Saddam' was competing with that of Jai Sri Ram."[47] This demonstration of Indian Muslims' solidarity with their co-religionists provided further evidence for the politically conscious Hindus that their primary loyalties lay with the Islamic world.

Inflexible and Orthodox Muslim Leadership

Both the Congress (I) leadership and the centrist parties have played into the hands of the BJP and the Hindu nationalists when instead of encouraging the moderate and enlightened Muslim leaders, they dealt with inflexible and orthodox leaders of the Muslim community. The rigid Muslim politicians, led by Sultan Salahuddin Owaisi, Shahabuddin and Ibrahim Sulaiman Sait, and orthodox clergy, led by Shahi Imam of Delhi, Maulana Abul Hasan Ali Nadvi (Ali Mian), as well as many entrenched clergy members, were unwilling to compromise on the emotionally charged issue of Ramjanambhoomi and even opposed the singing of "Vande

Mataram," a patriotic song sung widely during the independence movement.

The song was opposed on the grounds that it smacked of idolatry. Mohan Dharia, a former Congress member of Parliament and a central minister, observed that "those who are opposing Vande Mataram should not forget that they are supporting the fundamentalism from the other side at their own cost and also at the cost of their secular philosophy and national integration."[48] The Orthodox Muslim leaders, including the orthodox clergy, according to this view, have never repudiated the theory on which Pakistan was created. As a whole, the Muslim community stayed away from the independence movement. It would have helped in national reconciliation, the Hindu nationalists believe, if the Muslim leadership had denounced the basis on which Pakistan was created.[49]

The Muslim clergy's opposition to family planning and abolishing polygamy, as well as their insistence on rebuilding the Babri mosque on the same spot and the basic principle enshrined in the Constitution, are frequently cited as examples of obscurantist attitudes. The Muslim clergy draws its spiritual and cultural inspiration from the Islamic world. According to Iqbal Ansari, Hindus have been frequently termed *kafirs*, which is a socially and spiritually derogatory term. Since the *Koran* exhorts Muslims to fight *kafirs* to the finish until they submit to God's will, many Hindus believe that they are the targets of Islamic fundamentalism. Ansari believes that Muslim clergy, by presenting a glorified vision of past Islamic history, has bred arrogance and a false sense of pride among their co-religionists.[50] Given these conditions, in the words of Rajni Kothari, the rise of militant Hindu nationalism may be attributed to the "thoroughly mindless fanaticism of segments of Muslim leadership."[51]

V.P. Singh solicited help from Shahi Imam, whom Inder Malhotra described as "an unreconstituted bigot,"[52] in the 1991 electoral contest by seeking from him an edict asking Muslims to vote for the Janata Dal. This and Singh's subsequent unabashed support for the Jamia Milia Islamia students' demand for Mushirul Hasan's resignation were cited by Hindu nationalists as examples of pandering to the Muslim orthodoxy and fundamentalism.[53] Mohan Dharia was not off the mark when he said that "all parties, including Congress, Janata, Janata Dal or the Communists, on some occasion or other have conveniently given strength to the communal forces from this or that side to secure or to retain power."[54]

For a liberal there is no contradiction in being a Muslim and an Indian nationalist simultaneously. But the paradox of Indian politics is that liberal and modernist Muslims do not have any support base among the Muslim masses; they cannot deliver votes. Furthermore, it is the Muslim clergy and orthodox leadership which give the image of being concerned about maintaining the community's distinct cultural and religious identity.

Cultural Contents of the Indian State

Most Hindu nationalists are not opposed to the modernization or the industrialization of Indian society. However, they assert that Nehru's or the Marxist visions of modernization are not rooted in the culture of Indian society. Their concept of a secular state is so alien in its origins that it could not be meaningfully translated into Indian vernaculars. Particularly they undermine and downgrade the religious and cultural traditions of Hindus.

According to them, India's struggle for freedom and modernization was a quest for self-recovery, following the Hindus' military defeats at the hands of Islam and the British. Islamized or westernized Hindus reacted either by self-repudiation or wholesale imitation, surrendering themselves culturally to the conqueror. In fact, the cultural conquest of the country seems to have had a far deeper impact on the Hindus than the military conquest. It is for this reason that self-alienated Hindus, the products of Macaulay's English-medium educational system, not only deny the cultural basis of Hindu nationalism but are ashamed to call themselves Hindus. They dislike the use of Hindu cultural symbols to mobilize Hindus or express their cultural pride. For these self-alienated Hindus, Lord Ram and the issues related to the Ramjanambhoomi, the primary cultural symbols used for mass mobilization of Hindus, appear medieval and irrational.

Gandhi did not suffer from this type of self-alienation. This is why he said that he would "not like to live in an India which had ceased to be Hindu."[55] He was not afraid to idealize Lord Ram. And Ramrajya was Gandhi's version of an ideal polity. According to Hindu nationalists, this does not mean that they cannot borrow from other cultures. However, they believe, "we borrow what we can assimilate and transform in the light of our own *svadharma*. This keeps out bastardization of culture."[56]

Hindu nationalists believe that Nehru's version of secularism leads to the pursuit of amoral politics, and politics devoid of religion-based cultural contents in contemporary India has led to a steady decline in political morality. For Nehru and the Congress leaders the state is a public institution, which has nothing to do with religious or ethical values. It is primarily an agency seeking equitable distribution of material goods and services in the society. In other words, the rationalist ideologies of liberalism and socialism, developed in the context of the historical experience of alien societies, failed to provide substitutes for the norms of individual behavior and social traditions based upon the cultural values of the society which had ensured, in earlier periods, stability and order within the society. Hindu nationalists hold that it is the philosophy of Integral Humanism, developed in the context of Hindu culture and *dharma*, which would restore a sense of individual and social responsibility to the political culture of India. They tend to disagree with the positivist social science view of material progress resulting from industrialization held by westernized Indian political elites. Like the early Hindu nationalists, the philosophy of Integral Humanism tends to look back at the mythical Golden Age to denounce both capitalism and Communism.

There may be a need for reappraisal of the cultural contents of the Indian state, however. In the rhetoric of Hindu nationalists boundaries between India, Hindu religion, and Hindu culture are not clearly demarcated. In fact, for them India becomes identified with both Hindu culture and Hinduism as religion to the exclusion of all others. The efforts of the BJP-run Uttar Pradesh government to change Muslim names of such cities as Allahabad to the Hindu name Prayagraj, Mughal Sarai to Deendayal Nagar, Faizabad to Saket, and Lucknow to Lakshmipur were crude expressions of the cultural fanatacism of Hindu nationalists.[57] Consequently the imposition of this ideology of *Hindutva*, with an emphasis on the allegiance to the majority-dominated cultural values, in a plural and segmented society like India's could have grave consequences for the country's political stability and for the working of its democracy.

To ensure a minority its rightful place within a democratic society, not only does the majority community need to recognize the contributions of the minority to its culture but it also needs to provide constitutional safeguards for the preservation of its cultural identity. Forcible assimilation, the goal of the Hindu nationalists, is neither possible nor desirable.

The root cause of Hindu-Muslim tension in contemporary India, according to Hindu nationalists, is a false representation of the Muslim period in Indian history. They contend that under the auspices of the Congress party, Indian historians, deeply influenced by Marxism and European liberalism, concealed the records of atrocities committed on Hindu subjects by their Muslim rulers. Instead of exposing the Muslim rulers' hostility towards pagan Hindus, their forcible conversion to Islam, the destruction of their temples, slaughter of thousands of innocent civilians, and enslavement of their women, these historians "shamelessly rewrite history and conjure up centuries of Hindu-Muslim amity . . ."[58] Instead of suppressing this history, it should be openly discussed and debated by both Hindus and Muslims.

Hindu nationalists believe that the healing and reconciliation process between the two communities can start if the Muslims concede that Hindus suffered at the hands of the Muslim rulers. "By denying the vandalism of the Ghaznis, the Baburs and the Aurangzebs, or seeking to justify it, negationism contributed to an ideological regime based on a pathological disregard for Hindu sentiments."[59] It is this coverup of history by the Marxists and the liberal Hindu historians which prevents the Muslims from understanding the Hindu psyche. This has resulted in the internalization of falsehood and even self deception for Hindus as well as Muslims. A symbolic gesture, such as handing over the site where the Babri mosque stood to Hindus for the construction of the Ramjanambhoomi temple, as suggested by some liberal Muslims,[60] according to Hindu nationalists, could have gone a long way in assuaging the feelings of Hindus. Because of the support that they received from the liberal and secular Hindus, Muslims are unwilling to make even a minor gesture towards accommodation with the Hindus.[61]

Hindu Nationalism and the BJP Versus Indian Nationalism and the Congress (I)

Given the nature of contemporary debate on the ideological basis of the Indian state, the rise of militant Hindu nationalism at the center stage of Indian politics, and the place of the Muslim minority in the future of Indian politics, it becomes imperative to assess the major contenders for power at the national level.

In India's multi-party system, the Bharatiya Janata Party and the Congress (I) have emerged as the two primary contestants for political power at the national level. As noted in the preceding pages, the Congress (I) represents the ideological center and the traditions of Indian nationalism while the BJP, on the other hand, has been the representative of Hindu nationalism and the conservative right of India.

Given the organizational reach and the ideological approach of the two parties, they are most likely to determine the future course of Indian politics. The Janata Dal and the National Front are fragile coalitions of minor parties of different ideological shades but basically falling in the middle, close to the Congress (I). However, without having any mass-based organizational structure and with a limited support base, the Janata Dal and National Front are unlikely to emerge as major players in national politics.

The Samajwadi Janata Party of Mulayam Singh Yadav in U.P. and the Bahujan Samaj Party of Kanshi Ram, having their support base among the backward castes and schedule castes respectively among Hindus, do not have a well-thought-out ideological plank. Also, since both are heavily dependent upon the personalities of the two leaders and lack a stable organizational structure, the long-term survival of both the parties, at least at this stage, is uncertain. Furthermore, the history of coalition governments of various political parties in India in providing political stability is not very encouraging.

Left of center are India's two Communist parties. The Communist parties have regional support bases. Even though Communists in West Bengal and Kerala have been able to consolidate their power base by introducing land reforms and following pro-labor policies, they are unable to face the challenge of Hindu nationalism in the Hindi-speaking states of north India. The BJP has made slight inroads in West Bengal. The Marxists' collaboration with the Muslim League in Kerala is not looked upon favorably by the Hindus in the state.

Furthermore, with the fall of Communism in the former Soviet Union and the disintegration of Yugoslavia into different warring republics on cultural and religious bases, and thus the stark failure of their socialist utopia, Indian Communists are unable to parade their moral superiority or claim that history has been on the side of the working classes. Many of their leaders, being in their late seventies, are no longer in touch with contemporary political realities and are still stuck in ideological rigidities. They have failed to alter substantially their basic stand on economic and political issues. In a recent party congress they conceded the mistakes made in the past and declared they would "Indianize" their approach by adapting Marxism to the traditions and culture of India.

Communists have provided protection to the Muslims in both West Bengal and Kerala, where Muslims constitute 21.5 and 21.3 percent of the population, respectively. In turn the Muslims have voted for the Communist parties. It is, however, in states like U.P. and Bihar, where Muslims constitute 15.5 and fourteen percent of the population respectively, and where the real battle for power is to take place, that the Communists have very little influence.

To face the rising tide of Hindu nationalism even the Communists have started invoking the names of Swami Vivekananda and other Hindu reformers. Given their Marxist interpretation of Indian history and their negative perception of the cultural heritage of Hinduism, however, Communists are unable to offer an alternative ideology of Indian nationalism capable of attracting mass support. Furthermore, their ill-considered

support of the People's Republic of China's brutal suppression of the
democratic movement led by the Chinese students and their subsequent
criticism of Gorbachev's political reforms in the Soviet Union cost them
considerable good will with India's intellectual establishment.

There are a few regional parties like the DMK or AIADMK of Tamil
Nadu, the Akali party of Punjab, and others. They might play a role in the
formation of a coalition government at the national level, if no party is
able to obtain a clear majority. Since 1947, after the withdrawal of the
British from India, the country has been governed by the centrist parties
only, however.

The Congress (I), a broad-based coalition of different interests, classes,
religions, and caste groups, is a highly aggregative party. It has depended
heavily on the votes of minorities and low caste Hindus. With few excep-
tions the Muslims voted for the Congress leaders such as Nehru, Indira
Gandhi, and Rajiv, trusting in their ability to protect their interests.
Despite its flaws, the Congress received support from India's westernized
and vocal intellectual establishment. Given the current split in the Indian
intellectual establishment into secularists and pro-Hindu nationalist groups
and the decline of the Nehruvian consensus on the fundamentals of the
Indian state, the question can be asked: what are the prospects of the
Congress (I) in facing the challenge posed by the Bharatiya Janata Party
and the rising tide of Hindu nationalism?

P. V. Narasimha Rao, the president of the Congress (I) and the prime
minister of the country, made an effort to revitalize the party organization
in 1992 by holding organizational elections after more than twenty years.
However flawed the elections might have been, they showed that the
Congress party is no longer the fiefdom of the Gandhi-Nehru family. The
restoration of the inner party democracy brought to an end the fear and
sycophancy which were so prevalent in the past two decades. Also, even
though the new leadership structure did not terminate the oligarchic
character of the party, it gave considerable freedom to the local and state
leaders to stay in tune with the grass-roots. Lacking the charisma of his
predecessors, Rao also recognized and allowed, though grudgingly, the
existence of various oligarchies within the Congress at both the state and
national levels.

Paradoxically, however, the restoration of the electoral process within
the party also strengthened the power base of these oligarchies, especially
the ones led by two of his rivals, Arjun Singh and Sharad Pawar, both key
members of the top party leadership. Singh has his support base in
Madhya Pradesh, where the BJP ran the state government, and is trying to
extend his support base into other Hindi-speaking states. Pawar comes

from the state of Maharashtra, where the Congress (I) under his leadership is in power although it faces a major challenge from the BJP-Shiv Sena coalition. Rao's support base is in south India, where the Hindu nationalism of the BJP has little or only limited appeal.

The Congress is presently plagued by a power struggle between rival leaders guided by their political ambitions rather than by ideological considerations. There is also difference of opinion regarding the strategy which the party needs to follow in order to face the challenge posed by the BJP.

An overwhelming majority of Indians are Hindus. And in contemporary India, as Dileep Padgaonkar, the editor of *Times of India*, noted, there is drastic change in the mood of the majority population. He observed that "the mood, to describe it bluntly, is that feelings against 'actually existing Islam' run higher among Hindus of all shades of opinion than their revulsion for the shrill rhetoric of the BJP-VHP-RSS combine."[62] During the 1989 elections V.N. Gadgil, the general secretary of the Congress (I), spoke of the need to reorient the party's secularism in light of political reality, and he conceded that "somewhere along the line the Hindu mind is hurt. Somehow we will have to convince the Hindus."[63]

Rao, probably being aware of these political realities, initially followed a policy of consensus, avoided political confrontation, and sought political accommodation with the BJP, the votary of *Hindutva*. Rao was engaged in the drastic reorientation of India's economy and needed time to demonstrate the success of his economic policies. He was also unwilling to destabilize the BJP-run state governments. On the other hand, Arjun Singh and his supporters, while accepting only grudgingly his economic liberalization policies, sought confrontation with the BJP, demanded the dismissal of the four BJP-run state governments, and advocated use of force to protect the Babri mosque.[64] However, after the demolition of the mosque in December 1992 by the Hindu militants, while both factions became engaged in shadow boxing, they failed to present an ideologically coherent and politically practical program with mass appeal. While they dismissed the popularly elected BJP-run state governments and imposed a ban on Hindu militant organizations like the VHP and the RSS, they did little to denounce the communalism practiced by the minority communities. It was observed that "any attempt on the part of the Congress to denounce the communalism of one community without denouncing the others will once again expose the ruling party to the charge that it remains a prisoner of its moribund past."[65]

It is to the credit of Rao that as the prime minister of the country he held elections in Punjab despite the boycott of the Akalis, made a settlement with the Bodos in Assam, got the Panchayati raj Bill through Parliament, and decentralized the political and economic decision-making process.

Nevertheless, whatever his achievements as the prime minister of the country, he has failed to provide an alternate vision of India as the leader of the Congress (I) party.[66] The efforts of the Rao government to impose a legal ban on the use of religion in electoral politics or to prohibit parties organized on the basis of religion from entering the electoral contest show how the Congress (I) has run out of ideas to face the challenge posed by the Hindu nationalists and the BJP. There is little realization that the battle is ideological and can be fought only on ideological and moral levels and not through contrived legal methods.

Its organization being in shambles in the Hindi-speaking states of north India, the Congress (I) seems to have lost the support of both the majority and the minority communities. Presently the Congress leadership is counting on the success of its new economic policies. If they are able to generate jobs, increase productivity, and achieve significant economic growth, its leaders believe that the party will be able to face the challenge posed by the BJP and Hindu nationalism.

However, increased economic growth, a higher pace of industrialization, and even modernization alone, as believed by many liberal and Marxist intellectuals, are not likely to lead to peaceful coexistence between the members of the two communities. Increased competition for scarce jobs and resources between equally qualified members of the two communities is likely to increase further the tension between Hindus and Muslims. Increased economic and educational disparities and unfulfilled expectations could cause unrest, leading to greater political instability and violence.

R. K. Hegde, a former Congressman and now a leader of the Janata Dal, called for the formation of a united front of all secular forces. He observed that "the rise of the BJP has created a new situation and it calls for coming together of all secular forces to combat the BJP. There is hardly any difference in the policies of the Congress, JD and the Communist parties. The difference is one of emphasis and maybe priorities."[67] Such a joint front should recognize the need for a collective leadership, coalition government, and consensus on basic policies. Eventually such a joint front might emerge, but so far there have not been many takers for the proposal. In other words, the centrist parties have yet to come up with a valid political strategy and a new vision of India to counter the appeal of *Hindutva*.

Despite its many drawbacks, it is the Congress (I) alone, representing the traditions of Indian nationalism, which has the potential to meet the challenge of Hindu nationalism and the Bharatiya Janata Party. Rejuvenation of the Congress (I), under more dynamic leadership and with greater democratization within the party than provided by Rao, is a possibility which cannot be discounted. A large majority of Hindus are non-sectarian and they seek political stability. If the Congress (I) leadership pursues a policy of genuine secularism, it may be able to bring back the ideology of Indian nationalism to the center stage of Indian politics. Such an effort would be facilitated by a change in the leadership of the Indian Muslims.

Compared to the Congress (I) and other centrist parties, the Bharatiya Janata Party possesses a very effective organization. However, the BJP also suffers from its many external and internal limitations. Despite a steady increase in the percentage of votes polled by the party, the BJP has not yet been able to build a nationwide support base among the voters. Its primary support base is confined to Hindi-speaking states of north India. It has also been successful in building considerable support in two western states, Gujarat and Maharashtra. However, the BJP's support base is still soft. Even in north Indian states the party has not yet been very successful in converting the members of scheduled castes and socially and economically backward castes among Hindus to its ideology of *Hindutva*. The party seems to have underestimated the extent of the pluralism existing in the Hindu society. A political unification of fragmented Hindu society is not easy.

Evidently the use of religious and emotional issues can bring only short-term political gains. In order to build broad-based support among the voters, the party leadership would have to adjust both its ideology and electoral strategy. Furthermore, despite its gains in the southern state of Karnataka it has not had much success in other southern and northeastern states of India. The BJP still has a long way to go to become a party with nationwide support.

The BJP also has internal limitations. It is not a monolith organization. Along with ideological divisions, the party is plagued by factions based purely on personal political ambitions as well as on caste and class-based divisions. The BJP also faces the problem of maintaining discipline within its own ranks, although such a problem is far less serious in the BJP than in other parties of India. The BJP is likely to come under intense pressure from the Hindu revivalist and lumpen elements represented by such organizations as the VHP and the Bajarang Dal to adopt a belligerent approach on social and religious issues. Exercise of control on the activities of these organizations is essential for the BJP's survival as a responsible political party.

It is hard to predict the future of Hindu nationalism in Indian politics. It appears, however, that it is unlikely to disappear as a major political force in the near future despite the electoral setbacks that the BJP suffered in November 1993.

Notes

1. Romila Thapar, "Imagined Religious Communities? Ancient History and the Modern Search for Hindu Identity," *Modern Asian Studies*, Vol. 23, No. 2 (1989), p. 20.

2. Eric Hobsbawm and Terrence Ranger (eds.), *The Invention of Traditions* (Cambridge, Cambridge University Press, 1983), p. 1.

3. *Ibid.*, p. 9.

4. Liah Greenfeld, *Nationalism: Five Roads to Modernity* (Cambridge, Harvard University Press, 1992), p. 488.

5. Ernest Gellner, *Nations and Nationalism* (Ithaca, Cornell University Press, 1983), p. 7.

6. Benedict Anderson, *Imagined Communities: Reflection on the Origin and Spread of Nationalism* (London, Verso, 1983), p. 7.

7. *Ibid.*

8. Greenfeld, *Nationalism*, p. 16.

9. Ashis Nandy, "The Culture of Indian Politics," *Journal of Asian Studies*, Vol. 30, No. 1 (November, 1970), p. 59.

10. *Ibid.*

11. Ashis Nandy, "Three Propositions," *Seminar*, February 1993, p. 16, and interview with Girilal Jain, March 17, 1992.

12. Ashis Nandy, "Culture of Politics and Politics of Cultures," *Journal of Commonwealth and Comparative Politics*, Vol. 22, No. 3 (November, 1984), p. 277.

13. Prakash Chandra Upadhyaya, "The Politics of Indian Secularism," *Modern Asian Studies*, Vol. 26, No. 4 (1992), p. 826.

14. B.P. Singhal, "Who is Secular," *Organiser*, March 21, 1993, p. 34.

15. Bhabani Sen Gupta, "Ice on Summer Seas," *Economic and Political Weekly*, October 14, 1989, pp. 2285-2288.

16. Asghar Ali Engineer, "Common Civil Code: A Poser," *Hindu: International Edition*, March 20, 1993, p. 9.

17. Interview with Girilal Jain, March 17, 1992.

18. Max L. Stackhouse, "Fundamentalism Around the World," *Christian Century*, August 28-September 4, 1985, p. 770.

19. Gail Omvedt, "Hinduism and Politics," *Economic and Political Weekly*, April 7, 1990, pp. 723 -729.

20. Anil Nauriya, "Indian National Congress: Its Place in Politics," *Economic and Political Weekly*, November 23, 1991, pp. 2675-2682, and Victor S. D'Souza, "Roots of Present Communal Crisis," *Economic and Political Weekly*, May 25, 1991, pp. 1333-1335.

21. Quoted in Subramanian Swamy, *Building a New India: An Agenda for National Renaissance* (New Delhi, UPSPD, 1992), p. 41.

22. *Organiser*, May 23, 1993, p. 14.

23. Quoted in Dennis Dalton, "The Concepts of Politics and Power in Indian Ideological Traditions," in A. Jeyaratnam Wilson and Dennis Dalton (eds.), *The State of South Asia: Problems of National Integration* (London, C. Hunt and Company, 1982), p. 177.

24. Yogendra K. Malik, "Indira Gandhi: Personality, Political Power and Party Politics," in Yogendra K. Malik and Dhirendra K. Vajpeyi (eds.), *India: The Years of Indira Gandhi* (Leiden, E.J. Brill, 1988), pp. 7-21.

25. *India Today*, April 4, 1984, p. 38.

26. *Ibid.*

27. *Ibid.*

28. Inder Malhotra, *India : Trapped in Uncertainty* (New Delhi, UPSPD, 1992), p. 122.

29. Quoted in *Ibid.*, p. 88.

30. *Indian Express: Sunday Magazine*, May 3, 1992, p. 2.

31. *Times of India*, May 10, 1992, p. 14.

32. *Economist*, February 6, 1993, p. 22.

33. Louis Dumont, "Nationalism and Communalism," *Contributions to Indian Sociology*, Vol. 7 (1964), p. 54.

34. *Ibid.*

35. *Ibid.*, p. 56.

36. Girilal Jain, "Secularism and Nehruism," in M.M. Sankdher (ed.), *Secularism in India: Dilemmas and Challenges* (New Delhi, Deep and Deep Publications, 1992), p. 123.

37. G. Hossein Razi, "Legitimacy, Religion, and Nationalism in the Middle East," *American Political Science Review*, 84 (March, 1990), p. 76.

38. Quoted in Girilal Jain, "Secularism," pp. 125-126.

39. R.E. Miller, "Modern Indian Muslim Responses," in Harold G. Coward (ed.), *Modern Indian Responses to Religious Pluralism* (Albany, State University of New York Press, 1987), p. 261.

40. *Ibid.*

41. Girilal Jain, "Secularism," pp. 139-140.

42. Asghar Ali Engineer, "Liberal Islam Under Challenge," *Hindu: International Edition*, June 20, 1992, p. 9. Also see Girilal Jain, "Plight of Muslim Liberals: Implications for India's Future," *Times of India*, May 7, 1992, p. 8.

43. *Ibid.* Also see Dharma Kumar, "Jamia Blackmail: Not Minority Rights," *Times of India*, May 11, 1992, p. 8, and Saeed Naqvi, "Muslim Leaders Fiddle as Jamia Burns," *Pioneer*, May 3, 1992, p. 8.

44. *Pioneer*, May 10, 1992, p. 7.

45. Quoted in Jain, "Secularism," p. 128.

46. *Ibid.*, p. 129.

47. Inder Malhotra, *India Trapped in Uncertainty* (New Delhi, UPSPD, 1991), p. 106.

48. Mohan Dharia, "Only Secularism Can Save the Country," *India Abroad* (New York), January 29, 1993, p. 2. Recently a Muslim minister, a member of the Muslim League and a partner in the Congress (I) government in Kerala, refused to light ceremonial brass-oil wick lamps at a public function, calling it un-Islamic. *The Statesman* commented that such an "attitude would hardly promote secularism," *Statesman Weekly*, March 27, 1993, p. 8.

49. Mohan Dharia, "Only Secularism," p. 2.

50. Iqbal A. Ansari, "Hindus, Muslims and Inter-Communal Perceptions," *Islamic Times International* (Bombay), Vol. 1, No. 4 (1992), p. 10.

51. Rajni Kothari, "Secular Politics and Sectarian Strife," *India Abroad* (New York), February 6, 1993, p. 2.

52. Inder Malhotra, *India Trapped*, p. 83.

53. Asghar Ali Engineer, "Liberal Islam Under Challenge," *Hindu: International Edition,* June 20, 1992, p. 9.

54. Mohan Dharia, "Only Secularism," p. 3. Also, see Dharma Kumar, "Jamia Blackmail: Not Minority Rights," *Times of India,* May 11, 1992, p. 8.

55. Ram Swarup, "Hindu Response to Foreign Rule-1," *Times of India,* July 2, 1987. Also, see his "II-Hindu Self-Hate and Self-Recovery," *Times of India,* July 3, 1987, p. 8 and "Towards Conscious Hindu Identity-III," *Times of India,* July 4, 1987, p. 9.

56. Ram Swarup, "Hindu Response to Foreign Rule-1," p. 8.

57. *Illustrated Weekly of India,* January 9-15, 1993, p. 31.

58. "Concealing Record of Islam," *Organiser,* June 21, 1992, p. 13.

59. Swapan Das Gupta, "Present Imperfect: Those Who Deny the Horrors of History Will Repeat Them," *Sunday,* 10-16 May, 1992, p. 9. Also, see Koenraad Elst, *Negationism in India: Concealing the Record of Islam* (New Delhi, Voice of India, 1992) and David Washbrook, "South Asia in the World System, and World Capitalism," *The Journal of Asian Studies,* Vol. 49, No. 3 (August, 1990), pp. 479-508.

60. Akhtar Abbas Naqvi, "We'll pull down Babri Masjid because Ramjanambhoomi is for Hindus what Kaaba is for Muslims," *Sunday Observer,* August 13, 1989, p. 10.

61. *Organiser,* November 29, 1992, p. 13.

62. Quoted in *Organiser,* November 29, 1992, p. 13.

63. Quoted in Swapan Das Gupta, "Secularism and Hindu Nationalism," in M.M. Sankdher (ed.), *Secularism in India,* p. 206.

64. Inder Malhotra, "Political Commentary: Murky Manipulation Persists," *Times of India,* April 6, 1992, p. 10, and Girilal Jain, "Fall-out of CWC Elections: Validity of Congress Culture of Consensus," *Times of India,* April 23, 1992, p. 8.

65. Dileep Padgoankar, "Agenda for Tirupati: For a Democratic and Modern Congress," *Times of India,* April 23, 1992, p. 8.

66. Prem Shankar Jha, "Narasimha Rao's Lonely Battle," *Hindu: International Edition,* March 20, 1993, p. 9.

67. Madhu Limay, "An ECG of Indian Polity," *Sunday Hindustan Times Magazine,* March 22, 1992, p. 1.

BIBLIOGRAPHY

Interviews

Sundar Singh Bhandari (Vice-President, BJP) New Delhi, March 12, 1992.
T.N. Chaturvedi (Member, National Executive, BJP) New Delhi, April 24, 1992.
Jay Dubashi (Member, National Executive, BJP) New Delhi, March 3, 1992.
Babhani Sen Gupta (Author and Newspaper Columnist, Centre for Policy Research) New Delhi, March 8, 1992.
Girilal Jain (former editor, *Times of India*) New Delhi, March 17, 1992.
Hari Babu Kansal (Joint Secretary, Vishwa Hindu Parishad) New Delhi, February 27, 1992.
Promod Mahajan (MP Secretary, BJP) New Delhi, February 27, 1992.
K.R. Malkani (Vice-President, BJP) New Delhi, February 13, 1992.
J.P. Mathur (MP All India Secretary, BJP) New Delhi, March 4, 1992.
Brajesh Mishra (Member, National Executive, BJP) New Delhi, February 17, 1992.
Krishan Lal Sharma (MP and Vice-President, BJP) New Delhi, February 25, 1992.
Davinder Swarup (Vice-President, Deendayal Research Institute) New Delhi, March 9, 1992.

Newspapers

Economic Times
Hindustan (Hindi)
Hindustan Times
Hindu: International Edition
Indian Express
Pioneer
Statesman
Statesman Weekly
Times of India
Tribune

Fortnightlies and News Magazines

Economic and Political Weekly
Frontline
Illustrated Weekly of India
India Today
Probe India
Sunday
Telegraph

Party Papers

BJP Today
Organiser
Panchjanya (Hindi)

Bibliography

Abrahamsson, B. 1977. *Bureaucracy or Participation: The Logic Of Organization.*
    London: Sage Publications.
Advani, Lal Krishan. 1979. *The People Betrayed.* New Delhi: Vision Books.
_____. 1988. "Backward March: The Ban of Minorityism." *Statesman Weekly,* October
    28.
_____. 1989. *Ramjanam Bhoomi: Honour People's Sentiments.* New Delhi: Bharatiya
    Janata Party Publications.
_____. 1991. *Kuchh bunayadi samayiki.* New Delhi: Saruchi Prakashan.
Akbar, M.J. 1985. *India: The Siege Within.* New Delhi: Penguin.
_____. 1991. *Riot After Riot.* New Delhi: Penguin.
Alam, Javed. 1983. "Dialectics of Capitalist Transformations and National
    Crystallization: The Past and the Present of National Question in India." *Economic
    and Political Weekly,* January 29, pp. PE-29-PE-46.
Andersen, Walter K. and Shridhar D. Damle. 1987. *The Brotherhood in Saffron: The
    Rashtriya Swayamsevak Sangh and Hindu Revivalism.* Boulder, CO.: Westview Press.
Anderson, Benedict. 1983. *Imagined Communities: Reflection on the Origin and Spread
    of Nationalism.* London: Verso.
Ansari, Iqbal A. 1992. "Hindus, Muslims and Inter-Communal Perceptions." *Islamic
    Times.* Bombay, Vol. 1, No.4, pp. 5-6.
Aurobindo, Sri. 1965. *On Nationalism.* Pondicherry: Sri Aurobindo Ashram.
Bakker, Hans. 1991. "Ayodhya: A Hindu Jerusalem." *Numen,* Vol. 28, Fasc. 1, pp. 80-
    109.
Bakshi, S.R. 1992. *Syama Prasad Mookerjee: Founder of Jana Sangh.* New Delhi:
    Anmol Publications.
Banerjee, Sumanta. 1991. "Hindutva: Ideology and Social Psychology." *Economic and
    Political Weekly,* January 19, pp. 97-101.
Bardhan, A.B. 1990. *Appeal to All Countrymen.* New Delhi: Communist Party of India.
Basham, A.L. 1991. *The Wonder that Was India.* Delhi: Rupa and Co.
Baxter, Craig. 1969. *The Jana Sangh: A Biography of an Indian Political Party.*
    Philadelphia: University of Pennsylvania.
Bell, Daniel. 1977. "The Return of the Sacred? The Argument of the Future of
    Religion." *British Journal of Sociology* Vol. 20, No. 4 (December) pp. 419-450.
Bhambhari, C.P. 1980. *The Janata Party: A Profile.* New Delhi: National.
Bharatiya Janata Party. 1993. *Lal Krishan Advani ka adhyaksheeya bhashan 18-20 June
    1993.* New Delhi: B.J.P. Publications.
Bhardwaj, Surinder M. 1973. *Hindu Places of Pilgrimage: A Study in Cultural
    Geography.* Berkeley, University of California Press.
Bhat, S.R. 1990. *The Problem of Hindu-Muslim Conflicts.* Bangalore: Navakarnatka
    Publications.

Bhishikar, C.P. 1988. *Pandit Deendyal Upadhyaya: Ideology and Perception: Concept of Rashtra.* New Delhi: Suruchi Prakashan.

Binder, Leonard, et al. 1971. *Crisis and Sequences in Political Development.* Princeton: Princeton University Press.

Black, Cyril E. 1966. *The Dynamic of Modernization.* New York: Harper and Row.

Bose, Ajoy. 1987. "Interview Y.C. Chandrachud: The Supreme Court Interpreted Muslim Personal Law, It Didn't Interfere in It." In Asghar Ali Engineer (ed.). *The Shah Bano Controversy.* Hydrabad: A.P. Orient Longman, pp. 80-82.

Bottomore, T.B. 1964. *Elite and Society.* Harmondsworth: Penguin Press.

Brass, Paul R. *Ethnicity and Nationalism: Theory and Comparison.* New Delhi: Sage Publication.

_____. 1974. *Language, Religion, and Politics in North India.* London: Cambridge University Press.

Burke, Edmund. 1930. *Works*, Vol. 11. London: Oxford University Press.

Burke III, Edmund and Ira M. Lapidus (eds.). 1988. *Islam, Politics and Social Movements.* Berkeley: University of California Press.

Cardoso, Fernando Henrique and Enzo Faletto. 1979. *Dependency and Development in Latin America.* Berkeley: University of California Press.

Chagala, M.K. 1980. *Aik hee vikalap.* Bombay: Bharatiya Janata Party.

Chatterjee, Partha. 1965. *Nationalist Thought and the Colonial World.* London: Zed Press.

_____. 1986. "Transferring a Political Theory: Early Nationalist Thought in India." *Economic and Political Weekly*, Vol. 21, No. 3 (January 18) pp. 120-128.

Dalton, Dennis. 1982. "The Concepts of Politics and Power in India's Ideological Tradition." In A. Jeyaratnam Wilson and Dennis Dalton (eds.). *The States of South Asia: Problems of National Integration.* London: C. Hurst and Co., pp. 175-196.

Dasgupta, Swapan. 1989. "Hedgewar's Legacy: Limitations of Elitist Hinduism." *The Statesman Weekly*, April 8.

_____. 1992. "Secularism and Hindu Nationalism." In M.M. Sankdher (ed.). *Secularism in India: Dilemmas and Challenges.* New Delhi: Deep and Deep Publications, pp. 204-212.

Deendayal Research Institute. "Towards an Alternative Discourse: A Draft for Discussion." New Delhi: Deendayal Research Institute, n.d.

Deodhar, V.N. 1989. *Pandit Deendayal Upadhyaya: Ideology and Perception: A Profile.* New Delhi: Suruchi Prakashan.

Deoras, Bala Saheb. 1985. *Country's Unity A Must.* New Delhi: Suruchi Prakashan.

Deshmukh, Nana. 1979. *R.R.S.: Victim of Slander.* New Delhi: Vision Books.

de Toqueville, Alexis. 1945. *Democracy in America.* New York: Alfred A. Knopf, Inc.

Devi, Savatri. 1989. *A Warning to the Hindus.* Meerut: U.P. Hindi-Vikas Peeth.

Dharia, Mohan. 1993. "Only Secularism Can Save the Country." *India Abroad* (New York) January 29, p. 2.

Dixit, Prabha. 1986. "The Ideology of Hindu Nationalism." In Thomas Pantham and Kenneth L. Deutsch (eds.). *Political Thought in Modern India.* New Delhi: Sage Publications. pp. 122-141.

D'Souza, Victor S. 1991. "Roots of Present Communal Crisis." *Economic and Political Weekly*, May 25, pp. 1333-1335.

Dua, B.D. 1985. "Federalism or Patrimonialism: The Making and Unmaking of Chief Ministers in India." *Asian Survey*, Vol. 25, No. 8 (August) pp. 793-803.

Dubashi, Jay. 1992. *The Road to Ayodhya*. New Delhi: Voice of India.

Dumont, Louis. 1987. "Nationalism and Communalism." *Contributions to Indian Sociology*, Vol. 7 (March) pp. 30-70.

Dutt, Guru. 1966. *Dharm, samskriti aur rajya*. New Delhi: Bharatiya Sahitya Sadan.

_____. 1969. *Bharat: Gandhi aur Nehru ke chhaya main*. New Delhi: Bharatiya Sahitya Sadan.

Dutt, R.C. 1988. "Recipe for Unrest: Threat of Hindu Chauvinism." *The Statesman Weekly,* August 20.

Duverger, Maurice. 1954. *Political Parties*. New York: John Wiley and Sons.

Eisenstadt, S.N. 1966. *Modernization, Protest and Change*. Englewood Cliffs, NJ: Prentice Hall.

Elst, Koenraad. 1990. *Ramjanambhoomi Vs. Babari Masjid: A Case Study in Hindu-Muslim Conflict*. New Delhi: Voice of India.

_____. 1991. *Ayodhya and After*. New Delhi: Voice of India.

_____. 1992. *Negationism in India: Concealing the Record of Islam*. New Delhi: Voice of India.

Embree, A. 1990. *Utopias in Conflict: Religion and Nationalism in Modern India*. Berkeley: University of California Press.

Encarnation, Dennis J. 1989. *Dislodging Multi-Nationals: India's Strategy in Comparative Perspective*. Ithaca: Cornell University Press.

Engineer, Asghar Ali, ed. 1987. *The Shah Bano Controversy*. Hydrabad: Orient Longman.

Evans, Peter. 1979. *Dependent Development: The Alliance of Multi-National, State and Local Capital in Brazil*. Princeton: Princeton University Press.

Fox, Richard G. 1987. "Gandhian Socialism and Hindu Nationalism: Cultural Domination in the World System." *The Journal of Commonwealth and Comparative Politics* Vol. 25, No. 3 (November) pp. 233-247.

Frank, Andre Gunder. 1969. *Capitalism and Underdevelopment in Latin America*. New York: Monthly Review Press.

Freitag, Sandria B. 1980. "Sacred Symbol as Mobilizing Ideology: The North Indian Search for a Hindu 'Community.'" *Comparative Studies in Society and History* Vol. 22, No. 4, pp. 597-625.

Gadbois, George H. 1990. "The Indian Superior Judiciary: Help Wanted: Any Good People Willing to be Judges?" In Yogendra K. Malik and Dhirendra K. Vajpeyi (eds.). *Boeings and Bullock-Carts: Studies in Change and Continuity in Indian Civilization Vol. 3. Law, Politics, and Society in India*. Delhi: Chanakya Publications, pp. 16-51.

Galtung, John. 1971. "Structural Theory of Imperialism." *Journal of Peace Research* Vol. 8 (August) pp. 80-117.

Ganguli, Amulya. 1990. "Temple of Doom: Roadblocks Before Hindutva." *The Statesman Weekly* June 2.

Gellner, Ernest. 1983. *Nations and Nationalism*. Ithaca: Cornell University Press.

Goel, Sita Ram. 1985. *Secularism rashtradroh ka doosra nam*. New Delhi: Bharati-Bharat.

_____. 1987. *Defence of Hindu Society*. New Delhi: Voice of India.

_____. 1992. *Hindu Society Under Siege*. New Delhi: Voice of India.

Gopal, Sarvepalli, ed. 1991. *Anatomy of a Confrontation: The Babari Masjid-Ramjanmbhumi Issue*. New Delhi: Penguin Books.

Graham, B.D. 1987. "Challenge of Hindu Nationalism: The Bharatiya Janata Party in Contemporary Indian Politics." *Hull Papers in Politics*, No. 40. Hull, Department of Politics, pp. 1-29.

_____. 1990. *Hindu Nationalism and Indian Politics: The Origins and Development of Bharatiya Jana Sangh.* Cambridge: Cambridge University Press.

Green, Jarold D. 1985. "Islam, Religiopolitics, and Social Change." *Comparative Studies in Society and History* Vol. 27, No. 2, pp. 312-322.

Greenfeld, Leah. 1992. *Nationalism: Five Roads to Modernity.* Cambridge: Harvard University Press.

Guha, Amalendu. 1982. "The Indian National Question: A Conceptual Frame." *Economic and Political Weekly*, July 31, pp. PE-2-PE-12.

Gupta, Amalendu Das. 1990. "BJP in Perspective: Demystifying a Phenomenon." *The Statesman Weekly*, March 24.

Gupta, Bhabani Sen. 1989. "Ice on Summer Seas." *Economic and Political Weekly*, October 14, pp. 2285-2288.

Gupta, N.L., ed. 1965. *Nehru On Communalism.* New Delhi: Sampradayikta Virodhi Committee.

Haqu, Jalalul. 1992. *Nation and Nation-Worship in India.* New Delhi: Genuine Publications.

Hardgrave, Robert. 1984. "India on the Eve of Elections: Congress and the Opposition." *Pacific Affairs* Vol. 53, No. 3 (Fall) pp. 404-428.

Hasan, Mushirul. 1991. "Adjustment and Accommodation: Muslims After Partition." In K.K. Panikkar (ed.). *Communalism in India: History, Politics and Culture.* New Dehli: Manohar, pp. 62-79.

Hasan, Zoya. 1991. "Changing Orientation of the State and the Emergence of Majoritarianism in the 1980's." In K.K. Panikkar (ed.). *Communalism in India: History, Politics and Culture.* New Dehli: Manohar, pp. 142-151.

Heimssath, Charles H. 1964. *Indian Nationalism and Hindu Social Reform.* Princeton, NJ: Princeton University Press.

History Versus Casuistry: The Evidence of the Ramjanambhoomi Mandir. 1991. Presented by the Vishwa Hindu Parishad to the Government of India in December-January. New Delhi: Voice of India.

Hobsbawmi, Eric and Terence Ranger, eds. 1983. *The Invention of Tradition.* Cambridge: Cambridge University Press.

Hunnington, Samuel J. 1968. *Political Order in Changing Societies.* New Haven: Yale University Press.

_____. 1971. "The Change to Change: Modernization, Development and Politics." *Comparative Politics*, Vol 3, No. 3 (April) pp. 283-322.

_____. 1993. "The Clash of Civilization?" *Foreign Affairs*, Vol. 72, No. 3 (Summer) pp. 22-49.

Isaacs, Harold R. 1989. *Idols of the Tribe: Group Identity and Political Change.* Cambridge: Harvard University Press.

Iyer, V.K. Krishna. 1991. *Politics and Religion.* Delhi: Konark Publishers.

Jagmohan. 1991. *My Frozen Turbulence in Kashmir.* New Delhi: Allied Publishers.

Jain, Girilal. 1991. "A Turning Point in History." *Manthan*, Vol. 13, No. 1-2 (May-June) pp. 19-24.

_____. 1992. "Secularism and Nehruism." In M.M. Sankdher (ed.). *Secularism in India: Dilemmas and Challenges.* New Delhi: Deep and Deep Publications, pp 123-141.

Jain, S.N., S.C. Kashyap, and N. Srinivasan, eds. 1972. *The Union and the States.* Delhi: National.

Jayaprasad, K. 1991. *RSS and Hindu Nationalism.* New Delhi: Deep and Deep Publications.

Jha, Prem Shankar. 1980. *India: Political Economy of Stagnation.* New Delhi: Oxford University Press.

Jog, B.N. 1989. *Pandit Deendayal Upadhyaya Ideology and Perception: Politics for Nation's Sake.* New Delhi: Suruchi Prakashan.

Juergensmeyer, Mark. 1993. *The New Cold War? Religious Nationalism Confronts the Secular State.* Berkeley: University of California Press.

Kapoor, R.N. 1991. "Voluntary Organizations in Promoting Science and Technology in Rural Developments." *Manthan*, Vol. 12, No. 1 (January) pp. 9-14.

Karlekar, Hiranmay. 1991. "Hinduism and Indian Unity." *Manthan*, Vol. 13, Nos. 1-2 (May-June) pp. 59-61.

Kelkar, B.K. 1988. *Pandit Deendayal Upadhyaya: Ideology and Perception: Political Thought.* New Delhi: Suruchi Prakashan.

Khan, S. 1987. "Towards a Marxist Understanding of Secularism: Some Preliminary Speculation." *Economic and Political Weekly*, March 7, pp. 406-408.

Kochanek, Stanley. 1987. "Briefcase Politics in India: The Congress Party and the Business Elite." *Asian Survey* Vol. 27, No. 12 (December) pp, 1278-1301.

Kothari, Rajni. 1977. "Design for an Alternative." *Seminar* (August) pp. 12-20.

_____. 1988. "Class and Communalism in India." *Economic and Political Weekly,* December 3, pp. 2589-2592.

_____. 1988. "Integration and Exclusion in Indian Politics." *Economic and Political Weekly,* October 22, pp. 2223-2228.

_____. 1989. "Cultural Context of Communalism in India." *Economic and Political Weekly,* January 14, pp. 81-85.

_____. 1992. "Pluralism and Secularism: Lessons of Ayodhya." *Economic and Political Weekly*, December 19-26, pp. 2695-2698.

Lane, Robert. 1962. *Political Ideology.* New York: Free Press of Glenco.

Lawrence, Bruce B. 1989. *Defenders of God: The Fundamentalist Revolt Against the Modern Age.* San Francisco: Harper and Row.

Limaye, Madhu. 1992. *Decline of a Political System: Indian Politics at Crossroads.* Allahabad: Wheeler Publishing.

Macpherson, C.B. 1977. *The Life and Times of Liberal Democracy.* New York: Oxford University Press.

Madan, T.N. 1987. "Secularism in Its Place." *Journal of Asian Studies*, Vol. 46, No. 4 (November) pp. 745-780.

_____. 1989. "Religion in India." *Daedulas*, Vol. 118, No. 4 (Fall) pp. 115-145.

Madhok, Balraj. 1990. *Hindu rajya.* Delhi: Rajpal and Sons.

Malhotra, Inder. 1992. *India Trapped in Uncertainty.* New Delhi: UPSPD.

Malik, Yogendra K. 1988. "Indira Gandhi: Personality, Political Power and Party Politics." In Yogendra K. Malik and Dhirendra K. Vajpeyi (eds.). *India: The Years of Indira Gandhi.* Leiden: E.J. Brill, pp. 7-21.

_____. 1989. "Political Finance in India." *Political Quarterly*, Vol. 60, No. 1 (January) pp. 75-94.

_____ and Surinder M. Bhardwaj. 1983. *Politics, Technology, and Bureaucracy in South Asia.* Leiden: E.J. Brill.

_____ and Surinder M. Bhardwaj. 1990. "Ideology, Politics, and Technology Policy in India." In Dhirendra Vajpeyi and R. Natrajan (eds.). *Technology and Development: Public Policy and Managerial Issues.* Jaipur: Ravat.

_____ and Jesse F. Marquette. 1990. *Political Mercenaries and Citizen Soldiers: A Profile of North Indian Party Activists.* Delhi: Chanakya Publications.

_____ and V.B. Singh. 1992. "Bharatiya Janata Party: An Alternative to the Congress (I)?" *Asian Survey*, Vol. 32, No. 4 (April) pp. 318-336.

_____ and Dhirendra K. Vajpeyi. 1989. "The Rise of Hindu Militancy: India's Secular Democracy at Risk?" *Asian Survey*, Vol. 29, No. 3 (March) pp 308-325.

Malkani, K.R. 1980. *The RSS Story.* New Delhi: Impex.

_____. 1989. "EMS Versus BJP: Why Is The CPI (M) Leader Angry?" *The Statesman Weekly*, March 25.

Manor, James. 1983. "Anomie in Indian Politics: Origins and Potential Wider Impact." *Economic and Political Weekly* (Annual Number, May) pp. 725-734.

_____. 1988. "Parties and Party System in India." In Atul Kohli (ed.), *India's Democracy: An Analysis of State-Society Relations.* Princeton: Princeton University Press, pp. 62-98.

McClosky, Herbert, Paul J. Hoffmann, and Rosemary O'Hara. 1964. "Consensus and Ideology in American Politics." *American Political Science Review* Vol. 58, No. 2 (June) pp. 361-381.

Mernissi, Fatima. 1992. *Islam and Democracy: Fear of the Modern World.* Reading, MA: Addison-Wesley Publishing Company.

Miller, Barbara S. 1991. "Presidential Address: Contending Narratives-The Political Life of Indian Epics." *Journal of Asian Studies*, Vol. 50, No. 4 (1991) pp. 783-792.

Miller, R.E. 1987. "Modern Indian Muslim Responses." In Harold G. Coward (ed.). *Modern Indian Responses to Religious Pluralism.* Albany: State University of New York Press, pp. 235-268.

Mishra, Dina Nath. 1980. *RSS: Myth and Reality.* Shibabad (U.P.): Vikas Publishing.

Mitra, Subrata K. 1991. "Desecularizing the State: Religion and Politics in India After Independence." *Comparative Studies in Society and History*, Vol. 33, No. 4 (October) pp. 755-777.

Mortinar, Edward. 1983. *Faith and Power.* New York: Vintage Books.

Munshi, D.N. 1992. *Agony of Kashmir.* New Delhi: Suruchi Prakashan.

Muralidharan, Sukumar. 1990. "Mandal, Mandir aur Masjid: 'Hindu' Communalism and the Crisis of the State." *Social Scientist*, Vol. 18, No. 10 (October) pp. 18-30.

Nandy, Ashis. 1970. "The Culture of Indian Politics: A Stock Taking." *Journal of Asian Studies*, Vol. 30, No. 1 (November) pp. 57-78.

_____. 1972. "Making and Unmaking of Political Cultures in India." In S.N. Eisenstadt (ed.). *Post-Colonial Societies.* New York: W.W. Norton, pp. 115-137.

_____. 1979. "Myths, Persons, and Politics." *Seminar* (October) pp. 242-246.

_____. 1979. "Political Consciousness." A paper presented at the seminar held at the India International Centre. New Delhi, December 16.

_____. 1983. *The Intimate Enemy.* New Delhi: Oxford University Press.

_____. 1984. "Cultural Frames for Transformative Politics: A Credo." *Indian Philosophical Quarterly*, Vol. 11, No. 4, pp. 30-38.

_____. 1984. "Culture of Politics and Politics of Cultures." *Journal of Commonwealth and Comparative Politics*, Vol. 22, No. 3 (November) pp. 262-274.

_____. 1984. "Culture, State and the Rediscovery of Indian Politics." *Economic and Political Weekly* (December 8) pp. 2078-2083.

_____. 1985. "An Anti-Secularist Manifesto." *Seminar*, (October) pp. 14-24.

_____. 1986. *At the Edge of Psychology*. New Delhi: Oxford University Press.

_____. 1989. "The Political Culture of the Indian State." *Daedulas*, Vol. 118, No. 4 (Fall) pp. 1-26.

_____. 1993. "Three Propositions." *Seminar* (February) pp. 15-17.

Narayan, Harash. 1989. *Sammrishat sanskriti aur sarvdharm-samata apvad*. New Delhi: Bharat-Bharati.

Nauriya, Anil. 1991. "India National Congress: Its Place in Politics." *Economic and Political Weekly* (November 23) pp. 2675-2682.

Nayar, Baldev Raj. 1990. *Political Economy of India's Public Sector: Policy and Performance*. Bombay: Popular Prakadshan.

Nayar, Kuldip. 1986. "Separate Personal Law Would Not Dilute Secularism." *Telegraph*, March 15.

Nehru, Jawaharlal. 1946. *Discovery of India*. New York: Doubleday.

Nene, V.V. 1988. *Pandit Deendayal Upadhyaya: Ideology and Perception: Integral Humanism*. New Delhi: Suruchi Prakashan.

Omvedt, Gail. 1990. "Hinduism and Politics." *Economic and Political Weekly*, April 7, pp. 723-729.

Pandey, Gyandra. 1992. *The Construction of Communalism in Colonial North India*. Delhi: Oxford University Press.

Pandya, Anand. 1990. *Hypocrisy of Secularism*. Karnavati: Vishwa Hindu Parishad Prakashan.

Panelbianco, Angelo. 1988. *Political Parties: Organization and Power*. Cambridge: Cambridge University Press.

Pannikkar, K.N., ed. 1991. *Communalism in Indian Politics: History, Politics and Culture*. New Delhi: Manohar.

Pantham, Thomas. 1988. "Beyond Liberal Democracy: Thinking with Mahatma Gandhi." In Thomas Pantham and Kenneth L. Deutsch (eds.) *Political Thought in Modern India*. New Delhi: Sage Publications.

Parameswaran, P. 1978. *Gandhi, Lohia and Deendayal*. New Delhi: Deendayal Research Institute.

Parekh, Bhikhu. 1991. "Nehru and the National Philosophy of India." *Economic and Political Weekly*, January 5-12, pp. 35-47.

Parikh, Manju. 1993. "The Debacle at Ayodhya: Why Militant Hinduism Met with Weak Response." *Asian Survey*, Vol. 33, No. 7 (July) pp. 673-695.

Patel, Sujata and Krishna Kumar. 1988. "Defenders of Sati State." *Economic and Political Weekly*, January 23, pp. 129-130.

Pettigrew, Joyce. 1984. "Take Not Arms Against Thy Sovereign." *South Asia Research*, Vol. 4, No. 2 (November) pp. 102-123.

_____. 1987. "In Search of a New Kingdom of Lahore." *Pacific Affairs*, Vol. 60, No. 1 (Spring) pp. 1-25.

Pipes, Daniel. 1983. *In the Path of God: Islam and Political Power*. New York: Basic Books.

Pollock, Sheldon. 1993. "Ramayana and Political Imagination in India." *Journal of Asian Studies*, Vol. 52, No. 2 (May) pp. 261-297.

Prior, Katherine. 1993. "Making History: The State's Intervention in Urban Religious Dispute in the North-Western Provinces in the Early Nineteenth Century." *Modern Asian Studies*, Vol. 27, No. 1, pp. 179-203.

Puri, Balraj. 1990. "Can Caste, Region and Ideology Stem Hindu Wave?" *Economic and Political Weekly*, January 6, pp. 15-16.

Puri, Geeta. 1980. *Bharatiya Jana Sangh: Organization and Ideology*. New Delhi: Sterling Publishers.

Raje, Sudhakar, ed. 1972. *Pt. Deendayal Upadhyaya: A Profile*. New Delhi: Deendayal Research Institute.

_____. 1978. *Destination*. New Dehli: Deendayal Research Institute.

Rao, C. Rajeswara and Shameem Faizee. 1989. *Babri Masjid Ram Janam Bhoomi Controversy: Dangerous Communal Situation*. New Delhi: Communist Party of India Publication.

Rao, S.V. Seshagiri. 1991. *Collapse of Communist Oligarchy*. New Delhi: Suruchi Prakashan.

Ray, Anal. 1982. "From Consensus to Confrontation: Federal Politics in India." *Economic and Political Weekly*, October 2, pp. 1619-1624.

Ray, A.K. 1991. "Hinduism: A Geo-Cultural Concept." *Manthan*, Vol. 13, No. 1-2, (May-June) pp. 25-28.

Razi, Hossein G. 1990. "Legitimacy, Religion and Nationalism in the Middle East." *American Political Science Review*, Vol. 84, No. 1 (March) pp. 79-92.

Robinson, Francis. 1993. "Technology and Religious Change: Islam and the Impact of Print." *Modern Asian Studies,* Vol. 27, No. 1, pp. 229-251.

Rostow, Dankwart A. 1967. *A World of Nations*. Washington: Brookings.

RSS: Spearheading: National Renaissance: 60th Anniversary Year 1985. 1985. Bangalore: Prakashan Vibhag.

Rudolph, Lloyd and Susanne H. 1967. *The Modernity of Tradition: Political Development in India*. Chicago: University of Chicago Press.

_____. 1987. *In Pursuit of Lakshmi: The Political Economy of Indian State*. Chicago: University of Chicago Press.

The Saga of Ayodhya. 1990. Bangalore: Jagarana Prakshana.

Saman nagarik samhita:aik paricharcha. 1986. New Delhi: Suruchi Prakashan.

Sankhdher, M.M., ed. 1992. *Secularism in India: Dilemmas and Challenge*s. New Delhi: Deep and Deep.

Satyarthi, Vivek. 1988. *Kmunism benakab*. New Delhi: Suruchi Prakashan.

Saxena, Kiram. 1993. "The Hindu Trade Union Movement in India: The Bharatiya Mazdoor Sangh." *Asian Survey,* Vol. 33, No. 7 (July 8) pp. 685-696.

Sayed, Anwar Hussain. 1982. *Pakistan: Islam: Politics and National Solidarity*. New York: Praeger Publications.

Seal, Anil. 1970. *The Emergence of Indian Nationalism: Competition and Collaboration in the Nineteenth Century*. London: Cambridge University Press.

Seshadari, H.V. 1984. *The Tragic Story of Partition*. Bangalore: Jagaran Prakashan.

_____. et al. 1990. *Why Hindu Rashtra?* New Delhi: Suruchi Prakashan.

_____. 1991. *Universal Spirit of Hindu Nationalism*. Madras, Vigil: A Public Opinion Forum.

_____. 1991. *The Way*. New Delhi: Suruchi Prakashan.

Shah, Ghanshyam. 1991. "Tenth Lok Sabha Elections: The BJP's Victory in Gujarat." *Economic and Political Weekly*. December 21, pp. 2921-2924.

Sharma, R.S. *et al*. 1991. *Ramjanambhumi Babri Masjid: Historians' Report to the Nation*. New Delhi: People's Publishing House.

Sheth, D.L. 1992. "Movements, Intellectuals and the State: Social Policy in Nation-Building." *Economic and Political Weekly*, February 22, pp. 425-432.

Shouri, Arun. 1987. *Religion in Politics*. New Delhi: Roli Books International.

_____. 1991. *The State as Charade*. New Delhi: Roli Books International.

Singh, Khushwant. 1993. "India: The Hindu State." *New York Times* (August 3) Sec. A, p. 17.

Singh, Randhir. 1991. "Communalism and the Struggle Against Communalism: A Marxist View." In K.K. Panikkar (ed.). *Communalism in India: History, Politics, and Culture*. New Delhi: Manohar, pp. 109-131.

Singh, S. Nihal. 1989. "The BJP: Wanting its Share, and More." *Telegraph*, February 25.

Sisson, Richard and Ramashray Roy. 1990. *Diversity and Dominance in Indian Politics*. Vols. 1 and 2. New Delhi: Sage Publications.

Smelser, Neil J., ed. 1967. *Sociology*. New York: Wiley and Sons.

Stackhouse, Max L. 1985. "Fundamentalism Around the World." *Christian Century*, August 28-September 4, pp. 769-771.

Swamy, Subramanian. 1992. *Building a New India: An Agenda for National Renaissance*. New Delhi: UPSPD.

Swarup, Ram. 1985. *Hindu-Sikh Relationship*. New Delhi: Voice of India.

_____. 1987. *Cultural Self-Alienation and Some Problems Hinduism Faces*. New Delhi: Voice of India.

Tanham, George K. 1992. *Indian Strategic Thought: An Interpretive Essay*. Santa Monica: Rand.

Thakur, Janardan. 1977. *All the Prime Minister's Men*. New Delhi: Vikas.

_____. 1978. *All the Janata Men*. New Delhi: Vikas.

_____. 1979. *Indira Gandhi and Her Power Game*. New Delhi: Vikas.

Thakur, Ramesh. 1993. "Ayodhya and Politics of India's Secularism: A Double-Standard Discourse." *Asian Survey* Vol. 33, No. 7 (July) pp. 645-665.

Thapar, Romila. 1989. "Imagined Religious Communities? Ancient History and the Modern Search for Hindu Identity." *Modern Asian Studies*, Vol. 23, No. 2, pp. 209-231.

Thapar, Romila, Harbans Mukhia and Bipan Chandra. 1984. *Communalism and the Writing of Indian History*. New Delhi: People's Publishing House.

Thengdi, D.B. 1978. "Integral Humanism: One Concept, Many Facets." In Sudhakar Raje (ed.) *Destination*. New Delhi: Deendayal Research Institute, pp. 15-25.

_____. 1991. *Genocide of Hindus in Kashmir*. New Delhi: Suruchi Prakashan.

_____ and M.S. Golwalkar. 1991. *Deendayal Upadhyaya and Integral Approach*. New Delhi: Suruchi Prakashan.

Tripathi, Kamalapati, *et al*. 1989. *Three Eminent Personalities on the Ram Janam Bhoomi-Babri Masjid Controversy*. New Delhi: Communist Party Publication.

Tully, Mark. 1991. *No Full Stops in India*. New Delhi: Penguin Books.

_____ and Zareer Masani. 1988. *India: Forty Years of Independence*. New York: George Braziller.

Upadhyaya, Prakash Chandra. 1992. "The Politics of Indian Secularism." *Modern Asian Studies*, Vol. 26, No. 4, pp. 816-853.

Vajpayee, Atal Bihari. 1980. *India at the Crossroads*. New Delhi: Bharatiya Janata Party Publications.

Van Der Veer, Peter. 1987. "God Must be Liberated? A Hindu Liberation Movement in Ayodhya." *Modern Asian Studies*, Vol. 21, No. 2, pp. 283-303.

Varshney, Ashutosh. 1993. "Contested Meanings: India's National Identity, Hindu Nationalism and Politics of Anxiety." *Daedulas*, Vol. 122, No. 3 (Summer), pp. 227-261.

Vazirani, Gulab. 1991. *Lal Advani: The Man and His Mission*. New Delhi: Arnold Publishers.

Verney, Douglas V. 1986. "The Limits to Political Manipulation: The Role of the Governors in India's 'Administrative Federalism' 1950-84." *Journal of Commonwealth and Comparative Politics*, Vol. 24, No. 2 (July) pp. 169-196.

Virat Hindu Sammelan: Souvenir, 26th-27th August, 1989. London.

Vishwa Hindu Parishad. n.d. *Hindu parishad ke uddeshya, karya tatha uplabhdhiyan*. New Delhi: Vishwa Hindu Parishad.

Wallerstein, Immanuel. 1974. "The Rise and Future Demise of the World Capitalist System." *Comparative Studies in Society and History*, Vol. 16, No. 4 (September) pp. 387-415.

_____. 1974. *The World Capitalist System: Capitalist Agriculture and the Origins of the European Economy in the Sixteenth Century*. New York: Academic Press.

_____. 1980. *The Modern World System II: Mercantilism and Consolidation of European World Economy, 1600-1750*. New York: Academic Press.

Washbrook, David. 1990. "South Asia in the World System, and World Capitalism." *The Journal of Asian Studies*. Vol. 49, No. 3 (August) pp. 479-508.

Wilson, J.R., and Dennis Dalton, eds. 1982. *The States of South Asia: Problems of National Integration*. London: C. Hurst and Co..

Yang, Anand A. 1980. "Sacred Symbol and Sacred Space in Rural India: Community Mobilization in the 'Anti-Cow Killing' Riot of 1893." *Comparative Studies in Society and History*, Vol. 22, No. 4 (October) pp. 576-596.

Index

Deendayal Research Institute (DRI), 170–
172
Delhi, 34, 52, 64, 72, 87, 188, 189, 190, 191,
195, 201, 208
Democracy, 6, 15, 17, 18, 38, 43, 60, 73, 74,
165, 233
democratic socialism, 10
Deoras, Balasaheb, 77, 157, 160, 161, 163,
174
Dependency theory, 105
Desai, Morarji, 33, 34–35, 37
Deshmukh, Nanaji, 33, 40, 43, 159–160,
170, 172, 190
Deshpande, Bani, 160
Devilal, 66, 82, 88
Dharia, Mohan, 231
Dharma, 17, 19, 21
Distributive justice, 16, 18, 37, 86
Diu Union territory, 201
Diversity, 2, 15, 17, 23
DMKP. *See* Dalit Mazdoor Kisan Party
DRI. *See* Deendayal Research Institute
Dua, Bhagwan, 113
Dubashi, Jay, 50
Dumont, Louis, 227
Duverger, Maurice, 139

Ecological issues, 17, 18
Economic issues, 100–106, 131, 155–156,
237
centralization, 10, 17–18, 20, 38, 42, 89,
101, 194
crises, 90–91, 101–102
development, 5, 10, 16, 60, 61, 101, 102,
105, 238
foreign investments, 105
global economy, 126
planning, 10, 16, 20, 42, 101, 104
productivity, 37, 106, 156, 238
Economist, 224–225
Education, 107, 111, 164, 216, 232, 238
Egalitarianism, 10, 102, 117
Ekta Yatra, 91–92
Election Commission, 117
Elections
1946, 19
1952, 30
1967, 30, 31
1971, 32
1972, 32

1974, 180
1977, 34, 59
1980, 36, 63, 135(n73), 180, 181, 185
1982, 63, 179, 181
1983, 64
1984, 41, 67–69, 73, 74, 78, 186–
187(table), 188, 189–191
1987, 82
1988, 78, 82
1989, 41, 80, 83–85, 147, 179, 186–
187(table), 194–196
1990, 86, 208
1991, 41, 88–90, 147, 164, 186–
187(table), 198–201, 202(fig.), 204–
205(table)
1992, 93
1993, 208–212, 209(table)
Vidhan Sabha, 180–181, 182–184(table),
185, 188–189, 191–194, 196–198, 201,
203, 208, 209(table)
See also Muslims, Muslim vote
Elites, 3, 6, 10, 19, 20, 22, 36, 53, 71, 105,
112, 216, 217, 218, 233
Embree, Ainslie T., 21
Emergency Rule, 33, 38, 44, 112, 155, 156
Engineer, Asghar Ali, 220–221
Erickson, E., 21

Federalism, 6, 120
Five Year Plans, 106, 108
Foreign policy, 124–127
Freedom, 17, 18, 38, 117. *See also*
Independence movement
Fundamentalism, 29, 199, 229, 231. *See also*
Islam, fundamentalist

Gadbois, George, 117
Gadgil, V.N., 237
Gandhi, Indira, 32, 41, 60, 70, 116, 117, 120,
135(n73), 207, 223
assassination of, 67, 73, 189, 219
See also Congress (I) party; Emergency
Rule
Gandhi, Mahatma, 9, 10, 21, 30, 103, 160,
161, 218, 232
trusteeship concept of, 61
See also Socialism, Gandhian
Gandhi, Rajiv, 7, 8, 41, 72, 78, 80, 84, 116,
129, 189, 223
assassination of, 89, 90